Narrative Design in *Finnegans Wake*

The Florida James Joyce Series

The Florida James Joyce Series
Edited by Zack Bowen

The Autobiographical Novel of Co-Consciousness:
Goncharov, Woolf, and Joyce,
by Galya Diment (1994)

Shaw and Joyce:
"The Last Word in Stolentelling,"
by Martha Fodaski Black (1995)

Bloom's Old Sweet Song:
Essays on Joyce and Music,
by Zack Bowen (1995)

Reauthorizing Joyce,
by Vicki Mahaffey (paperback edition, 1995)

Joyce's Iritis and the Irritated Text:
The Dis-lexic Ulysses,
by Roy Gottfried (1995)

Joyce, Milton, and the Theory of Influence,
by Patrick Colm Hogan (1995)

Jocoserious Joyce:
The Fate of Folly in Ulysses,
by Robert H. Bell (paperback edition, 1996)

Joyce and Popular Culture,
edited by R. B. Kershner (1996)

Narrative Design in Finnegans Wake:
The Wake *Lock Picked,*
by Harry Burrell (1996)

Narrative Design in *Finnegans Wake*

The *Wake* Lock Picked

Harry Burrell

University Press of Florida
Gainesville, Tallahassee, Tampa, Boca Raton,
Pensacola, Orlando, Miami, Jacksonville

Copyright 1996 by the Board of Regents of the State of Florida
Printed in the United States of America on acid-free paper
All rights reserved

01 00 99 98 97 96 6 5 4 3 2 1

Library of Congress Cataloging-in-Publication Data

Burrell, Harry.
        Narrative design in *Finnegans Wake:* the *Wake* lock picked /
by Harry Burrell.
        p.   cm.—(The Florida James Joyce series)
        Includes bibliographical references and index.
        ISBN 0-8130-1465-4 (acid-free paper).
        1. Joyce, James, 1882-1941. *Finnegans Wake.* 2. Joyce,
James, 1882-1941—Techniques. 3. Bible. English—Language,
style. 4. Rhetoric in the Bible. 5. Narration (Rhetoric). 6.
Bible—In literature. I. Title. II. Series.
        PR6019.O9F568   1996
        823'.912—dc 20   96-24031

The University Press of Florida is the scholarly publishing
agency for the State University System of Florida, comprised of
Florida A & M University, Florida Atlantic University, Florida
International University, Florida State University, University of
Central Florida, University of Florida, University of North
Florida, University of South Florida, and
University of West Florida.

University Press of Florida
15 Northwest 15th Street
Gainesville, FL 32611

To Carol
whose "days of youyouth are evermixed mimine"

Contents

Foreword

While the honor of introducing Harry Burrell's extraordinary study of *Finnegans Wake* falls to me as Bernard Benstock's editorial successor, nothing I could say would do the book any more justice than Berni's remarks—written when he enthusiastically approved the book for publication, and now reproduced for this foreword.

Zack Bowen, University of Miami

A certain amount of historical background is necessary if one is to demonstrate how important an achievement this book is, how significant a contribution to *Finnegans Wake* scholarship. The assumption of a "central thesis" or "contained narrative" in *Finnegans Wake* existed almost as a given in the early days of scholarly explication of the work, but except for rumors about the possibility, nothing emerged in the 1950s and 1960s, and it has since been assumed that no such overextensive pattern would ever be uncovered. Harry Burrell has returned *Wake* scholarship to the possibility of such a pattern and has based his reading of Joyce's text on the Adam-and-Eve portions of Genesis. What he has achieved is a consistent reading along these lines, accounting for the omnipresent God and Adam, Eve, and the Serpent as the primary characters throughout the *Wake,* with all the extenuating or conflicting or corroborative personae aspects of the basic Four, and purposeful obfuscations by Joyce to hide the total significance of the Four. It is an ingenious theory, fully documented and persistently detailed in *Narrative Design in "Finnegans Wake,"* and the explications cut across Joyce's text in numerous directions, weaving and reweaving the pattern that Burrell discerns.

No book like it has as yet been published, unless one goes back to 1944 to the Campbell and Robinson *Skeleton Key to "Finnegans Wake,"* with its cultural anthropological approach—although without a stated central thesis as such. Nor will there be any rival to it in the near future, but future books on the *Wake* will concentrate on coming to grips with Burrell's ground-breaking study.

Preface

Apology

This is not an expression of regret or atonement. I choose the word *apology* deliberately, as a reminder that the words of *Finnegans Wake* are not what they seem to be. *Apologia* is the Latin and Greek etymological antecedent (*apo* meaning "from" and *logos* meaning "speech") of the word, which has developed different connotations in English. One of the accepted definitions does remain close to its derivation: an explanation or justification, but not an excuse. That is the sense I intend.

Joyce tells us to "look at this prepronominal *funferal* [which is the *Wake*] . . . sentenced to be nuzzled over a full trillion times for ever and a night till his noddle sink or swim by that ideal reader suffering from an ideal insomnia" (120.09–14). I qualify as ideal in perseverance but not in insomnia. Rather, "after years upon years of delving in ditches" (108.17), I accept Joyce's advice "and remember patience is the great thing" (108.08).

Finnegans Wake was first published in 1939, and I have been reading it for more than fifty years. This book is *apo logos* an explanation of "what *Finnegans Wake* is all about." Even before its publication, the *Wake* was the subject of conjecture. Ever since then, numerous enthusiasts and scholars have endeavored to enlighten puzzled readers. Yet the mystery of the work's meaning and significance remains. Academics such as William York Tindall were hopeful that a code to the cryptography of the work could be found. Tindall once wrote that the *Wake* "seems an arabesque—the elaborate decoration of something so simple that it evades us. This simple text . . . is lost in the design" (13). More recent scholars have given up in despair. In her brilliant analysis, *The Decentered Universe of "Finnegans Wake,"*

Margot Norris writes, "The greatest critical mistake in approaching *Finnegans Wake* has been the assumption that we can be certain of who, where and when everything is in the *Wake* if only we do enough research. . . . The formal elements of the work, plot, character, point of view and language are not angled to a single point of reference, that is, they do not refer back to a center." The *Wake* "represent[s] a decentered universe, one that lacks a center that defines, gives meaning, designates and holds the structure together." Remembering Tindall, she concludes that "there is no such thing as a 'simple text' in *Finnegans Wake*" (120).

I have found the "simple text." This book shows how it is embodied in *Finnegans Wake* and how its recognition can bring sense and understanding to the chaos.

Besides the two above-mentioned books, there are a few others that have been indispensable in my reading.

A Skeleton Key to "Finnegans Wake," by Joseph Campbell and H. M. Robinson (1944), is often considered outmoded and at times misleading, but it still contains gems of insight and background information. If used with discretion, it can still be illuminating.

The Books at the Wake, by James S. Atherton (1960), is awesome in its erudition. Adaline Glasheen's *Census, Second Census,* and *Third Census* of *Finnegans Wake* (1956, 1963, and 1977) are excellent. The *Third Census* is probably the only reference book one needs for biographical information on persons mentioned in the *Wake,* but Glasheen's earlier prefaces and synopses still provide some insight and record the struggle—with which I sympathize—of a devoted and unpretentious mind groping toward understanding.

It is impossible to read the *Wake* without Roland McHugh's *Annotations to "Finnegans Wake"* (1980; rev. ed., 1991) alongside. Clive Hart's *Concordance to "Finnegans Wake"* (1963) is the road map for locating the territory. I have followed its typographical conventions. Both the original and revised editions of Richard Ellmann's biography of Joyce (1959; rev. ed., 1982) are essential. Page number citations are to the first edition, indicated by the abbreviation JJ1. Of all of Joyce's books, the *Wake* is probably the most autobiographical; it cannot be understood without some knowledge and appreciation of Joyce's travails and foibles.

The Gideon edition of the King James Bible is the most readily available and least corrupt rendition of the 1611 text. *The Other Bible,* edited by Willis Barnstone (1984), contains a satisfactory collection of carefully translated Gnostic texts. And no Joyce reader should tackle *Finnegans Wake* without a Webster's unabridged dictionary close at hand.

All citations of *Finnegans Wake* in the text are to the pages and lines of the seventh printing of the 1939 Viking edition, with Joyce's corrections.

A final note about the text: in order to avoid unnecessary duplication and to interweave the explication of various sections of the *Wake,* I have occasionally placed cross-references in bold type in the text so that the reader will be aware of the connections. These refer to the index entries in the back of the book.

Chapter One

Background

Title

Finnegans Wake is so controversial that even the meaning of the title is the subject of dispute (see Simpkins for a review of the debate). As Richard Ellmann has explained, it comes from an Irish music-hall ballad about a hod carrier who fell from a ladder and whose funeral was celebrated at a wake, where he revived after being splashed with whiskey. The song title (appearing in the *Wake* at 607.16) contains an apostrophe which Joyce omitted in his title, thereby suggesting an altered meaning. Ellmann comments that "the apostrophe [was] omitted because it means both the death of Finnegan and the resurgence of all Finnegans" (JJ1, 556). While this may be true, it only complicates the mystery because it is not apparent who Finnegan or Finnegans are in the *Wake*. Joyce writes, "who guesse his title grabs his deeds" (137.10–11), but only an understanding of the book will reveal the title's meaning. As will shortly become clear, Finnegans are Joyce's Irish compatriots (as Maria Jolas suggests), whose conscience he intends to arouse from torpid slumber.

So the title *Finnegans Wake* may be taken as a plea or a command for Irishmen to awake from their centuries of outmoded ideas of religion, sex, and the treatment of women.

Style

Few other books have been written in a style quite like that of *Finnegans Wake,* a work the author has taken great pains to make so obscure, enigmatic, perplexing, and labyrinthine that it is unintelligible at first reading. Still, the human mind is so constructed that puzzles and riddles are an entertaining challenge, particularly when presented to be such. It is safe to say that most people consider the novel unreadable, and yet a few persist in trying to discover a solution. Understanding some of the work's idiosyncrasies will help the unscrambling.

The first frustration to overcome is the neologism. In his effort to reorganize the English language, Joyce invented thousands of new words, almost all of which are based on the same etymological principles as standard English. It is well known that he read etymological dictionaries for pleasure; his addiction to word derivation resulted in word synthesis. His artifices have been compared to Lewis Carroll's *portmanteau* words, which carry a briefcase full of meanings. Joyce's usage is slightly different, however. First of all, the sheer volume of them presents an overwhelming assault on the reader's comprehension. To pause to decipher an occasional word is stimulating, but to be confronted with page after page with no clue as to what is intended is exhausting. The neologisms are not frivolous or merely stuck in as decoration. They all have meaning that is directly connected with the subject matter. The problem, of course, is to discern the topic of discussion, and that is what this book sets out to explain.

An example will illustrate the rewards of an effort to unravel the enigmas. "Painapple" is obviously not exactly a pineapple although its rough exterior could be imagined to cause pain if rubbed hard on the skin. As used at 167.15, it is compared to a bomb, so it might be considered a hand grenade, for which "pineapple" is a slang equivalent. But at 246.28–29, we find "the devil took our hindmost, gegifting her with his painapple," and here we can recognize that it is the apple with which the Serpent tempted the woman. In other words, sex. The gift resulted in the pain of God's curses and expulsion from Eden. But also, as the first usage reminds us, there is the pain of death that resulted from God's refusing access to the Tree of Life.

Most of the problem words involve a far more complicated deciphering. There is a process of Wakean logic, which consists of a string of associations mirroring actual brain activity. Without intending a technical discussion, one can say that memory requires neuron connections which the mind records as association of ideas. Improper or false connections are normally discarded by an acculturated screening process so that we usually strive for a logical mental image which projects the "real world." When "unreal" associations remain, they may be labeled insane, creative, or artistic. Somewhere in this latter category the language of *Finnegans Wake* allows formation of an image which may be dream-like and unscreened by logic processes. Often the associations are only klang words—that is, words which when pronounced sound similar but whose meanings are logically unrelated. Common figures of speech involve simple one-step associations, but the Wakean figures require successive associations through several steps, each suggesting that which follows. An example of this is "The only man was ever known could eat the crushts of lobsters" (624.35–36). This seems like a straightforward sentence except for "crushts," which—if it means that crusts are lobster shells—does not express a likely behavior of the "man." Now whenever eating or food is mentioned in the *Wake,* it is a reference to the forbidden fruit; and as will be shown in Chapter 5, a lobster is equated to an earwig, which in turn represents the biblical Serpent. The implication is that the Serpent "crushed" the fruit, despoiled it by having sex with the woman before the first man Adam did, as some old myths claim. Furthermore, eating crushed fruit seems somehow sinful and therefore results in the Fall.

If all this sounds unnecessarily complicated and oblique at this point, it will become clearer as this book develops. To borrow a metaphor from the computer trade, the difficulty you experience in attempting to understand *Finnegans Wake* arises from the conventional programming of your brain. It is necessary to reprogram it with Joycean software.

A word of caution must be offered regarding neologisms: Joyce's vocabulary was so extensive that what often appear to be invented words are actually legitimate, although frequently they are rare or obsolete ones. Therefore unfamiliar words should advisedly be checked in an unabridged dictionary. For example, at 572.24, the phrase "practising for unnatural coits" would suggest that "coits" means "coitus," but it is actually a dialect variation of "coat" and refers to the coats God made for Adam and Eve (Genesis 3.21). Another example is "awn" (154.05), which only a zoologist would know refers to a barbed appendage to a snake's penis.

A second obstacle to comprehension is the ubiquitous use of foreign words. They are usually chosen because they sound as though they might be neologisms or merely English. An example is "Malmarriedad he was reversogassed by the frisque of her frasques and her prytty pyrrhique" (20.31–32). This clause uses the French terms *mal maridade, frisque, revergasse,* and *pyrriche* (all referring to dances); and *frasques,* which means "prank" or "trick." An additional reference is to Pyrrha of Greek myth, who, with her husband Deucalion, repopulated the world after the flood (thus a parallel to Noah and his wife). With these clues we can understand the sentence to imply that although "dad" (Adam, our first forefather) had an unfortunate marriage to Eve, she reversed his discontent by her pranks and dances, and together they populated the world. This example also illustrates the necessity of Roland McHugh's *Annotations,* which translates many of the foreign expressions found in the *Wake.*

A third frustration is the lack of quotation marks. Often we can tell that someone is speaking by the indented paragraph beginning with a dash, but only occasionally is the speaker identified. Sometimes the speech may be interrupted by a second speaker in the middle of a paragraph with no punctuation so indicating, as in the middle of ALP's letter at 616.35 (see Chapter 8). At other times there is not even a dash—as in Book I, Chapter 7, where Shem and Shaun and sometimes Joyce, the author, speak. In the Norwegian captain episode we are fortunate because each of the characters can be identified by the way the word *said* is spelled ("sayd," "sagd," and so on; see Chapter 7). Book III, Chapter 3, offers a challenge because the four evangelists converse with St. Patrick as well as the other characters. It is not always possible to ascertain whether Matthew, Mark, Luke, or John is speaking, but this is of little importance because they all have the same quest, and it is usually clear that it is either one or the other. We can know who else speaks by what or how they say or ask, once we understand what *Finnegans Wake* is about. Joyce was well aware of the deliberate dilemma he had caused. At 108.33–36 he cautions the reader not to infer "from the nonpresence of inverted commas (sometimes called quotation marks) on any page that its author was always constitutionally incapable of misappropriating the spoken words of others."

One beneficial characteristic of Joyce's style is what Hilary Clark refers to as "networking": the repeated use of categories of words to bring to the mind of the reader one of the themes of the book. For example, whenever eating food of any sort is mentioned, it embodies Adam's accepting the fruit of the tree of knowledge from the woman. Likewise the well-known inclusion of falls of all kinds, from Humpty Dumpty's to Finnegan's, is intended to incorporate Adam's fate. Other categories—which include clothes, time, and the Bible—are discussed in subsequent chapters. As *Finnegans Wake* itself reminds us, "the scheme is like your rumba round me garden" (309.07). One of the fundamental particulars of the style is the literary use of the psychology of multiple personalities, which is the subject of Chapter 5.

Finally, one of the most overworked ideas is that *Finnegans Wake* is about a dream. It is not, and there is no dreamer. This has been a favorite topic of previous critics stymied by the difficulty of comprehending the novel and the search for some kind of understanding of it. While it may be true that the language resembles the confused remembering of dreams and that the episodes are repetitive, the *Wake* has a straightforward message that is developed from beginning to end. The language is far more elaborate, comprehensive, poetic, and artistic than any dream could be. The obsession with *Finnegans Wake* as dream was fostered by Joyce as part of his publicity efforts, but his own testimonials must be accepted with extreme caution. As Adaline Glasheen comments, "Joyce told other people that *FW* was 'about' other things. I doubt he ever absolutely lied, but I am sure he equivocated like crazy" (*Second Census*, 81). He even confesses to misleading his friends and helpers while writing *Work in Progress* by "giving unsolicited testimony . . . unconsciously explaining . . . with a meticulosity bordering on the insane, the various meanings of all the different foreign parts of speech he misused and cuttlefishing [blackening] every lie unshrinkable about all the other people in the story, leaving out, of course, foreconsciously, the simple worf and plague and poison they had cornered him about until there was not a snoozer among them but was utterly undeceived in the heel of the reel [in the end] by the recital of the rigmarole" (173.30–174.04).

Esthetics

With all these difficulties why should anyone be attracted to *Finnegans Wake*? Why do some of us spend a lifetime rereading, puzzling, and writing about it? Why has it occupied academics and scholars already for fifty years, and continues to do so, as Joyce predicted it would? The answer has to be that it is esthetically satisfying as no other form of literature has ever been. It is perhaps the epitome of twentieth-century artistic endeavor in all the fields of the arts.

The key word of all twentieth-century art is ambiguity. Picasso, Kandinsky, and a hundred other painters have changed the way we look at the world by making us wonder about, and pay attention to, what we are looking at. Brancusi, Caro, Cornell, and their contemporaries have replaced the imitation of nature in sculpture by invention of previously unconceived forms and juxtapositions. Stravinsky, Poulenc, and all those Americans who created jazz have introduced new pleasure into the way we hear sound. The one element common to all these art forms is uncertainty, an obfuscation of sense messages which engages our minds.

No one will argue that *Finnegans Wake* is not ambiguous. It passes the twentieth-century esthetic test because it not only intrigues a serious reader but continues to delight and refresh with each rereading: never the same, always new, eternally seductive.

Much has been written about Joyce's esthetic theory, its supposed foundation in Aquinas and its sublimation in epiphanies. Without wishing to enter into the controversy about its validity or whether the theories he held "As a Young Man" were abandoned as he grew older, it seems evident that epiphanies constitute an important element in the style of *Finnegans Wake*. The word remained in his repertoire: HCE is called "*Father Epiphanes*" (341.27), and St. Patrick responds to a comment by HCE with "How culious [curious] an epiphany!" (508.11).

It is unfortunate that Joyce chose the word *epiphany* to express the sudden insight in which the mind comprehends unexpected associations prompted by a sensory input. His religious training that provided the word also offers *revelation,* which is perhaps more accurate. In any event a strong element of esthetic pleasure is contained in the intuitive, effortless activity of the mind that results in an unexpected insight. The dawning light of discovery is the psychological basis of esthetic pleasure. When we are fortunate enough to experience such a surprise, whatever activity we are engaged in is reinforced so that esthetic comprehension subsequently becomes easier. This is especially true in the cases of the appreciation of humor and the attraction of puzzle solving, two common human attributes.

Joyce created thousands of opportunities for esthetically satisfying epiphanies in the *Wake*. The neologisms, misdirections, puns, puzzles and riddles, the obscurity of the characters, and apparent lack of cohesion and plot all set us up to search for known associations which we call meaning. The fact that they are deliberately obscure and ambiguous makes them all the more challenging and thus the more satisfying when solved.

There is a legitimate question of whether all of the obscenity and blasphemy is necessary and productive. Modern readers can probably no longer be shocked, but the censorship and rejection *Ulysses* received in the 1920s and 1930s may have made Joyce cautious as well as defiant. We do not find the forbidden English four-letter words (with a single exception) in *Finnegans Wake,* but practically every foreign equivalent—as well as multitudinous puns and innuendos, and covert sexual descriptions—is there. It is heterosexual and blasphemous because both support the theology.

The problem of enjoying *Finnegans Wake* arises because we do not have access to Joyce's mind from which to select his intended associations. He used the book as a storage disc for all the bytes of information he accumulated over a lifetime. Previous readers have slowly revealed a wealth of data and recorded it in the literature. McHugh's *Annotations* assembles a software window to enter the *Wake* computer. The password is *Bible*.

Finnegans Wake and the Bible

The idea that *Finnegans Wake* is related to the Bible is by no means new. Almost every commentator recognizes its presence. In *Joyce and the Bible* Virginia Moseley expounds on all of his earlier books but says, "I attempted no more than an introductory explication of *Finnegans Wake*." James Atherton, however, devotes a chapter of *The Books at the Wake* to each of the Old and New Testaments and demonstrates that all of the books of the Old Testament and eight of the New Testament are named. He says, "This shows, I think, that Joyce was intending to contain the Bible in his book by this method" (179); "It was to contain within itself all the sacred books which had ever been written. The method which Joyce adopted to make his book subsume all others was his customary one of selecting fragments from all he could find and distributing the fragments in his own pages" (169).

Joyce, however, goes far beyond just incorporating the Bible along with all other literature. He actually rewrites it, creating a new text and a new theology. Furthermore the third chapter of Genesis, reinterpreted and repeated hundreds of times, is the narrative base of *Finnegans Wake*. All of the events are simply reenactments of the Fall story. There is no action which does not contain Adam and Eve's travail in the Garden of Eden. All conversation relates to it. All of the characters are united into the four mentioned in Genesis 3 except St. Patrick and the evangelists, who merely discuss the actions of the four.

It has, of course, always been known that *Finnegans Wake* is "about" the Fall of Man. Joyce's admission from the beginning can be accepted as one of his completely true statements, although much of his explanation was misdirective and diminuating. What has not been realized is that that is *all* it is about. Virtually every page has the Bible story as its basic level of communication. To understand *Finnegans Wake* readers must maintain a mind set that what they are apprehending is fundamentally nothing but the Fall story with all the other levels of meaning and reference grafted onto and embellishing it. This approach allows us to understand who HCE and Earwicker are and why there are earwigs; the connection among the prankquean, ALP, Issy, and Kate; the relationship of Shem, Shaun, and the ass; and how the Greek fables of the ant and the grasshopper, and the fox and the grapes; and the episodes of Buckley and the Russian General, and the Norwegian Captain are related to the story of Adam and Eve. The rest of this book shows how this was done.

Narrative?

Wake criticism has worked itself into a position of denying that there is a basic narrative but does not give up the plaintive hope that one exists. David Hayman, Bernard Benstock, John Bishop, and Margot Norris, for example, have all concluded that there is no underlying narrative and have evolved different systems of dealing with the dilemma. Others, particularly those older scholars who have devoted a lifetime to *Wake* studies, such as Fritz Senn, still yearn for some "unknown design, matrix, concept, blueprint, *gestalt*, configuration . . . some *germinal deep structure*" (27, 31). Clive Hart pleads, "We are still in need of a satisfactory perspective which will allow us to respond more fully to the whole . . . a thread of English meaning. . . . I plead for a simple meaning because I should like to pay as much attention as possible to the surface . . . its colour, wit and pathos, achieved through the immediacy of image and pattern" (158–61).

Two other early commentators intuited the deep structure but were unable to bring it to full expression because they looked for the same pattern that Joyce had used for *Ulysses*. Adaline Glasheen said, "The story of our first parents in 'Milton's Park' underlies all falls in *FW*. It does not, however, dominate *FW* as the *Odyssey* dominates *Ulysses,* making events assume a predetermined form and sequence" (2). Atherton ventured, "No single book serves the same purpose [as the *Odyssey* for *Ulysses*] in *Finnegans Wake;* perhaps the Bible comes nearest to it, but it is Joyce's bible" (73). He further noted that even though "the parallels between sections of Homer's *Odyssey* and Joyce's *Ulysses* are also occasionally labored and doubtful we have Joyce's authority for their existence" (184). Actually, any connections one can find with Homer are tenuous at best and provide but little help in understanding Joyce's work. Nevertheless, no one has pursued these leads to *Finnegans Wake*. Furthermore, Joyce does provide the authority for the biblical parallel, but until now, it has not been recognized.

Chapter 2 of this book details the evidence showing how the Bible was rewritten. Joyce carefully followed a series of structural parallels that call attention to the form of the *Wake* as being similar to the Bible's. There is also a wealth of internal evidence supporting this proposition. A considerable portion of the *Wake* is devoted to asides to the reader, purporting to instruct him or her on the book's content, structure, and intent, and to explain (or obfuscate) the stories. One group of such recurring asides points out that *Finnegans Wake* should be read as the rewritten Bible. These are collected in the second part of Chapter 2.

The search for "a simple text" as well as a "germinal deep structure" is revealed in the second and third chapters of Genesis, which tell the Judeo-Christian version of the Fall of Man. Although "everybody" knew and Joyce admitted that such was the basis of his novel, he did not discuss it and invariably diverted attention away from the idea, focusing on all the surface subterfuges and misdirections incorporated into the text. All his letters and comments to helpers carefully wove a tapestry of mystery so that the public relations diffusion effectively screened away the core. "Your exagmination round his factification for incamination of *a warping process. Declaim!*" he writes in the *Wake* (497.02–03; my italics), disclaiming the 1929 book he had inveigled his friends to write. Unfortunately critics then and now have fallen for the publicity effort.

Joyce's rewriting the Bible does not mean that he reworks the entire text. Rather, taking the simple Fall story, and repeating it again and again with embellishments and interweaving fables, bits of history, jokes, and personal biography, he rewrites it in the sense of creating a new Bible with its own theology and rules of ethics. Indeed he does not often take the whole Fall story in sequence from the creation of man and woman through the Temptation, their confrontation by God, their being cursed by him, and then exiled. Most of the repetitions utilize the individual episodes either alone or in whatever order suits his purpose—as is demonstrated in Chapter 6 of this study. Furthermore, he uses ancient mythological sources or Gnostic variants of Genesis to support his New Theology.

Genesis 3 is utilized completely differently from the way the *Odyssey* is related to *Ulysses*. In *Finnegans Wake* the Fall story underlies, generates, and is fundamental to all of the action on virtually every page. It is the basic level of narrative. The Bible story is not used as a vague parodic source but is quoted and modified directly, verse by verse. It provides the covert meaning which every reader intuitively seeks. It is the polar gnosis required to guide the novice or the devotee through the delightful surface embroidery and embellishment. It is the purpose of this book to explain how this was accomplished.

Part of the critical denial of narrative involves the claim of circularity, the idea that there is no beginning or end in *Finnegans Wake*. This conception is reinforced by the apparent jointure of the first and last sentences, but this artifice serves the quite different purpose of pointing to a biblical similarity. Repetition rather than circularity establishes the pattern, but it is a special kind of repetition. It never becomes monotonous. It is the type where the more things change, the more they remain the same. The superposition of other stories, events, and points of view onto Genesis 3 produces a narrative that moves from beginning to end to reveal the essence of Joyce's Theology.

In order to accomplish this he utilized Vico's theory of history. Nearly every critic going back to before *Finnegans Wake* was even published has recognized Vico's importance, and it is not the purpose here to add to or dispute these learned discussions. Indeed, Atherton cites Vico's cyclical history to support the cyclical theory of *Finnegans Wake* (29), and I do not argue against the proposition that in a space-time continuum Joyce held with Vico. Atherton also writes: "The book itself is written in cyclic form not because it has no beginning and end—there is an obvious development as the book progresses . . . but because when it has finished *it* has to begin all over again in accordance with Vico's theory" (18; my italics). The *it* which must "begin all over again" is human history and life itself; the *it* is not the book. The sense in which I urge Joyce's use of Vico is in the "development as the book progresses." *Finnegans Wake* is not circular in the sense that, as some have held, one can enter at any page and read randomly without paying attention to a first and last page. Such a haphazard approach can be enjoyable and enlightening, but it will not produce the narrative fulfillment. The narrative pattern is linear and follows Vico's enumeration of successive ages of society.

The authority we have for this approach is no less than Samuel Beckett, who wrote the first essay in the *Exagmination,* ostensibly at Joyce's direction. Vico held that the history of man proceeds in four stages: theocratic, heroic, human, and divine providence. Beckett claimed that Joyce adapted this structure by dividing *Finnegans Wake* into four books with similar themes.

The point is that Joyce clearly divided his book into parts intended to develop as a progression. The embellishments he grafted onto Genesis 3 are intended to provide a series of modifications of the narrative which show how his New Theology overcomes and replaces the encumbering Irish Catholic religion. This encompassing plan is not, however, the enlightening "simple text." That remains the repeated story of God's relationship to his creatures as told in Genesis 2 and 3. All of this will become clearer herein in Chapter 4.

It should be noted that there is much in *Finnegans Wake* which is not narrative. There are many digressions that are comments on the book itself, some apparently intended to aid the reader's comprehension. Others are asides venting Joyce's wrath about Irish life and the clergy or repenting his own behavior.

The New Theology

Perhaps the most quoted phrase Joyce ever wrote is the one at the end of the *Portrait* when Stephen says he intends to forge the uncreated conscience of his race. There is plenty of evidence Joyce intended this autobiographically, and in fact all of his works encompass this theme. *Finnegans Wake* is the ultimate effort.

It is generally agreed that the *Wake* is a religious book, perhaps because of its blasphemy and heresy. This was early commented on by Beckett, who devotes most of his essay on the application of Vico's theories to Joyce's theology in the reference already mentioned. The matter was put succinctly by Atherton: "In a way Joyce is replacing the Old Testament by *FW* and substituting his theology for the religion of the Bible" (179). The same concept was proposed in some detail almost ten years earlier by L. A. G. Strong in his almost forgotten *The Sacred River.* This intuitive clue to meaning was never adequately followed up. Chapter 8 of the present study explores the New Theology and relates it to the text.

Very briefly, the wrathful and vengeful Yahweh was unjustly and unnecessarily cruel. He played a practical joke on Adam by giving him a woman and then exiling him for fulfilling the purpose for which he was created. God instituted death by exiling Adam and Eve, created all wars and calamities, killed his own two sons, and cursed and subjugated women. In the *Wake* he is vanquished, buried, and replaced by a Mother Goddess, who foils death by sex and procreation.

Summary and Method

All of the foregoing propositions are discussed in detail in the following chapters.

Chapter 2 presents the evidence that *Finnegans Wake* is indeed the rewritten Bible. The correspondences are of two kinds: the first are structural similarities common to both books, and the second are specific statements in *Finnegans Wake* supporting the contention.

Chapter 3 carefully goes over Genesis 2 and 3, pointing out the elements of the Fall story which receive so much elaboration in the *Wake.* The various segments are often modified, twisted, and subverted so that they are barely recognizable, and that is why it is necessary to retain a clear image in the mind of the exact wording and event that will promote the formation of a meaningful association. It should be noted that the narrative of Genesis 3 is seldom used in its entirety in any one passage. Rather, the four segments of the Temptation, the encounter with God, God's curses, and the exile all serve separately as motifs. These are considered further in Chapter 6. Sometimes the adaption assumes additional mythological antecedents of the Genesis story. Also there is a whole class of antecedent and competitively contemporaneous literature that is not very well known: the Gnostic texts, which still retain ancient Eastern sources discarded by the Bible compositors. These are used by Joyce as though they were valid Bible references, particularly when he impugns the wrathful God of the Old Testament or seeks to validate the Mother Goddess. For that reason the Gnostic texts are briefly reviewed.

Chapter 4 is a Generic Synopsis. This is a condensed summary of *Finnegans Wake* in which the gist or theme of each page is interpreted briefly in a couple of lines. The word *generic* here means generated from Genesis. The abridgment displays the narrative continuity previously discussed. It should also alert the reader to the Genesis connections and to Joyce's frequent asides and authorial comments. There have been several synopses published since Campbell and Robinson's *Skeleton Key.* This one differs in attempting a guiding interpretation rather than a "translation." Like the others, it proposes titles to the chapters Joyce avoided naming. These seek to indicate the continuity and the theological and biblical relations to be extracted from the text. It is hoped that readers can retain a two-line summary while reading a page in the novel so that the full surface texture of *Wake* language can be appreciated. The more complete Generic Paraphrases will be discussed shortly.

Chapter 5 presents what is probably the most unifying literary device that Joyce uses: the multiple personality. As he seeks to combine all the histories, stories, and books of the world with Genesis, so he subsumes his hundreds of mentioned characters into just four personalities: God, Adam, Eve, and the Serpent. Since these are the players who enact the story of Genesis 3, they must also provide all of the action in *Finnegans Wake.* No matter who seems to be doing what to whom, at the skeletal narrative level all the action is among these four, and they behave as prescribed by Genesis 3. The apparent exception of St. Patrick and the four evangelists (who, incidentally, have the four Irish master historians as their split-personality counterparts) is allowed in the scheme by their being merely commentators on the actions of the principals. With this ingenious invention Joyce is able to condense and unify all the variety and apparent confusion which coalesce in the *Wake*. The failure to recognize the full extent to which he incorporates the device is responsible for much of the present state of *Finnegans Wake* criticism. Every previous writer has been unable to separate HCE from Earwicker when, in fact, they are two separate and opposing personalities. Chapter 5 explains how to rationalize, as Glasheen put it, "who is who when everybody is somebody else" (lx).

Genesis 3 is the codebook for *Finnegans Wake*. It contains the elements and information necessary to decode the deep infrastructure, the underlying basic narrative. Using it to "translate" *Wake* language results in what I call a *Generic Paraphrase*. This term has a specialized meaning herein. *Generic* signifies that the origin of meaning derives from what is recorded in Genesis; it simultaneously means that the paraphrase *generates* the basic level of cognition. This generation is not only of the meaning produced in the mind of the reader; it is generated from the Genesis precursor, with which Joyce undergirds his final expression. *Paraphrase* implies that the intrinsic English meaning is being stated but suffers, as all paraphrases do, from being incomplete and deficient in esthetic satisfaction. Elegance must be sacrificed to comprehension.

Chapter 6 uses Generic Paraphrases to examine how the episodes of Genesis 3 are incorporated, the fragmentary use of which does not normally follow the same sequence in which they occur in the Bible. No doubt this disjunction aides Joyce in his disguising their presence, but his primary purpose is to support his development of a new theology. The Fall story is essentially a simple one; it is not difficult to recognize the episodes if you know they are there or to accept them as part of the narrative in either *Finnegans Wake* or Genesis order. Many but by no means all of these fragments have been collected and are presented, restored to biblical sequence.

Chapter 7 is devoted to a line-for-line explication of some of the most significant passages in *Finnegans Wake*. It is likewise a demonstration of the power of a Generic Paraphrase to render intelligible the densest and most difficult pages. What is required is the proper mind-set. Readers must approach the text with the resolute conviction that Joyce intended his basic level of narrative to be his own peculiar transcription of Genesis. If they seek, they will find. The apparent or surface message must be subverted until the underlying association can be made. Usually the easiest approach is to connect with one of the four principal personalities. Many clues are given in Chapter 5, below.

In Chapter 7 the previous discussions are exemplified with six Generic Paraphrases. It is hoped that they will produce some epiphanies. We start with "The Ballad of Persse O'Reilly," in which it becomes clear that Hosty is God cursing Adam and Eve and defending His own actions. Then comes the "prankquean," one of the most studied yet enigmatic sections. This is presented in great detail because, together with ALP's letter, it is crucial to understanding ALP and her role. The famous triple riddle (Patrick A. McCarthy reviews the surface aspects and previous attempts to solve it in *The Riddles of "Finnegans Wake"*) can be solved by applying the generic paraphrase technique. All previous attempts were thwarted by the inability to identify the characters properly. The "Mookse and the Gripes" is the first of two well-known fables that Joyce combines with Genesis; it provides a devastating portrait of God and His ultimate fate as well as a censorious attack on the Catholic church. The episode of the "Norwegian Captain" is an ingenious blending of a joke with the entire Fall story, which explains the identification of God as the tailor and the earwig as the Serpent. The episode of "Buckley and the Russian General" is perhaps the most difficult to unscramble. This generic paraphrase stretches the limits of Joyce's convolutions in his indictment of God and the resolution of the problems he created. The second fable—so obvious in "The Ondt and the Gracehoper"—shows that Adam, who hoped for God's grace, was denied it in the same way the grasshopper was: both were turned out to die in the cold. There are also, in Chapter 8, sections titled "ALP's Letter" and "ALP's Trial."

Chapter 8, which interprets the New Theology, starts with a selection of passages showing Joyce creating the conscience of the Irish race. He is merciless in his condemnation of his contemporary society and lyrical in his restoration of it. The Joycean heresy that God sinned by creating both death and its philosophical reckoning, time, are extracted from the literary maze. The recurring problem of the Trinity provides comic relief but also some difficulty in resolving into the new scheme; Joyce's solution is revelatory. The wicked God of the Old Testament is replaced by the Mother Goddess, who is, of course, ALP. This startling but logical conclusion is supported by the account of her trial and the decipherment of her letter. The letter and its origin have occupied and mystified *Finnegans Wake* critics since it was first read. The explication here should clarify much of its obscurity. It should also prompt Joycean expounders of feminist criticism to rethink their position.

Chapter Two

The Bible Rewritten

Structural Correspondences

One of the reasons for postulating that *Finnegans Wake* is the rewritten Bible is that Joyce carefully leaves clues of a parallel structure between them. While any one of these correspondences could be considered trivial in itself, their combined effect augments the other evidence to show that the Bible is rather closely followed.

First Word

From the very first word, there is a suggestion that the Genesis story of the Fall has started. It has generally been accepted that *Finnegans Wake* begins in the middle of a sentence—although that is debatable. In any event, the book ends in a verbless phrase, which in turn ends with the definite article and without a period, thus suggesting that the rest of the sentence is lost, to be found elsewhere. The first word, "riverrun," although indented to start a paragraph, is not capitalized—a suggestion that there are previous words. The implication is overwhelming that the first and last words of the book are to be joined. It is certainly meant to appear that *Finnegans Wake* starts in the middle of a sentence as the Genesis story of the Fall actually does.

In the King James Version, the story starts in the middle of verse 4 of Chapter 2. The original compilers who adapted the chapter and verse system continued the Genesis 1 account of Creation into verse 4 and then, after a comma (not a period), started the second lection, which combines with Genesis 3 to tell the parable of Adam and Eve. Joyce not only contrives the similarity but to insure its discovery immediately writes "past

Eve and Adam's" to alert the reader with a double allusion. Lest we forget, we are reminded at 122.03–04 that *Finnegans Wake* has "the vocative lapse from which it begins and the accusative hole in which it ends itself."

Multiple Books

The derivation of the word *Bible* is the Greek *biblia*, "books," and the Bible is, of course, a collection of books. All of the books of the Old Testament, and at least seven of the New Testament, are named in the *Wake*—a fact certified by James Atherton, whose *The Books at the Wake* cites hundreds of books, secular and nonsecular. A common assumption is that by merely mentioning an author or a title, Joyce intended that the entire work would be incorporated; he made no secret of his use of quotations, ideas, and bits of his vast literary sources. In a sense *Finnegans Wake* is a collection of other books.

Multiple Stories

The Bible tells a multitude of stories about a profusion of characters, many of them odd. What are we to make of the many miracles such as the burning bush, getting water from a rock, parting the sea, raising the dead, and all the other unnatural phenomena? What about the talking Serpent and Balaam's ass? Did the sons of God come down and take daughters of men as wives? There are many accounts of sexual activities with varied orientations and frequently with disastrous consequences. Personal struggles, battles, and slaughters abound.

Ostensibly the *Wake* seems to be a similar collection of strange, disconnected stories; it also seems to have enough personalities to warrant a *Census*.

Digressions

Biblical narrative is sometimes interrupted by the insertion of unrelated material. For example, the history of Joseph is split by Chapter 38 of Genesis, a charming account of Tamar, who went to extraordinary lengths to conceive a child. It has nothing to do with Joseph, whose adventures resume in Chapter 39. In other cases events are buried in a plethora of related but divergent data. The history of Moses obtaining the Tablets of the Law, on which the Ten Commandments were written, starts at Exod. 24.12–18 where he ascends Mount Sinai to receive them from God. There is an interval of seven chapters, or 242 verses, before God gives him the tablets at Exod. 31.18. Fifteen verses later, Moses comes down from the mountain, and at 32.19 he sees the people dancing and rejoicing; this makes him so angry that he breaks the tablets. Two chapters, or 58 verses, later he goes up the mountain the second time, and at Exod. 34.1–10 God writes out another set; this time it takes only seventeen verses to get Moses down from the mountain, at 34.28–29.

Following continuity in the *Wake* is equally challenging. Tedious listings such as the "Begats" (Gen. 5.6–32 and 11.11–27) or the excruciatingly detailed description of the ark of the covenant (Exod. 25.2–26.37 and again at 37.1–29) are as effective in diverting attention as Joyce's favored device of cataloging or his asides to the reader on how to read *Finnegans Wake*.

Repetition

The fundamental method of narrative in *Finnegans Wake* is the continual restructure of Genesis 3. There are a wealth of examples of repetition in the Bible where each succeeding version is slightly varied.

The statement that God created man is made three times: at Gen. 1.27, 2.7, and 5.1. Moses's problems with his tablets are told again at Deut. 9.9–10.5. The Ten Commandments are given first in Exod. 2.3–17. They are repeated in Deut. 5.3–21, but the wording in Deuteronomy is identical with that in Exodus in only three commandments, and it varies by one word in four others. Commandments 2 through 5 and 8 and 9 are given for the third time in Lev. 19.3–14, differing slightly in language and adding some others such as "thou shalt love thy neighbor as thyself" (Lev. 19.18) and "Ye shall not round the corners of your heads, neither shalt thou mar the corners of thy beard" (Lev. 19.27).

It is twice reported that Adam had a third son, Seth (Gen. 4.25 and 5.3). God promises Sarah a son at Gen. 17.16–19 and again at 18.10–15. Since "Abraham and Sarah were old and well stricken in age," they thought the idea of Sarah's conceiving was funny and are said three times to have laughed (Gen. 17.17, 18.12, and 21.6). Abraham dug a well and named the place Beersheba, as mentioned at both Gen. 21.31 and 26.33. Abraham passes his wife, Sarah, off as his sister to make her available to the Pharaoh of Egypt and save his own life at Gen. 12.10–20 and does so again at 20.1–2 for the King of Gerar; Isaac, his son, repeats the cowardice at Gen. 26.6–11. At Gen. 6.19–20 the generally agreed number of animals Noah stored in the ark is two, but in Gen. 7.2–3 it is said he took seven of the birds and clean beasts.

Repetition also occurs in the New Testament. Mark, the oldest of the Gospels, was probably compiled around A.D. 70. Matthew and Luke, written about twenty years later, repeat much of their content from Mark. All of the New Testament borrows heavily from Isaiah.

Word Usage

The usage of foreign words in *Finnegans Wake* is an indication of its linkage with the Bible. The English Bible is a translation from foreign languages—from Hebrew and Greek, by way of Latin, into English. The multitude of languages in the world is explained as resulting from the wrath of God in Gen. 11.1–9. The descendants of Noah built a tower at Babel whose top they hoped would "reach unto heaven." To prevent this, God proposed to his cohorts (angels?), "let us go down, and there confound their language that they may not understand one another's speech." This is referred to at least thirteen times in *Finnegans Wake*—notably "babble towers" (354.27) and "the turrace of Babble" (199.31). As explained below, the word *Babel* meant "Babylon" but was also a pun on the Hebrew word for "confusion," a fact which is acknowledged at 15.12: "The babbelers . . . (confusium hold them!)." There is a *Wake*-style pun at 258.11, "And shall not Babel be with Lehab?"; *Lehab* not only is *Babel* spelled from right to left in Hebrew fashion but also means "hearts" in Hebrew. It is appropriate in this rewritten Bible for Joyce to oppose God's action by reabsorbing all the foreign words into the English syntax to make a single language again.

The frequent use of the conjunction *and* to begin a sentence or verse is a characteristic of Genesis and in fact all of the Pentateuch. Such usage is carried into *Finnegans Wake* as a subliminal reminder of the Bible. Likewise *thou* and *shalt* frequently occur when HCE/God is speaking or when He is being ridiculed, as when Jaun amplifies the Seventh Commandment: "First thou shalt not smile. Twice thou shalt not love. Lust, thou shalt not commix idolatry" (433.22–23). When God is announced just before the Gracehoper poem, he is "Thou-who-thou-art" (418.7) to mock the Exodus "I AM."

Masoretic Consonants

All of the original manuscripts of the Old Testament were written with the classical Hebrew alphabet (including brief portions in Aramaic, a cognate language that used the same letters), which consists of only twenty-two consonants. The vowel sounds that made the words intelligible were transferred orally through generations of rabbis. Such a practice compounded the many mistakes made by the copyists of the writings over a thousand years. Around A.D. 200, the Jewish leaders compiled the Old Testament from those manuscripts still available, and their document is known as the Masoretic ("traditional") text. In order to preserve what they regarded as the correct pronunciations, the rabbis added diacritical signs to the consonants. Apparently there were several such schemes, but after the sixth century, those developed at Tiberias prevailed (recognized in *Finnegans Wake* at 123.30: "Tiberiast") and are still used in Hebrew Bibles.

The rabbis did not always agree with the text and would frequently write a different vowel sign in the margin to alter a word in the text. One word they universally avoided was the name of God, which was forbidden to be spoken aloud. This was written as *YHWH,* which they wrote in the margin with vowel signs that made it mean "My Lord." Over the years the original pronunciation, which was probably Yahweh, was forgotten, and the translators into Greek and Latin, and subsequently English, read *YHWA* as *LORD.* The *Wake,* however, remembers "Yawhawaw" (619.34).

Joyce parodies this system of writing to disguise the name of his God with the letters HCE. The results are explained in detail in Chapter 5. He also used the scheme to alter *Jesus* into *ass* (see **Adam**). Joyce's following the Hebrew shorthand is another indication of *Finnegans Wake*'s ties to the Bible.

Puns

There has been some unfavorable criticism of Joyce for his liberal use of puns—comments relying on the old saw about its being the lowest form of humor. But "punns and reedles" (239.36) are an essential part of his esthetic and literary technique and add to the sublime hilarity of the *Wake.*

The biblical pun generally recognized in *Finnegans Wake* is the one at 307.02: "When is a Pun not a Pun?" The answer "Isaac" in the left margin refers to Gen. 17.16–19, where God told Abraham that He would give him a son: "Then Abraham fell upon his face and laughed and said in his heart, Shall a child be born to him that is an hundred years old? and shall Sarah, that is ninety years old bear? . . . And God said, Sarah thy wife shall bear thee a son indeed; and thou shall call his name Isaac." *Isaac* means "He laughed." Other puns occur when God changes the name *Abram* ("high father") to *Abraham* ("father of a multitude") and *Sarai* ("mockery") to *Sarah* ("princess"). Puns are very common in the Old Testament, a fact not generally realized by *Wake* readers. The Masoretic text makes punning almost inevitable when mistakes or changes in the vowel sounds automatically change the meaning of a consonantal word. The pun was therefore widely used as a mnemonic device. Pun usage in *Finnegans Wake* is another of its structural correlations to the Bible.

Below is a sampling of puns from Genesis:

2.7 "And the Lord God formed man from the dust of the ground." The pun is on *adham,* meaning "man," and *adhama,* meaning "ground" or "dirt."

3.20 "And Adam called his wife's name Eve; because she was the mother of all living." *Hawwah,* meaning "mother of all living," is a pun on *hayah,* "to live."

3.21 At this point in the Hebrew manuscripts, Adam is called by name for the first time. Although the King James Version names him freely from Gen. 2.19 on, this was an error corrected in the Revised Version. The error can be excused as a pun because when *adham* is used with a definite article, it means "man"; without the definite article the word is a proper name: Adam. Wakeans contemplating the final "the" should think about this.

5.29 "And he called his name Noah saying, This same shall comfort us concerning our work and toil." *Noah* is derived from the Hebrew verb meaning "to rest."

10.25 ". . . the name of one [son of Eber] was Peleg for in his days was the earth divided." *Peleg* means "division."

16.11 The angel of the Lord told Hagar that she should call her son "Ishmael; because the Lord hath heard thy affliction." *Ishmael* means "God heard."

29.32–30.24 In all, four women bore eleven sons to Jacob, each of whom was named with a pun. Leah, who had six of the sons, also had a daughter, but they must have run out of puns; the girl was called simply Dinah.

21.30–31 Abraham had dug a well on Abimelech's territory, an act to which Abimelech objected. Abraham gave him seven ewe-lambs, and the men took an oath of peace. They called the place *Beersheba,* a name that is a pun: it means both "Well of Seven" and "Well of an Oath."

3.1 "Now the Serpent was more subtil than any beast of the field." *Subtle* here means "crafty," which in Hebrew can be punned for "naked."

2.22 "And the rib, which the Lord God had taken from man, made he a woman." In ancient Sumerian, *rib* is the same word as that meaning "to make alive."

11.9   "That is why they called it Babel because the Lord there made a Babel of the language of all the world." Babel was *Babylon,* a word which in Babylonian meant "the gate of the gods." The pun is on the Hebrew *balal,* meaning "to confuse."

Internal Correspondences

Joyce devotes a significant portion of *Finnegans Wake* to asides and instructions to the reader that show he intended it to be understood as a rewritten Bible. The following is a collation of such passages. In some places, Generic Paraphrases are provided in brackets.

4.20–25   The clues start almost immediately, indicating that Finnegan's history began before the old Bible books of Joshua, Judges, Deuteronomy, Numbers, or Leviticus were written "and all the guennesses [the people in Genesis] had met their exodus [Adam and Eve had been exiled] so that ought to show you what a pentschanjeuchy [Pentateuch + Punch and Judy as man and woman] chap he was!" It ought to show us that Finnegan is Adam and this is his Bible.

18.17–24   The "claybook paragraph" indicates that *Finnegans Wake* is a version of the Bible. "Claybook" is an acknowledged neologism, but it suggests an ancient book; "what curios of signs" connotes (among other things) cuneiform writing on clay tablets. The Gilgamesh story and other precursors of Bible myths were so written. The statement "this claybook . . . in this allaphbed!" indicates that *this* claybook is *Finnegans Wake* and that *Finnegans Wake* is also this aleph resting place. Now *aleph* is not only the first letter in the Hebrew alphabet; it also means the Codex Sinaiticus, a fourth-century manuscript of the Bible. [Can you read its word-world?] shows that *Finnegans Wake* is to be read as the Bible. "It is the same [as the Bible] told of all" the characters, Adam, Eve, the Serpent, and God, but with "Miscegenations on miscegenations." "Many . . . Tieckle . . . Meades and Porsons" refers to the biblical writing on the wall in Dan. 5.25–28.

597.04   [Of all the strange things that ever happened, it was not to be anticipated in a hundred and one pages of eddas or odes found in tombs or caves. The entirety of life's living being the one theme of this riverrun book . . . totally within the old story but told in a new language. Why?

.10 Because, grace be to God, whose words were the beginning, there are two sides to turn to, the past and the present, the right and wronged side, and so forth. Why? . . . One is

.16 a story about a bride and eating fruit and fighting with the Father but the other is of suffering, tombs, old clothes {Gen. 3.21}, cursings and chafing heat, war and enmity. Why? Every speaker has his day to bring his thoughts to life with all his dreams, perhaps, with luck,

.20 to be made known.]

614.27 After the discussion of Joyce's New Theology and just before ALP's letter is the claim of *Finnegans Wake* as the rewritten Bible:

[Our whole undermining, mill-wheeling, measured-by-Vico's-cycles, four-dimensioned, guiding-light creation (the "Mother Goddess Gospel" known to every scholarly critic); self-provided with an applauded, coupling, lascivious, old fashioned process (for the common man and his descendants and their common sense morals); known as

.32 birth, coitus, death, and regeneration; receives through the idea of the Fall of Man the meticulously separated elements of the preceding biblical divulgence; for the purpose of subsequent recombination so that the heroic eroticisms, catastrophes, and eccentricities transmitted

.36 from the ancient legacy of the past, by type and place,

615.01 by collecting, editing, and translating, with emphasis on primitive religions such as sun worship; since the days of Pliny and Columella when hyacinths, periwinkles, and daisies symbolized Aphrodite's ancient rite; all this cross connected, assimilated, and identified by esoteric

.06 knowledge; in fact the same old Adam personality of our Finn character structured and composed in the image of HCE/God may be there for you, fellow Irishmen, at the

.10 fertility feast as sure as ALP writes in her letter.]

107.08 "The proteiform graph itself is a polyhedron of scripture" equates *Finnegans Wake* with an image of the Bible. The text continues: [There was a time when naive literary scholars would have dismissed it as the rewriting by an all wet,

.10 incorrigible criminal, writing both sides of the dogma, unjustly critical and presenting a strange multicolored view. To the hardly curious student of lust-love it has shown a mosaic of immature sexuality in which the eternal

.15 hunter of scapegoats, God/HCE, beloved of assaults, sequesters and persecutes his female creation {Gen. 2.16}. Closer inspection of the stories {*Finnegans Wake*} would reveal the multiple personalities inflicted on the documents {Bible and related myths}; and some interpretation of a virtual

.25 crime might be made by anyone unwary enough. In fact the traits featuring their differences coalesce into one personality, eliminating their contrarieties; for example, similar to the providential warring of the heartshaker {ALP/woman} with the housebreaker {HCE/God,

.31 who exiled Adam and Eve}.

.36 Who in hell wrote the darn thing anyhow? An erect,

108.01 seated charlatan with a turbid or pellucid mind . . . interrupted by helpers . . . or a too-pained

.07 whittlewhit laden with stolen learning {both Joyce}.]

118.12 [Somebody named Cock or Bull wrote it . . . but one who thinks deeply will bear in mind that it is all in his

.18 mind's eye. Why? Because in the "So for him," that is, the writer's Bible if it comes to that (and subsequent commentators will cry it from the housetops, as sure as the writing on the wall {Dan. 5.5}, to the common man); every person, place, and thing in the cosmos connected with the story was changing all the time: the continually "intermisunderstanding minds" of the characters will be variously inflected, differently pronounced, and otherwise spelled, and will be

.28 changing their speech characteristics.]

20.04–16 "But the horn, the drinking, the day of dread . . . a ramskin" refers to the Talmud, the Jewish Bible; "chip them, chap them, cut them up allways [always and all ways]" indicates that the ancient text has already been edited, rewritten [including by Gutenberg and as the

Koran] until the newer versions contain "hides and hints and misses in prints" [hidden and obscure meanings and misprints]. "So you need hardly spell me how every word will be bound over to carry three score and ten toptypsical readings throughout the book of Doublends Jined," says Joyce, meaning that the word of the Bible will be carried over into the upset and obscure readings of *Finnegans Wake.*

256.14–23   "For here [also hear] the holy language. Soons to come . . . Too soon are coming tasbooks and goody, hominy bread and bible bee [textbooks are coming testing *Finnegans Wake* as Bible {as in a spelling bee} as well as taste tests for bread, honey, sugar, and jam {all suggesting the forbidden fruit}] . . . from the Four Massores [four masters but also Masora, the Hebrew language of the Bible] . . . and what happened to our eleven in thirtytwo antepostdating the Valgur Eire [and what happened to Adam and Eve with the Serpent and exile in the Vulgate Bible and the vulgar Ireland as Eden]." (See **Time: 1132**)

189.28–31   Shaun/Brawn castigates Shem/Joyce for writing *Finnegans Wake:* "seeker of the nest of evil in the bosom of a good word" can be read: seeker of an evil God in the words of the Bible; "you, who sleep at our vigil and fast for our feast" is Joyce, the lapsed Catholic; "you with your dislocated reason, have cutely foretold" is the writer of *Finnegans Wake;* "a jophet in your own absence" is Joyce, a joker who was not a prophet in his own country.

374.16–36   This passage clearly establishes *Finnegans Wake* as the New Bible written by Joyce, "the Boy of Biskop" [the Boy Bishop]. It is "Epistlemadethemology for deep dorfy doubtlings" [*Finnegans Wake* epistle made theology for doubting Dubliners]. "Hence counsels Ecclesiast" [Joyce the preacher counsels like HCE/God]. "The find of his kind! An artist, sir! . . . How you fell from story to story" shows the story of the Fall repeated in *Finnegans Wake.*

424.32–35   "Every dimmed letter in it is a copy and not a few of the silbils and wholly [holy] words. . . . The last word in stolentelling [stealing and retelling the story of Genesis]."

464.02–05 In this passage Jaun/Shaun is commenting about Shem/ David/Joyce: [Monsieur David/Shem as Christ and God's son is a close equivalent. Take notice how I employ your crib {translation of the Bible}. Be aware as you and I {Shem and Shaun aspects of Adam} fall while you copy the Bible].

113.18–22 [It is an old story, the tale of Tristan and Isolde {as well as Adam and Eve}, of a mountain {God} holding the earth down and his pal the Serpent let loose and on the run; of what God could do but the Serpent wouldn't; of all rivalry and battles; and why Kate (ALP/Eve) takes charge of the world.]

212.32–36 "Foul strips of his chinook's bible I do be reading [heretical parts of Adam/Joyce's primitive or native bible], dodwell disgustered but chickled with chuckles at the tittles is drawn on the tattlepage" [theologically disgusting but filled with chuckles at the jokes on *Finnegans Wake;* such jokes as "God said, 'Let there be man!' And man was. Ho! Ho! God said, 'Let there be Adam!' Adam was. Ha! Ha!"].

293.16–18 "And, heaving alljawbreakical expressions out of old Sare [Sarai was Sarah's name before she conceived Isaac] Isaac's universal of specious aristmystic [false ruling mysticism = Bible] unsaid. . . ."

293.F2 "O, Laughing Sally, are we going to be toadhauntered by that old Pantifox Sir Somebody Something [unnamed God], Burtt, for the rest of our secret stripture [*Finnegans Wake* as the secret Bible]?"

350.31–32 "raiding revolations over the allbegeneses" [in addition to referring to massacres caused by God's edict of death, it also suggests that reading *Finnegans Wake* involves reading the revelations of a book which is all Genesis].

489.28–34 Yawn is talking to St. Patrick about: "my shemblable!"

[Shem/Joyce, the blabber who wrote a Bible], and St. Patrick replies, "That letter selfpenned to one's other, that neverperfect [Joyce made constant revisions even after publication] everplanned [and planned writing it at least since *Portrait*]?"

123.30–35 "The unmistaken identity of the persons in the Tiberiast duplex [Talmud] came to light in the most devious of ways . . . on holding the verso against a lit rush this new book of [Moses]."

579.10–21 In a series of pseudo proverbs we find "Renove that bible" [Remove the old Bible and replace it with the renovated version, *Finnegans Wake*. {See also 71.16, where one of the names that Earwicker/Adam is called is "*Remove that Bible*"}]. Another proverb is "Herenow chuck english and learn to pray plain."

110.16–20 [Nobody having studied the subject in Aristotle or the Bible will go out of his way to applaud the author,] "for utterly impossible as are all these events they are probably as like those which may have taken place as any others."

Chapter Three

The Origin

The Genesis Narrative

It might be presumed that every reader of *Finnegans Wake* has already read the Genesis story of the Fall of Man. But the Bible is the most published and least read book ever written. It is more likely that they have read Milton's or Dante's variation, at least more recently, than Genesis. It is a mistake when approaching *Finnegans Wake* to assume that you know and remember the Bible story unless you reread and consider the exact details and wording, for this is the framework on which the *Wake* is constructed.

There is no copy of the Bible in the remnants of Joyce's Paris library (see Connolly), so we do not know for certain which edition he used while writing *Finnegans Wake*. However, he left behind four copies in Trieste when he moved to Paris in 1920 (Gillespie). He claimed ownership of three of these by stamping "J. J." on the flyleaves. The fourth copy, an 1825 Authorized Version apparently rebound, was the only one showing signs of having been read, but there is no stamp on the flyleaf. Michael Patrick Gillespie reports, however, that "Joyce told Arthur Power that he felt the English version of the Bible more poetic, more powerful than the French" (48). This "English Version" would have been the Authorized or King James Version, so-called because it was first published in 1611 as the result of the work of Anglican theologians convened by James I. It is the version divided into chapters and verses, and uses language that has perhaps become archaic but still remains poetic and is typified by "thee," "thou," and "thy." This is to be distinguished from the Revised Version written in contemporary English, first published in 1884 as an attempt to make the Bible more understandable; containing numerous "corrections," its text is divided into chapters and paragraphs. It is important to recognize the distinction between "version" (of which there are primarily the two Protestant ones mentioned, although there are of course Jewish, Catholic, Adventist, and other versions) and "editions," of which hundreds have been and continue to be published. Editions vary in content as well as form. The Gideon edition of the King James Version is recommended for *Finnegans Wake* correlation as being readily available and the least corrupt, and the Oxford Study Edition of the New English Bible (a Revised Version) is recommended for Bible explication.

James S. Atherton (and others) have discussed biblical references in *Finnegans Wake,* pointing out that almost every book of the Bible is incorporated by name, and direct quotations are prolific. The purpose here is not to establish the well-known fact that Joyce made extensive use of the Bible, but to review those portions of Genesis which he used directly to produce the narrative and format of the *Wake.*

Joyce makes little use of the first chapter other than verse 27:

So God created man in his own image, in the image of God created he him; male and female created he them.

Since God created man in His own image, God and Adam are so confused in the *Wake* as to be separated only with great difficulty. It is to be noted that a distinction is made in the case of the female. Although she was created by God, the text does not say she was made in His image. This fact allows Joyce to create a special relationship for ALP.

The story of the Fall of Man begins in the second chapter of Genesis, and significantly it begins in the middle of the sentence in verse 4:

These are the generations of the heavens and of the earth when they were created, in the day that the LORD God made the earth and the heavens,

The part of this verse preceding the first comma belongs with and is the summation of the story of the Creation in Genesis 1. The second phrase, after the comma, is the start of a different version of the Creation, which establishes the situation for the Fall. The Revised versions of the Bible "correct" the mistake of ancient compilers by replacing the comma with a period and starting a new paragraph with the phrase "In the day that the LORD God. . . ." One reason for holding that Joyce used the King James

Version is that he adopted the same "mistake" by apparently beginning *Finnegans Wake* in the middle of a sentence.

In Genesis 2, when God creates man, the woman is conspicuously absent:

> 2.7 And the LORD God formed man of the dust of the ground, and breathed into his nostrils the breath of life; and man became a living soul.

Having created man God gave him a heavenly place to live and work:

> 2.8 And the LORD God planted a garden eastward in Eden; and there he put the man whom he had formed.
> .9 And out of the ground made the LORD God to grow every tree that is pleasant to the sight, and good for food; the tree of life also in the midst of the garden, and the tree of knowledge of good and evil.

The man was such an exact image of God that he was also immortal, being allowed to eat from the tree of life. Only one food was forbidden:

> 2.16 And the LORD God commanded the man, saying, Of every tree of the garden thou mayest freely eat:
> .17 But of the tree of knowledge of good and evil, thou shalt not eat of it: for in the day that thou eatest thereof thou shalt surely die.

Now God noticed His error in creating Adam and decided to correct it:

> 2.18 And the LORD God said, It is not good that man should be alone; I will make an help meet for him.
> .21 And the LORD God caused a deep sleep to fall upon Adam and he slept: and he took one of his ribs, and closed up the flesh instead thereof;
> .22 And with the rib, which the LORD God had taken from the man, made he a woman, and brought her unto the man.

Adam could now be happy forever if it were not for God's practical joke, which Joyce detected:

> 2.23 And Adam said, This is now bone of my bones, and flesh
> of my flesh: she shall be called Woman, because she was
> taken out of Man.
> .24 Therefore shall a man leave his father and mother, and
> shall cleave unto his wife: and they shall be one flesh.
> .25 And they were both naked, the man and his wife, and were
> not ashamed.

One other verse from the second chapter of Genesis is significant: Gen.
2.10 is connected to the extensive use of the number four and relates
especially to the four evangelists and the Four Masters in view of the pun
on the word *head;* the verse is also a source of Joyce's enumeration of rivers
in Book I, Chapter 8, of the *Wake:*

> And a river went out of Eden to water the garden; and from thence it
> was parted, and became into four heads.

The events of Genesis 3 are the generic basis for the narrative in *Finnegans
Wake.* The individual segments are not often used sequentially; that is, the
story in Genesis 3 is not often told in its entirety in any one passage, nor are
the segments necessarily used in the same order in which they occur.
Instead, these various sections are what David Hayman (1978, 135) refers to
as "nodes": they supply the implied action onto which is grafted apparently
extraneous events and personalities. Nevertheless they can always be detected as the basic level of narrative. The first segment tells of the woman's
temptation:

> 3.1 Now the serpent was more subtil than any beast of the
> field which the LORD God had made. And he said unto
> the woman, Yea, hath God said, Ye shall not eat of every
> tree in the garden?
> .2 And the woman said unto the serpent, We may eat of the
> fruit of the trees of the garden:
> .3 But of the fruit of the tree which is in the midst of the
> garden, God hath said, Ye shall not eat of it, neither shall
> ye touch it, lest ye die.
> .4 And the serpent said unto the woman, Ye shall not surely
> die:
> .5 For God doth know that in the day ye eat thereof, then
> your eyes shall be opened, and ye shall be as gods, knowing
> good and evil.

Then comes Adam's seduction. It is to be noted that sexual intercourse is not mentioned but only implied by metaphor, nor is the fruit of the tree named an apple. Both of these accepted readings have come down to us through ages of interpretation and repetition.

> 3.6 And when the woman saw that the tree was good for food, and that it was pleasant to the eyes, and a tree to be desired to make one wise, she took of the fruit thereof, and did eat, and gave also unto her husband with her; and he did eat.
>
> .7 And the eyes of them both were opened, and they knew that they were naked; and they sewed fig leaves together, and made themselves aprons.

The encounter of Adam with God is the segment used most frequently, from the Mutt and Jute episode to ALP's recollection of "that hark from the air" (624.28):

> 3.8 And they heard the voice of the LORD God walking in the garden in the cool of the day: and Adam and his wife hid themselves from the presence of the LORD God amongst the trees of the garden.
>
> .9 And the LORD God called unto Adam, and said unto him, Where art thou?
>
> .10 And he said, I heard thy voice in the garden, and I was afraid, because I was naked; and I hid myself.
>
> .11 And he said, Who told thee that thou wast naked? Hast thou eaten of the tree, whereof I commanded thee that thou shouldest not eat?
>
> .12 And the man said, The woman whom thou gavest to be with me, she gave me of the tree, and I did eat.
>
> .13 And the LORD God said unto the woman, What is this that thou hast done? And the woman said, The serpent beguiled me, and I did eat.

With God's curses, the vengeful, angry God of the Old Testament becomes evident. While He specifically cursed only the Serpent and the ground, the fate to which He sentenced both Adam and the woman is generally considered to be the curse on mankind. Focal points often repeated in *Finnegans Wake* are the snake's crawling on his belly and getting his head bruised by a heel; the woman's sorrow, her desire for her husband, and his dominance over her; and Adam's working in sweat and returning to the dust.

3.14 And the LORD God said unto the serpent, Because thou hast done this, thou art cursed above all cattle, and above every beast of the field; upon thy belly shalt thou go, and dust shalt thou eat all the days of thy life:

.15 And I will put enmity between thee and the woman, and between thy seed and her seed; it shall bruise thy head, and thou shall bruise his heel.

.16 Unto the woman he said, I will greatly multiply thy sorrow and thy conception; in sorrow thou shalt bring forth children; and thy desire shall be to thy husband, and he shall rule over thee

.17 And unto Adam he said, Because thou hast hearkened unto the voice of thy wife, and hast eaten of the tree, of which I commanded thee, saying, Thou shall not eat of it: cursed is the ground for thy sake; in sorrow shall thou eat of it all the days of thy life;

.18 Thorns also and thistles shall it bring forth to thee; and thou shall eat the herb of the field;

.19 In the sweat of thy face shalt thou eat bread, till thou return unto the ground; for out of it wast thou taken: for dust thou art, and unto dust shalt thou return.

Poor Eve finally gets a name after being sentenced to bear children, and God becomes a tailor. Joyce makes salient use of God's coats as a symbol for the preparation for banishment by Kersse the tailor.

3.20 And Adam called his wife's name Eve; because she was the mother of all living.

.21 Unto Adam also and to his wife did the LORD God make coats of skins, and clothed them.

Finally comes the exile. Details of special relevance are God's conversing with others, possibly angels, saying "Behold, the man is become one of us" suggesting He was not alone; his exiling Adam from the Garden of Eden to prevent him from eating of the tree of life; and his placing Cherubims with flaming swords at the east portal:

3.22 And the LORD God said, Behold, the man is become as one of us, to know good and evil: and now, lest he put forth his hand, and take also of the tree of life, and eat, and live for ever

.23 Therefore the LORD God sent him forth from the garden of Eden, to till the ground from whence he was taken.

.24 So he drove out the man; and he placed at the east of the garden of Eden Cherubims, and a flaming sword which turned every way, to keep the way of the tree of life.

Examples of how these specific segments turn up in *Finnegans Wake* are given in Chapter 6.

The Gnostic Texts

We know that Joyce was familiar with some of the pagan Gnostics. He associated "Trismegistus" with Shaun in his letter of August 14, 1927, to Harriet Shaw Weaver; and he mentions "Hermes" twice in *Finnegans Wake* (81.07, 263.22). Hermes Trismegistus, "Thrice-greatest Hermes," is the fictitious name attributed to the author of a second-century Egyptian Gnostic treatise. Plotinus ("plantainous" in the *Wake* at 470.20), also Egyptian but from the Greek sector of Egypt, writing in Rome in the third century, and Dionysus the Areopagite ("aeropage," 206.01), a Syrian from the sixth century, were two other pagan Gnostics. The Hermetic writing was known and used from Augustine to Giordano Bruno. There were also Jewish Gnostics and Christian Gnostic sects—one of the latter being that of the Manichaeans, founded in Persia in the third century by Mani (Glasheen [165] finds him in the word *manipulator* in the *Wake* at 472.20). Since Augustine was a Manichaean before converting to Christianity, it is likely Joyce knew something of their teachings.

The known Gnostic manuscripts comprise an exceedingly complex body of theogony and creation myths. They are often illogical, difficult, and inconsistent. Yet there is internal evidence in *Finnegans Wake* that their teachings are an abundant and dominant source of *Wakean* theology.

The strong religious ferment occurring in Judaism about the time of Jesus gave rise not only to the sect which has come down to us as Christianity but to a number of others collectively known as Gnostic. These were sometimes, but not always, Christian in that they discussed Christ and his origin in aspects which varied from the New Testament. They differed in detail but generally agreed that the Jewish God Yahweh was evil and corrupt and that the origin of the world arose from a struggle of Light and Darkness which resulted in good and evil. They all retained a dominant Mother Goddess (derived from Astarte, Cybele, and the Syrian Aphrodite) who was generally known as Sophia.

The Greek word *gnosis* means "knowledge," and the various Gnostic cults had esoteric and mystical systems for self-knowledge which were necessary for salvation. The esteem for *gnosis* was accompanied by a disdain for *pistis* (faith), which was associated with ignorance and held to be a biased belief imposed by the clergy. Gnosticism was defiantly opposed to traditional Jewish and Christian beliefs. The God worshipped in church and synagogue was not good and was associated with the Zoroastrian devil. Adam and Eve were heroic in their disobedience, aided by the beneficial Serpent, who gave them knowledge. The biblical God was the one who brought misery and corruption to the world by his evil act of creation, which was an attempt to catch spiritual light and hide it in ignorance and darkness. Such were the general tenets of the Gnostics, and such theology is embraced in *Finnegans Wake* by the antipathy between HCE with Adam and ALP.

The Manichaean creation myths (see Barnstone, 1) provide background which explicates the dialog between HCE and ALP in her letter. These myths hold that the highest member of the divine hierarchy is the Father of Light, and from him emanates Sophia, the Mother of Life. Sophia wanted to bring forth a likeness out of herself but did so without the consent of the Father of Light. The result was not a likeness but an ugly and imperfect monstrosity. To conceal it from the other immortals, she pushed it down into the darkness and it became Ialdabaoth, Prince of Darkness. The Gnostics held that Ialdabaoth was the Christian Yahweh, a "jealous God" because He knows He is not the sole divine power.

Another text, *On the Origin of the World,* has a section "The Raising of Adam from the Mud by Eve," which contains essential information for understanding the prankquean. With the help of six angels Ialdabaoth/ Yahweh created a man out of mud, but the man had no spirit in him because Yahweh had no light, so He left the body for forty days without a soul. Sophia, Mother of Life, saw this and sent her breath of life into the man. He began to crawl about but was not able to rise up. When Yahweh and the six angels [are these whom He addressed in Gen. 3.22?] saw the man, they rejoiced and left him to behave like an animal.

Then Sophia sent her daughter, Zoë-Eve (this could be the prankquean), as an instructor to raise up Adam, in whom there was no soul. Zoë-Eve said:

I am the portion of my mother and I am the mother. I am the woman and I am the virgin. . . . My husband is the one who begot me and I am his mother and he is my father and my lord.

When Eve saw her "co-likeness" (Barnstone, 70) cast down, she pitied him and she said, "Adam, live! Rise up on the earth." Adam rose up, and when he saw her, he said, "You will be called 'the Mother of the Living' because you are the one who gave me life."

In the next section, called "The Rape of Eve by the Prime Ruler (God) and by His Angels" (70), Yahweh sent seven archangels to investigate, and when they saw what had happened, they said, "Let us seize this female light-being and cast our seed on her so that when she is polluted she will not be able to ascend to her light but those she will beget will serve us." But they did not tell Adam that she was not derived from them but put him to sleep and had him dream that she was made from his rib so that he would rule over her.

But Eve laughed at them, darkened their eyes, and left her likeness there stealthily beside Adam. She entered the tree of knowledge and remained there and became the tree. The blinded archangels ran away in fear; but when they came back, they saw the likeness and thinking it to be the true Eve, raped her, even though "her first voice, which before spoke with them, 'What is it that exists before you?'" [This could be the source of the idea of a prankquean riddle.]

Then the seven archangels took counsel and warned Adam and Eve not to eat from the tree of knowledge. But the God of Darkness came as the Beast and tempted them. This Gnostic account is contained in the sentence in *Finnegans Wake* at 32.06–12 (with added Irish and other characters), which can be paraphrased: Put aside the fallacy that it was not God the king Himself but Zoë-Eve (inseparable sisters) who came down into the world when God's angels attacked Adam and who were presented by Sophia as Issy and Lilith.

The section ends in a kind of apocalypse anticipating ALP's dominance over HCE, in which Sophia "will put on a senseless wrath. Then she will drive out the gods of Chaos. . . . She will cast them into the abyss. They will be wiped out by their own injustice" (Barnstone, 74).

A Gnostic sect which is specifically included in *Finnegans Wake* is the Ophite—a group who included the Serpent in their worship, holding that he redeemed humanity by imparting knowledge of disobedience to the curse of the laws of Yahweh. The branch of the cult in Ireland was banished by St. Patrick, thus establishing the legend of his casting out the snakes. We find "ophis workship" in the *Wake* in a discussion of ancient Irish pagan worship (289.07); St. Patrick calls attention to Ophicus, which is the Serpent constellation (494.09); and HCE/God claims "Obeisance so their sitinins is the follicity of this Orp!" (494.22). The Ophites believed in a reformed concept of the Supreme Being as a trinity which consisted of (1) Primal Man, (2) the Son, equated to intellect or reason, and (3) the Spirit, a female principle equated with the waters and personified by Sophia, known for her prudence and wisdom. Their version of the Creation and the Fall was typically Gnostic. The Spirit let fall upon the waters a ray of light, which was Sophia, and from the contact came Ialdabaoth the "demiurge." He produced Six Powers and the Serpent and then announced himself as the Supreme Being. The Six Powers created man, who gave thanks to Primal Man and not to Ialdabaoth. This made Ialdabaoth so jealous that he created a woman to destroy man. Sophia foiled the destruction by sending the Serpent to persuade Adam and Eve to eat of the tree of knowledge, but Ialdabaoth/Yahweh banished them from paradise to earth.

Another associated text is *The Secret Book of John* from the second century (Barnstone, 51). It relates a conventional Gnostic theogony, holding that the highest deity is the Father of Light and that Yahweh is below him. Sin and evil came about, not through Adam and Eve's disobedience, but through Yahweh's act of creation, which He did with arrogance, vanity, and ignorance. Yahweh took light from His mother, Sophia, and trapped it in His human creations. As a result mankind struggled to return to the Father of Light, beginning the process of redemption by eating from the tree of gnosis (knowledge). Not only does the treatise reflect Joyce's view of original sin; it is written as a dialogue between John and Christ, a format which Joyce uses in *Finnegans Wake* in Book III, Chapter 1, for the development of the Shaun personality.

The last Gnostic book to be mentioned was not discovered until 1945, two years before the Dead Sea Scrolls, when a Coptic translation from the original Greek was found in Egypt; it was not published in English until 1977. Obviously Joyce could not have seen it, so we must relish it as one of those correspondences of which Joyce himself was so fond. It is called *The Paraphrase of Shem!* (101). To read it is an eerie experience, for it sounds as though the events happened to the Shem of *Finnegans Wake,* although it was written almost 2,000 years ago. The following quotations establish its flavor.

Shem has an ecstatic experience; he says, "My mind . . . snatched me away from my race. . . . And my mind separated from the body of darkness as though in sleep." In this condition he receives a revelation from Derdekeas, who is the Son of the God of Light and therefore a Gnostic Christ. These are some of the messages from Derdekeas:

Shem, since you are the first being upon the earth, hear and understand what I shall say to you concerning the great Powers who were in existence in the beginning. . . .

And from the Darkness the water became a cloud. And from the cloud the womb took shape. . . . And when the Darkness saw the womb he became unchaste . . . and he rubbed the womb . . . and when nature had taken to herself the mind . . . of the dark power, every likeness took shape in her. . . . Nature rose up to expel it; she was powerless against it . . . she brought it forth in a cloud. And the cloud shone. A mind appeared in it like a frightful harmful fire.

For the Hymen of Nature was a cloud which cannot be grasped; it is a great fire.

Return henceforth, O Shem, and rejoice greatly over your race and Faith. . . .

And in order that the sin of Nature might be filled, I made the womb, which was disturbed, pleasant—the blind wisdom. . . .

O Shem, no one who wears the body will be able to complete these things. But . . . when his mind separates from the body, then these things will be revealed to him.

A demon will come forth from the belly of the Serpent. . . . Many will loathe him. A wind will come from his mouth with a female likeness. Her name will be called Ab*alp*he [my italics].

So Adam was called Shem and talked with Christ two millenniums before Joyce thought of the idea.

Chapter Four

A Generic Synopsis of *Finnegans Wake*

The following is a one- or two-line synopsis of each page of *Finnegans Wake*. It is *generic* in that it emphasizes the derivation from Genesis and also gives the gist of a page's content. The summary does not attempt to cover the apparent allusions or surface meaning but seeks to look for the underlying message. It provides a clue as to the intent of each page. To discover the detailed narrative action requires the application of the Generic Paraphrase technique as shown in Chapter 7. This synopsis indicates the continuity of the narrative line and the development of the New Theology. It also serves to distinguish Joyce's comments from the narrative.

Book I, Chapter 1: The Fall in Ireland

3. Long before history the Fall took place in a Dublin park in east Ireland (Genesis 2 and 3).

4. What arguments there have been about that Fall.

5. There are 1,001 versions of what the original sin actually was.

6. Anyway, the result was death for mankind, which can be celebrated only at an Irish wake.

7. In those days there was a woman, lovely as a river, and a mythical man, now dead.

8. In a museum you can see relics of battles that remind you

9. of the disagreement between the man and woman and God which resulted in the Fall.

10. Though it happened in Eden, in this book the locale is hidden in more than fifty other places.

11. The woman was afraid of thunder and lightning, but when the rainbow appeared, she gathered all the fruits of the garden, including the forbidden one to which we fall heir.

12. Regardless, the union of man and woman is what makes life worth living, even in

13. one of the fake locations like Dublin.

14. According to ancient history two sons were born, but the records were then lost

15. until St. Patrick Christianized the Ireland of the Vikings and the races were mixed. A legend tells (Gen. 3.8–19)

16. how prehistoric man (Jute) met God (Mutt) in the garden and

17. how God rebuked Adam, sentenced him to death and cast him out, because

18. Adam and Eve sinned. From prehistory through ancient history, people kept on loving and

19. fighting. This book illustrates the history of mankind by telling what happened in Ireland

20. up to modern times. Before any books like the Bible or the Koran were printed our story begins with Eve.

21. In Ireland this is like Grace O'Malley, who was turned out of Howth Castle as Adam and Eve were expelled from Eden.

22. Eve and her descendants liked to sin, but God tried to "save" them twice with a flood and Christ.

23. But the sin was more fun than the saving. Except for this happy Fall, there would be no clergy.

24. Adam, cursed to till and toil, invented whiskey and the wake ritual to ease the pain of death. Finnegan's

25. Wake as celebrated in Ireland commemorates man's virtues, the release from Adam's toil

26. and his entry into heaven. Life goes right on after one dies.

27. Your children will carry on. Don't worry, your family will get by with the aid of some whiskey.

28. Your wife will remain as happy as you made her. Finnegan reminds us

29. of Adam, whose descendants we are. We too will produce offspring because of Adam's Fall.

Book I, Chapter 2: What Adam Did

30. The origin of man is given in Genesis, where we are told how Adam heard God walking in the Garden of Eden.

31. Adam admitted he had sinned, induced by the Serpent [the earwig in Ireland], and God turned Adam out.

32. Whether truth or myth, we all bear the stamp of Adam and continue his passion with woman.

33. Some would have you believe his affair with Eve in Eden was immoral.

34. Many interpretations are put on the "forbidden fruit," but the eating was only natural.

35. Another version of the story tells of the encounter of our ancestor with God, a cad, who started the conversation by asking the time

36. and telling Adam he may live in Eden and eat everything except the forbidden fruit (Gen. 2.16–17).

37. Adam thanked Him for the warning but forgot when he ate his wife's delicious supper.

38. Eve remembered the Serpent's recommendation and persuaded Adam that eating the fruit was

39. worth the risk. They should steal it like Tom, the piper's son, who stole a pig.

40. Adam in a drunken sleep talks of his coitus and is heard by Hosty, the hostile God.

41. Hosty/God and some priests woke early, crossed Dublin by the underworld, savoring the fruit,

42. had some drinks, and sang a ballad that was taken up by a

43. motley crowd and subsequently printed [as the Bible]

44. and publicly repeated or sung as Hosty wrote it:
45. Like Humpty Dumpty, Adam fell and was kicked out of Eden. Why?
46. He lost paradise and left us Ireland. From "knowing" Eve,
47. he acquired death. Now he's buried with other legendary ancestors.

Book I, Chapter 3: Sex Is Not a Sin

48. Everyone who heard the Ballad is dead now too. Of Hosty no end is known.
49. His prophets fought, wrote, and dramatized His message. Later prophets
50. —including Christ, Bruno of Nola, and the Catholic church— continued and confused it.
51. Now no one knows the facts. An explanation was asked of St. Patrick one evening
52. as he drank some stout. He showed on television God's first worker in the park (Gen. 2.15),
53. and now the Irish people talk of the Fall and how man/Adam met God; of history
54. illustrated; and directions to the toilet in many languages. Likewise *Finnegans Wake*
55. tells no single story but retells the theme of the biblical Fall with mythical equivalents,
56. copying other religions and their prophets. For example, In the beginning a poet lived in paradise, but where was it and why should he be there?
57. It has disappeared. Some think it is Ireland, but this is an illusion. A cursed tempter
58. persuaded him to accept the fruit with its consequences. Another version is that the first woman did it. Other opinions come from
59. ALP, a talker, an undertaker, a rewrite man, a gourmet, a tennis player,
60. a barmaid, a hero, a martyr, a missionary, a bookie, a bullfighter, a choir leader, two authors,
61. a girl detective, a politician, and a sailor. But are any of these fables true?
62. He fled to a refuge with his wife, but trouble followed him. As God had taught him in Eden, so man fought
63. man, and Cain killed Abel. Although God insisted on His own innocence,

64. the gate to Eden was closed (Gen. 3.24). Even the movies tell the story.

65. Daddy Browning and Peaches had intercourse and suffered the shame.

66. It goes on all the time. Will Eve ever tell her side of the story? She overcomes death

67. with sex. She told God He was wrong in condemning man to death. When Lilith left, Eve

68. attracted Adam. Though naive, he coupled with her. God's curse has

69. followed Adam, and that is the story. It concerns the expulsion at the east gate of Eden (Gen. 3.24). Joyce's

70. retelling the myth as *Finnegans Wake* reflects that he, like Adam, was outcast, threatened, and reviled,

71. being called many damning names,

72. but he remained silent and left Dublin,

73. retaliating with his books. Like Adam and HCE/God he will become immortal

74. through *Finnegans Wake*.

Book I, Chapter 4: Joyce Rewrites the Bible

75. Reminiscing of the joys of Eden, Adam fathered descendants,

76. founded civilization, died

77. and was buried and given a wake.

78. His descendants became wicked, and brothers fought each other.

79. Women also played their role—comforting, marrying,

80. restoring peace, and bearing children. God condemned the wickedness

81. and caused the Flood (Genesis 6).

82. Then God gave man another chance with Noah and the ark (Genesis 7).

83. Noah's family as well as birds and beasts were saved (Genesis 8).

84. But the rest of earth-life was destroyed (Gen. 7.17–24). The waters receded

85. and the dove showed the Flood was over.

86. Noah's family and the animals emerged and sacrificed to God.

87. God provided food (Gen. 9.3) and forbade the shedding of human blood (Gen. 9.6).

88. But Noah got drunk (Gen. 9.21) and fell asleep naked

89. and was covered by his two sons. God confused Noah's descendants' language (Gen. 11.7)

90. and scattered them over the face of the earth (Gen. 11.8), including Ireland.
91. God told Abram, "Go from your country . . ." (Gen. 12.1). Abram built an altar on his way to Egypt,
92. where his beautiful wife posed as his sister and married the pharaoh (Gen. 12.11–19).
93. The pharaoh exiled Abram, his wife, and removed his wealth from Egypt. These Bible tales are in *Finnegans Wake,*
94. where the stories are told anew, a new testament to exile.
95. Adam finds woman again and prefers her to God.
96. This theme of forbidden fruit has been used repeatedly. We are its heirs,
97. as the history of Parnell's
98. and Joyce's lives demonstrates.
99. Both were reviled in Ireland. But Joyce will rise again
100. and, though exiled across the ocean, will get his revenge by writing the story of God's murdering Adam;
101. also the story of Eve, who comforted and defended fallen Adam
102. and protected his grave and reputation, and who, as ALP, becomes the metaphor
103. of a flowing river.

Book I, Chapter 5: How to Read This New Bible

104. Eve's version of the Fall and the defense of Adam
105. have been told many times
106. under many titles.
107. *Finnegans Wake* is a many-sided Bible about multiple personalities fused into one character.
108. Patience is required to read this history, which incorporates all previous literature.
109. To appreciate it, one must look beneath the appearance of the words.
110. A myth from China to Ireland starts with the Creation by a hen on a dump [the Creation by the Gnostic Sophia].
111. But the truth is, mankind was created by man's ejaculating into woman.
112. So even if you don't understand, let us continue with the myth by the hen/ALP.
113. It is the old story of man and woman, temptation, good and evil,
114. told in all languages, starting with Albanian and mixing up all the world's literature.

115. When Adam mated with Eve, was it incest when she was his daughter made from his body?

116. The Serpent promoted their sin, which the Church mitigates with the sacrament of marriage.

117. The sin is known in all languages, but stimulated by wine, mating continues.

118. Though this happened before the Flood, the myth has been preserved by retelling right up to this book,

119. which defines the sin, supported by philosophy and organized tautology,

120. disguised by transposed letters, misspelled words, and so forth, requiring an ideal reader to decipher it

121. like an obscure ancient manuscript such as *The Book of Kells*

122. or a red-lettered *Rubaiyat*

123. or even *Ulysses.* This New Bible

124. offers communion, confession, and the state of grace before the Fall

125. and is written as an Irish myth by Shem/Joyce.

Book I, Chapter 6: A Catechism of Riddles

126. Q1. Which of the many names of Adam—who was made in the image of,

127. and is here confused with, HCE/God—should be selected from Irish geography, plants, food, people (rich, poor, rulers, servants), literature, songs, sayings, plays, myths (some fake), history, old religions, politics, plots,

138. battles, and wars?

139. A. Finnegan. Q2. Did Eve know Michael, whose name means "looks like God"? A. She did know Adam (Gen. 3.6). Q3. Where is Eden?

140. A. Dublin. Q4. Just Dublin? A. Also Belfast, Cork, Galway, and all Ireland.

141. Q5. Who did evil deeds there? A. J = Jahweh = HCE/God. Q6. How did He treat the woman? A. He cursed her.

142. Q7. Who did those original occupants of Eden become? A. Sleeping Irishmen. Q8. How are the women? A. Contrary.

143. Q9. If the reader were to dream all this, what would he dream? A. *Finnegans Wake* Q10. How did the love match occur?

144.– A. Issy/Eve/ALP/and others tempted

48. Adam/Swift/Joyce/and others (Gen. 3.6).

149. Q11. Did Adam sin, and should he have been exiled? A. No. Consult Bergson, Einstein,

150. Wyndham Lewis, Lévy-Bruhl, Darwin,
151. Pythagoras, Spangler, and the space-time controversy.
152. A parable will explain. Adam in the form of Mookse (the pope who gave away Ireland-Eden) took a walk in Eden
153. by a river like ALP and met God [Gripes].
154. God said, "Tell me all." The pope said, "All popes have pronounced Your word." God: "I am bound by what you say?"
155. Pope: "That is what I tell all my believers. I excommunicated all Dubliners
156. and proposed bulls, heresies, and schisms for a thousand years." God: "Still there are Mohammedans and pagans."
157. God and the pope cursed each other and ignored the first woman [Issy] as they quarreled.
158. "Stupid men," said Issy. God was silent, and the pope composed a new edict. Issy took the pope back to Eden, and ALP took God to heaven.
159. So God was wrong. However, Eden and woman were left. We continue, but
160. you still don't understand. Let us talk some more.
161. Here is another parable. From milk you can make *either* butter *or* cheese.
162. Thus, Burrus and Caseous are so opposed that they are a metaphor for enemies
163. and all kinds of opposites. Truth lies in the union of opposites. Consult Nicholas of Cusa and Giordano Bruno.
164. Consider the woman's point of view.
165. As depicted by [Joyce's enemy/opposite] Wyndham Lewis,
166. as a thoroughly modern woman, fond of men and babies,
167. she likes butter *and* cheese, that is, *all* men, but one man best, only if she is united with him.
168. But men continue to be enemies. Q12. Are they accursed? A. We are (Gen. 3.17–19).

Book I, Chapter 7: Biblical Brothers

169. Consider an accursed man like Shem/Adam or James Joyce.
170. Cursed man is like an imitation man, poverty stricken,
171. an Irish [Eden] exile, a drunk, a whoremaster, non-photogenic,
172. a debtor, a scrounger,
173. a prig, a heretic, an author of scurrilous and obscure books, and
174. an obsequious coward. In the beginning, before the Fall,
175. before woman was made and tempted, before the curse and expulsion from Eden,

176. man played in Eden-Dublin and avoided fights,
177. as did cursed Joyce—studying, writing, drinking, fucking,
178. getting educated (in school and out)—that is, eating the fruit of the tree of knowledge (Gen. 2.17)
179. and being found out (Gen. 3.9). To justify his actions
180. he wrote out his confession [*The Portrait of the Artist as a Young Man*]
181. and left Dublin-Eden, with the help of a woman (Gen. 3.12) and new clothes (Gen. 3.21),
182. to earn his living abroad. He was ashamed of his old home
183. but wrote lovingly and critically of it in *Finnegans Wake*.
184. He enjoyed his new clothes and exotic food (Gen. 3.6),
185. but his caustic writings were censored and criticized at home (Gen. 3.10–11),
186. so he rewrote the whole story [*Finnegans Wake*-Bible]. But God found them hiding (Gen. 3.8–9),
187. and they left Eden. Shaun/Brawn tells his version.
188. Shaun (innocent, uncursed, clerical) reprimanded Shem (cursed, God-hating)
189. for contraception, blasphemy, avoiding marriage, and writing *Finnegans Wake*,
190. and also for abandoning home and family.
191. God promoted enmity between the brothers (Gen. 4.4–5), and Cain killed Abel (Gen. 4.8).
192. James Joyce alienated his brother Stanislaus,
193. and Stanislaus [Abel] concluded that James [Cain] was mad,
194. but they were still brothers (although opposites) born of the same mother.
195. Since Eve is the mother of us all, we are all brothers.

Book I, Chapter 8: The River as Woman and Mother

196. The washwomen tell the parable of Adam and Eve (Genesis 3)
197. in metaphors of heroes and a feminine river [ALP].
198. ALP procured the fruit for Adam although he first kept the garden alone (Gen. 2.15).
199. Then God made a woman (Gen. 2.22) as Adam's helpmeet (Gen. 2.18),
200. and she did her best to please him.
201. But she got bored and wanted babies.
202. She flirted at first,
203. then gave kisses to Michael [in Hebrew, "who is like God" = Adam],

204. though she was just a young and not-so-innocent girl,
205. whose original name was Lilith or Issa. HCE/God was like a cold snowy mountain at the river's source, condemning Adam.
206. She made a plan to seduce Adam. First she bathed,
207. then put on her jewels and her makeup
208. and dressed.
209. She started out like a river with rivulet tributaries,
210. distributing appropriate presents in sorrow to her children according to God's curse (Gen. 3.16) and, like
211. Pandora, loosing evils on the world but also giving hope.
212. It's all in the Bible,
213. but the version you hear is just their dirty laundry,
214. especially from the Irish clergy. But God's edict of death persists (Gen. 2.17), and
215. in the end the River/ALP merges with the sea to begin the life cycle again,
216. for we are her children and heirs (Gen. 3.20).

Book II, Chapter 1: The Mime of Adam, Serpent, and Woman

219. The Adam and Eve story is recast as a mystery play with charades of children's games. GLUGG is Adam played by Shem;
220. CHUFF is HCE/God played by Shaun; HUMP is the exiled Adam played by Michael/Adam; IZOD is the innocent woman played by Issy; ANN is the fallen Eve played by ALP; a female chorus;
221. a male chorus; SAUNDERSON is the Serpent; and KATE is the exiled Eve. These are the announced [but mostly unused] cast.
222. God prohibited eating the fruit (Gen. 2.17), but Adam was possessed by the Devil and wanted a helpmeet (Gen. 2.20).
223. So God created one (Gen. 2.21), and Adam named her "woman."
224. The tempted GLUGG/Adam wanted the woman (the chorus dances out his desire),
225. but he only masturbated. He heeded God's warning, but IZOD/Issy did not understand why.
226. She sits depressed while the rainbow chorus dances out her desire.
227. The Serpent/Devil comes to tempt her, but the chorus girls repulse him with a game plus Catholic sacraments.
228. The Devil escapes back to hell
229. and contemplates writing an exposé of Ireland like Joyce wrote *Ulysses* about the Irish;
230. and like other historical affairs. As a result she would be sorry. Or he might write

231. juvenile poetry! That gave him such a toothache that he exorcised himself

232. out of hell to try to tempt her again.

233. Again the girls repulse him, and he slinks away.

234. Now the chorus dances to Shaun/CHUFF, alluring him

235. and sings a psalm praising the Garden of Eden,

236. which Ireland resembles.

237. Then they pray, exalting Shaun's innocence

238. but forecasting his Temptation and Fall,

239. with its consequences to mankind. The Serpent frets

240. in hell, then rose in defiance of God

241. and tempted the woman,

242. saying "you shall not die . . . you shall be as gods" (Gen. 3.4–5).

243. The woman persuaded Adam to eat the fruit (Gen. 3.6).

244. They knew they were naked like the animals Adam had named, and they hid in the garden

245. from God (Gen. 3.7–8).

246. Then God called Adam (Gen. 3.9) and the woman.

247. He discovered their sin (Gen. 3.12) and gave them clothes (Gen. 3.21).

248. The woman admitted her guilt (Gen. 3.13),

249. and Adam did too (Gen. 3.12).

250. The chorus dances a celebration of their happy fault.

251. Adam was afraid (Gen. 3.10). [Joyce here encourages the reader to believe that *Finnegans Wake* is about Adam and Eve.]

252. God cursed him (Gen. 3.17–19), and Adam was dejected.

253. He knows his Fall has unfairly damned mankind.

254. Mythology and the Bible tell stories of man's struggles as *Finnegans Wake* does those of Adam,

255. who starts as an Irish hero and ends up as a pub keeper. The woman produced from Adam's rib becomes the seductive ALP.

256. The hen will rewrite the holy word as *Finnegans Wake,* with its hodgepodge of people, things, and places, especially Dublin.

257. The play ends with the lightning of the flaming sword and the thunder of the slamming door of Eden (Gen. 3.24).

258. The exile of Adam and Eve started history; their children will learn by hearing the story [Book II, Chapter 2].

259. Pray to God and hope for his grace.

Book II, Chapter 2: The Lesson of Creation

260. In the beginning the earth was void and without form (Gen. 1.1–2).

261. God made the earth and heaven (Gen. 2.4). But who, where, and which god?
262. This history studied by the children will give the details. There are other theories of creation such as the Greek,
263. Egyptian, Persian, Europane, Scandinavian, and so on—besides the scientific and biblical ones.
264. This history will be of all mankind started in the garden in Dublin
265. at Chapelizod, a place similar to the one
266. where the children now study. The conflicting natures of man
267. and his desire for woman will result in big trouble
268. as well as great pleasure. Woman has been the great uniter of opposites and solver of problems
269. with her feminine understanding and love.
270. All mankind are comforted by Eve's daughters, although Eden is lost forever.
271. The history of wars from Punic to Irish started with God's prohibition of the fruit (Gen. 2.17) and the Serpent's interference (Gen. 3.1–5).
272. The Serpent tempted Eve, saying: "Don't deprive your husband. Think of the future.
273. Don't worry. Things will get better." It was a convincing speech, but it led to war—
274. like the Cherubims with the flaming sword (Gen. 3.24) and like the Celts held off the Vikings.
275. Later the English invaded Ireland.
276. But what does God care? We practice religious rituals derived from Greek myths,
277. but woman's role remains the same while history repeats itself,
278. and God's imposition of death continues in spite of Christ and the Bible.
279. Issy resents God's curse on women and prefers the old Norse gods.
280. The children must memorize the Genesis story of the Fall.
281. The ancient classical world has fallen, overcome by Christianity
282. even though it cursed man. The catechism is taught to children from infancy
283. like arithmetic, but it is not the truth.
284. Higher mathematics proves the combination of Adam and Eve to be a complex equation.
285. Permutations of the affair produced historical repetitions beyond comprehension.
286. So let's start a new creation myth. The first problem is to construct the earth from chaos

287. and put some rivers there (Gen. 2.10–14). The second, to make man (Gen. 2.7). Note that the feminine river is needed, not just dust.

288. Also study the average comings and exits from Ireland by St. Patrick,

289. who converted that country to Christianity by eliminating snakes and preaching hell's fire; and of Tristan

290. and Isolde with their forbidden affair, which was

291. like the first one (but he had two Isoldes) or the Irish version of Dermot and Grania.

292. Clothes won't prevent it (Gen. 3.21). Persist with the *Finnegans Wake* litter of times, languages, and people.

293. The third problem: construct woman, not from Adam's bones as he slept (Gen. 2.21–22), but by algebra

294. and geometry, and put her in Eden-Dublin. History will repeat itself

295. like a dream-vision

296. of the mating and Fall of Adam and Eve. The vision of Eve and the mating

297. is a metaphoric fusion of geometric forms and rivers

298. with some calculus, logarithms, and trigonometry thrown in.

299. So we learn the facts of conception and life.

300. Would you support a clergy that serves a God who cursed man

301. and posted the flaming sword (Gen. 3.24), who conducts masses with the fear of the Devil

302. and extracts the tithe? Adam wouldn't.

303. Lots of Irishmen didn't. Cain didn't (Gen. 4.3–8).

304. It makes more sense and it is certainly more fun to

305. read *Finnegans Wake*. Joyce forged it for years, hoping for reader support, waiting for recognition

306. and maybe a Nobel Prize. It covers all subjects

307. with lessons from ancient characters.

308. It explains the Creation and its repetition throughout space and time.

Book II, Chapter 3: Parables of Adam's Fall

309. In a modern version Adam is a Norwegian captain

310. of Viking heritage. The God (Host) of the Viking-Irish-Eden is about to

311. expel Adam/captain and his wife. First, God hailed them (Gen.

3.9), then cursed them (Gen. 3.16–19), and then tailored clothes for them (Gen. 3.21).

312. They wanted to stay in God's grace but

313. He expelled them (Gen. 3.22–23). The curse has continued to all men

314. from God through the Fall. But what about God's curse on woman? A second version says

315. the Serpent tempted her (Gen. 3.1–5). She ate the fruit and gave to her husband (Gen. 3.6)

316. that which God had forbidden. They hid, afraid; but God forced a confession (Gen. 3.8–13)

317. that Adam ate (and drank) and was naked and afraid (Gen. 3.10–11), and the woman gave him the fruit (Gen. 3.12).

318. With the eating they consummated the marriage sacrament.

319. Adam confessed they had sinned and were naked. God made them clothes and drove them out (Gen. 3.21–24).

320. The captain did not like God's clothes, curses, or banishment. His wife comforted him, but they were driven away by the flaming sword.

321. A third version comes from the drunks in a bar inspired by the [Holy?] spirits:

322. The Trinity said, "Show obeisance." But that is just dialectic. The vengeful God brought about the Fall.

323. God said, "Where art thou? [Gen. 3.9] You sailed with the woman. I'll make you fall and give you clothes" (Gen. 3.17–21).

324. Adam: "I was afraid and naked." God: "You sinned" (Gen. 3.11). His curse (Gen. 3.17–19) is forecast as bad weather ahead.

325. God sentenced the man and his wife but with reservations to forgive and save their descendants through Christ

326. and St. Patrick (in spite of the Vikings). Adam heard God's voice (Gen. 3.10). God said to the Serpent,

327. "Curse you, go on your belly. Woman and her descendants (including St. Patrick's mother) shall bruise your head" (Gen. 3.14–15).

328. God said to Eve, "To overcome your temptation, marriage will be instituted" (Gen. 3.16).

329. In Ireland this sacrament became a great celebration,

330. with many mixed marriages. Marriages produce children,

331. who fight like Cain and Abel, the Ondt and the Gracehoper, or the Mookse and the Gripes.

332. After the Fall, Adam and Eve continued to have intercourse.

333. Why did God open the door to sex (Gen. 2.24) and then curse woman to monogamy, submission, and painful births (Gen. 3.16)

334. yet have liturgies about Virgin Mary? Why promote war between brothers?

335. The story of Buckley and the Russian general is a metaphor of the confrontation of Adam by God (Gen. 3.10–19).

336. The story starts again in the garden which Adam tended (Gen. 2.8), eating fruit (Gen. 2.16), once improperly (Gen. 3.6).

337. In this *Finnegans Wake* version God, a Trinity, played an unfair prank on Adam and Eve.

338. As for war, God/TAFF expelled Adam/BUTT (Gen. 3.22–24), sad and disgraced. Using holy symbols, God promoted war.

339. God rejected Cain's sacrifice (Gen. 4.5). He demanded animal sacrifice like Abel's (Gen. 4.4), Montezuma's, and the Light Brigade's.

340. The vengeful God made a scapegoat of Adam (as the Russian general)

341. and made a virtue of murder by encouraging war. Buckley was Irish, thus trained in this religion

342. with its public confession, absolution, collecting money, horse racing, gambling, and breeding.

343. God challenged Adam/general (Gen. 3.11), and he confessed (Gen. 3.12) and was afraid (Gen. 3.10).

344. God cursed Adam and the Russian general; Adam sympathized with the general

345. and prayed for mercy. God offers hurt and sorrow and the mass, which offers forgiveness.

346. God/TAFF: "Both you and the general must die."

347. Adam/BUTT: "There has been defeat and death in Ireland always in spite of St. Patrick and his religion."

348. God: "Liquor helps." Adam: "Yes, from ancient heroes right up to modern battles."

349. God: "I gave fighters women." (His vicars also offer extreme unction to dying soldiers.)

350. Adam: "You support terrible fighters with massacres,

351. guns, promises, cigarettes, drinks, and whores. I did no wrong until

352. the Serpent tempted." God: "You get the same treatment as the Russian general." Adam: "He's doomed."

353. In the name of God, for the detriment of man, die, and be damned. (Man is destroyed.)

354. God: "I shot my own son?" Adam: "Sure enough." God and Son merge [two-thirds of the Trinity] and promise peace and forgiveness.

355. So man wins over God and enemies by merging opposites. This universal truth

356. must be told in *Finnegans Wake* although unrewarded, suppressed, and censored like *Lysistrata*

357. or the *Arabian Nights,* which treat sex humorously; *Finnegans Wake* reveals man's relationship

358. to God like some old theological heresies such as the Pelagian

359. by retelling the Old Testament story. Like the artificial sound of radio,

360. church bells and organ music suggest the Holy Spirit, the other third of the Trinity. Adam and Eve

361. had fun and laughter until the Trinity and the Serpent ended it. A funny story.

362. Their subsequent curse of poverty (Gen. 3.17–19) can be seen in Dublin.

363. Who can blame Joyce from escaping it?

364. His exile became part of the retelling of the story, using biographical

365. and fictional counterparts for Adam and Eve.

366. Joyce wrote the story of the Fall while being persecuted and criticized.

367. Man has survived throughout Egypt, Ireland, the Flood, and Vico's ages, and will in the future

368. in spite of guns if we remember the beatitudes and teachings of Christ—

369. not, however, as interpreted by Catholic theologians (but rather the *Finnegans Wake*

370. versions) especially in Dublin.

371. Dubliners escape such religion in pubs, where they are

372. pushed out at closing time (like Adam and Eve from Eden), fearful of retribution of God.

373. Better to read the edification in *Finnegans Wake.*

374. Study it. It is the Bible rewritten

375. especially for Dubliners, using old Irish folk tales and other Irish stories.

376. We think of Eve in the garden making love to Adam and God's betrayal

377. and take communion knowing God killed his own Son as told in the Gospels.

378. The Serpent in the guise of an earwig caused the Fall,
379. and we hear the echoes in *Finnegans Wake.*
380. When the last king of Ireland fell to the English,
381. he got drunk,
382. and Irishmen have upheld the tradition to this day.

Book II, Chapter 4: The Parable of Eve's Fall

383. The story of Tristan and Isolde is also a parable of the Fall. The primeval waters
384. surrounded Irish Eden, where Adam/Tristan and Eve/Isolde made love and were found out,
385. as has often happened since. The love-kiss carried the key to the escape.
386. Historians and biblical authors aside, Ireland was formed by volcanic eruptions
387. by chance where Dublin is now. Then came Adam and Eve and God and the other stories
388. including those of Tristan and Isolde and King Mark. There have been other Marks and other falls,
389. which you can learn about in college. It all goes back to the four: Adam, Eve, Serpent, and God.
390. God expelled Adam from Ireland-Eden and cursed the Serpent to go on his belly (Gen. 3.14)
391. because he tempted Eve. They fell, were naked, heard God, and confessed (Gen. 3.4–12).
392. God, ignoring that He had made them, accused and cursed them (Gen. 3.11–16).
393. He later tried to give grace through Christ and Noah. Adam and Eve in fig leaves hid from God (Gen. 3.7–8),
394. and Tristan and Isolde trysted on the boat, but God knew.
395. He peered, listening and spying. They defied his grace and had intercourse which was
396. oral [that is, "eating"]. Who could blame Isolde or Eve?
397. The Evangelists, the Four Masters, or *The Book of Kells* do not tell this.
398. It would be better to remember the experience of Tristan and Isolde than the taught Irish history.
399. So Joyce and his wife, Nora, experienced and escaped Dublin.

Book III, Chapter 1: The New *Finnegans Wake* Theology

403. A midnight dream of Tristan and Isolde is censored. The scene switches to Ireland

404. and what appears to be Sean the Postman but is really

405. innocent Adam (Shaun) being created by God (Gen. 2.7) in the garden of Eden (Gen. 2.8–9),

406. where food was plentiful (Gen. 2.16).

407. Adam/Shaun was unhappy so God promised him a helpmeet (Gen. 2.18).

408. Adam labored in the garden (Gen. 2.15). [Here the two stories of the Fall and the Stations of the Cross merge the two sons God killed: Adam

409. and Christ.] Adam heard the voice of the Lord asking, "Did you disobey?" (Gen. 3.8–11).

410. Adam answered: "You gave me the woman and I had the power and desire to breed [Gen. 3.12].

411. The woman helped me and I don't think it was wrong."

412. God: "Now you are going to sing about it?" Adam: "I will

413. praise woman as did Swift." God: "What does she say for herself?" Adam: "Nothing—

414. With woman and song goes wine." God: "So you ate!" (Gen. 3.12). Adam: "It happened like a fable."

415. Adam as the Gracehoper was busy as an insect in the garden, dancing and hopping on other insects.

416. He had eaten the forbidden fruit and everything else. Winter was coming, and he had no food or shelter.

417. He went to the Ondt/Ant/God, who had plenty of food and females,

418. and pleaded with a song: "As one of your creatures, please give me shelter and a wife. Why did you abandon us

419. and sentence us to death?" God asked Shaun: "Is this kind of fable like *Finnegans Wake*?" Adam/Shaun: "It is the theory of God's actions.

420. It gives all the details of the Fall" (Gen. 3.6–24). Joyce moved around like a prophet in Dublin/Eden.

421. God: "Didn't you plagiarize your brother's [Stanislaus's] theology?" Shaun/Joyce: "I doubt it.

422. My brother is not my keeper. These ideas are old but they are partly my own.

423. I invented a private language to reveal the world's literature, promoting woman even though God killed Adam and Eve and denied their rights.

424. Why? To understand God's curse. I repeated the world's schismatic literature.

425. I stole God's pen and rewrote the Bible, defending woman."

426. Nevertheless, Adam accepted God's curse and fell from heaven like Satan,

427. out of Eden. Thus Adam fallen becomes Shem, who continues to love Eve

428. and turns into the hope for Ireland.

Book III, Chapter 2: Genesis Revised

429. We begin again with Christ like Adam (as Jaun), tending Eden (Gen. 2.15) in Ireland.

430. This version starts apparently in a girl's school

431. where Adam recognizes his sister-daughter (Gen. 2.22–23) and proposes they leave (Gen. 2.24).

432. Before leaving he says Mass and preaches to the girls:

433. "Do not eat forbidden fruit. Avoid temptation [Gen. 3.4–6].

434. Do not promote the Fall of Man, even though it has been glorified in fiction

435. and art. Pornography is temptation of the Serpent.

436. Illicit sex is promoted by brothels and liquor.

437. Keep clean and use perfume to counteract God's curse.

438. Do not allow a man to fondle you, and don't fondle him.

439. Remember God's prohibition and resist the Serpent's temptations,

440. for God promises death for transgression [Gen. 2.17, 3.19]."

441. Now Eve remembered (Gen. 3.2–3), but the Serpent persuaded her:

442. "God is just trying to frighten you. You won't die [Gen. 3.4].

443. Your eyes will be opened [Gen. 3.5]. I'll take care of that father God," said the Serpent.

444. God cursed the Serpent above cattle, bruised his head and made him eat dust, go on his belly, and so on (Gen. 3.14–15).

445. Though Adam and Eve hid in the trees, they heard God, who found them (Gen. 3.8–11).

446. Adam enjoyed the fruit Eve gave him. Such love is better

447. than Dublin Catholic hypocrisy. [Joyce is rewriting the

448. Bible and "forging the uncreated conscience of his race."]

449. Adam would rather stay in Eden with Eve than die. Will the music + birds = Holy Spirit overcome death?

450. Making love to Eve/ALP is like fishing in a river but death lurks in the trees (Gen. 2.17).

451. It is worth everything to make love, and they should not be ashamed [rejecting Gen. 3.11].

452. But Adam was cold, wet, and afraid when he heard the voice of God (Gen. 3.10), and so he confessed (Gen. 3.12).

453. *Finnegans Wake* will overcome God's curse and shameful clothes (Gen. 3.21).

454. However, Adam and Eve knew they were naked (Gen. 3.7) before God told them so (Gen. 3.11) and banished them (Gen. 3.23).

455. God's clothes (Gen. 3.21) do not hide His curses or the banishment from Eden (Gen. 3.16–19, 23–24),

456. and His sacrament of communion does not compensate His forbidding eating from the tree of life (Gen. 3.22).

457. Having children is the consolation for death (Gen. 4.1). Issy [Eve innocent] says:

458. "It was nice to eat" (Gen. 3.6). Eve fallen: "We are naked and must veil ourselves [Gen. 3.7]. God sees us [Gen. 3.8–11]."

459. The transformation of Issy into Eve is completed with Eve clothed (Gen. 3.21) and named (Gen. 3.20).

460. God's curses (Gen. 3.16) included that she desire her husband and serve him,

461. which she loves to do. Jaun/Adam

462. drinks to that. Adam innocent now transforms into Shem, Adam fallen.

463. Although they look alike, Shem [Joyce] is anti-Irish Catholic, but

464. he uses ideas from St. Patrick, Christ, and the Holy Spirit to rewrite the Bible as *Finnegans Wake*.

465. Sex is to be enjoyed since the Fall, which God did not prevent.

466. Lack of sex promotes rape and masturbation, so sing of it!

467. *Finnegans Wake* will interpret Genesis as God's prank

468. or jest. His action was not logical. Cast out of Eden with a curse of thorns (Gen. 3.18), so

469. people also leave Ireland with the benediction of a thorny God, and Cherubims prevent return (Gen. 3.24).

470. So a Maronite rite mocks God's other killed son.

471. Though offering peace, Haun [Joyce] also left Ireland.

472. By rewriting the story of Adam and reorienting Irish morals,

473. *Finnegans Wake* will overcome the long dominance of Catholicism although it may take centuries.

Book III, Chapter 3: *Finnegans Wake* as a New Testament

474. Yawn/Adam lay asleep (Gen. 2.21), sad without a helpmeet (Gen. 2.20). The river in Eden

475. "became into four heads" (Gen. 2.10), who in this dream version are the four evangelists looking for Christ.

476. They see God's other son asleep in the lush garden (Gen. 2.9), mistaking him for Christ in his crib.

477. They see him giving birth to a woman (Gen. 2.21–22). They had intended to write of Christ's divinity and crucifixion. They ask: "Why do you have a woman?" Adam: "To provide your ancestors."

478. St. Patrick says: "I don't understand your words of salvation" and appears to proclaim the Trinity.

479. Keep me away from women. They associate with snakes."

480. Yawn: "Our Viking ancestors wanted women." St. Patrick: "Do not teach that to children."

481. Yawn: "God killed his sons three times" [the Fall, Flood, and Crucifixion]. St. Patrick: "That is why we fear God."

482. Yawn: "What's His name?" St. Patrick: "Rumor has it that it's Serpent." John and Matthew now ask Yawn about the author of *Finnegans Wake,*

483. who is forging a new conscience. Yawn: "What good are your Gospels when my Father caused the Fall?

484. He gave me woman, then unredeemed me. Believe in this New Gospel. I vow to rescue you."

485. Luke: "Believe in the Trinity. Don't listen to Yawn/Shem/Joyce." Yawn: "Please, Luke, the woman/ALP is boss now."

486. To stop this sob story St. Patrick arrives in Ireland and attempts conversions. He produces the triple sign of man, woman, and the Fall.

487. St. Patrick: "Think of your life after death." Yawn: "God put me to sleep, took my rib, gave me woman, and drove me out. I am a lover, not a Catholic."

488. St. Patrick: "Atone and seek salvation." Yawn: "Opposites reconcile. Adam and Joyce were expelled.

489. Joyce should get the Victoria Cross for rewriting the Bible to free mankind."

490. St. Patrick: "Why is he so good? Because he incorporates Bruno as Irish, should Irishmen read him?

491. He turns around the story of the Fall. Let's hear the woman's version." ALP: "The Serpent, who is an earwig, happened along [Gen. 3.1–5]. Adam was ashamed [Gen. 3.7], confessed [Gen. 3.10], and was clothed [Gen. 3.21]."

492. St. Patrick: "You seduced him." ALP: "I did give him forbidden fruit and

493. we exposed our genitals." St. Patrick: "You were naked and God said, 'What have you done?' [Gen. 3.11]."

494. ALP: "God promised a rainbow." St. Patrick: "More likely a volcano. The Serpent controls you." ALP: "I confessed.

495. The Serpent is cursed by a God, who killed His own Son, but I still have joy with a penis."

496. St. Patrick: "That is why Adam was sent forth." The Bible is recounted with an Irish slant in *Finnegans Wake,*

497. especially Dublin with its predators, St. Patrick, drunkenness, horror of condoms,

498. horse racing, politics, perverted religion, and English betrayal. No wonder Joyce escaped.

499. The death, pain, murder, and shit are overcome by the writing of *Finnegans Wake*. Like the song,

500. it sounds incomprehensible, the noise of a brawl at an Irish wake.

501. To start again, Adam awake from his sleep (Gen. 2.21) is like his brother, Christ. He saw the woman.

502. Christ's birth is confused with the woman's (Gen. 2.22). Adam's sleep is followed by his desire for the woman (Gen. 2.24–25).

503. In the Garden of Eden, God made man from dust and brought woman to cleave to him (Gen. 2.22–24). He also made the tree of life (Gen. 2.9, 17; 3.22), now embodied in woman.

504. He made a scapegoat of Adam, but the fruit of the tree of life is still woman.

505. Conception through intercourse is the source of life. Woman was made in God's image.

506. The Serpent is the phallic symbol, therefore cursed by God (Gen. 3.14) and absent from Ireland.

507. Thomas the Agnostic must have been Irish, doubting Christ's divinity.

508. Adam was God's son too. He fell, tempted by Eve's fruit, and was clothed an killed by God (Gen. 3.21).

509. *Finnegans Wake* differs from Genesis. Thomas and Joyce doubt divinity and equate the Russian general with Adam.

510. *Finnegans Wake* recycles the tale, justifies love and marriage (Gen. 2.24), and relates Ireland to the Fall.

511. But was the Serpent really responsible? Adam and Eve were innocent when God made them (Gen. 2.25).

512. Woman was made from and named for man (Gen. 2.22–23). They were one flesh (Gen. 2.24) and married (Gen. 2.20).

513. The evangelists are joined by Joyce, who dances through a metamorphosed version of Genesis as a New Testament.

514. Adam and Eve, whom God made, were kicked out of the garden as Joyce and Nora were out of Dublin.

515. Although Adam did not complain, God's sentence was not justified. What was God's purpose? A New Testament should explain that.

516. The Serpent tempted the woman, contradicting God (Gen. 3.1–5). So they ate (Gen. 3.6).

517. Adam met God (Gen. 3.7–12), who cursed (Gen. 3.17–19) and exiled him (Gen. 3.23). Time started then.

518. That should have been the armistice but God still found fault (Gen. 6.5–11).

519. He was sorry he made man (Gen. 6.6, 13) and sent forty days of rain to destroy all life (Gen. 7.4).

520. The four evangelists and four Masters agree God saw the wicked ways and it was woman's fault.

521. But Noah was saved in the ark (Gen. 7.5).

522. Did you know God killed two sons, cursed woman, and was a tailor (Gen. 3.21)? Could that be Irish?

523. It may be that God sinned against Adam. He established moral turpitude, disease, and poverty, and prompted

524. the Serpent to convince the woman, against God's warning, that the act was good (Gen. 3.5).

525. In Ireland sex is a curse although they breed like fish.

526. Women are still protected from temptation (and earwigs/Serpents) but still find ways to make love.

527. Joyce writes his version of Gen. 3.6—". . . tree was good . . . gave also to her husband . . ."—in which

528. woman's love compensates for death. God's prohibition of sex requires a laughable immaculate conception.

529. Dublin's leaders still sanction the exile (Gen. 3.24) although God clothed them (Gen. 3.21),

530. having found them naked. Dublin torpedoes the ark, kills the sons,

531. and makes slaves of woman. So say *Finnegans Wake* and Joyce. Now comes the version by the Irish Adam, Finnegan:

532. "I'm Adam. Here we are again." Adam was innocent. He did not take Eve's fruit. He loved her as his descendants judge.

533. Eve gave him the fruit. God gave Adam woman; Protestants and Christ defend that as does church service and music. Adam, God's image, bids for grace.

534. Irish Anglicans and Joyce join Adam as a protestant against God's actions.

535. God sent forth Adam, His own image. The Serpent lied (Gen. 3.4–5) and was cursed like Oscar Wilde,

536. who had to bear his burden of shame, punishment, and exile like Adam. Sex will continue

537. to be defended by protestors and promoters like *Finnegans Wake* in spite of the Bible, which sanctions the sale of women (Exod. 21.7)

538. and prostitution (Deut. 23.17–18) resulting from God's curse.

539. The first sex was innocent. Adam did his best to keep God's garden (Gen. 2.15, 19–20),

540. but after the Fall, God changed the rules, allowing death, evil, and shame.

541. The cities grew, and so did conquests, battle, accidents, and pestilence;

542. running water, tea, and coffee; and aids to indigence, childbirth, and hunger.

543. God brought woman to man (Gen. 2.22) and multiplied the Dublins and the churches

544. but cursed man to toil, sweat, and poverty,

545. thorns and thistles, slavery and death (Gen. 3.18–19).

546. This is man's inheritance. The woman knew better but was tempted

547. and gave her husband the heaven of sex (Gen. 3.6). They covered themselves and hid (Gen. 3.7–8) from God.

548. Adam named his wife Eve (Gen. 3.20), cleaved to her (Gen. 2.24), and cherished her above God and himself.

549. Joyce and *Finnegans Wake* will bring the light of this conscience to Dublin.

550. So Adam provided Eve with domestic bliss according to God's instructions (Gen. 2.24),

551. revered God, and behaved like Christ as Dublin teaches—Dublin (as Eden)

552. having been rebuilt by the Vikings in all four directions after the Flood,

553. to be the Seventh Wonder of the World with statues, parks, streets,

554. and horses, to the shame of the evangelists.

Book III, Chapter 4: Sex the Redeemer

555. In this modern Dublin/Eden of four parts (Gen. 2.10) the dream starts again with innocent baby Adam,

556. Issy, the Serpent (Gen. 3.1), and woman, all of whom were cursed (Gen. 3.16).

557. God called Adam, accused him, cursed them all (Gen. 3.9–19),

558. and "sent them forth from the garden" (Gen. 3.23). Adam named Eve "mother of all living" (Gen. 3.20).

559. In a house on the outskirts of Dublin "Adam knew Eve his wife . . . and she bare Cain" (Gen. 4.1).

560. Now known as the Porters, they lived near the garden portal. Mrs. Porter bore Abel (Gen. 4.2).

561. As in Eden she hid her nakedness; she was woman, made by God, flesh of Adam's flesh.

562. She had innocently talked to the Serpent. They knew they were naked and left Eden.

563. God cursed woman to bring forth children, desire her husband, and obey him (Gen. 3.16).

564. Phoenix Park, like Eden, has trees where Adam and Eve hid, were tempted by the fruit, and were murdered.

565. Adam heard God's voice and was afraid and ashamed. The expulsion (Gen. 3.23–24) was a bad dream.

566. The tempted, innocent woman had sex with her husband (Gen. 3.6). Their eyes were opened; they were afraid and naked (Gen. 3.10).

567. The phallic Serpent tempted woman, who gave good and pleasant sex to her husband,

568. an act which should have produced peace and patience but instead led to death and killing by God the murderer.

569. The Dublin churches may bless all, but in the new world the Serpent will promote sex, pleasure, food and wine,

570. music, dance, and fun. Killing goes back to Adam and Eve and their children. They were unluckily killed like Lot's wife.

571. They hid by the tree of life (Gen. 3.8), and though legally united (Gen. 2.24), God accused them

572. of having sex. His prohibition was unclear but Adam admitted it,

573. saying his wife (Gen. 3.12) was only fulfilling her conjugal duty (Gen. 2.24–25).

574. God then accused the woman, and she blamed the Serpent (Gen. 3.13),

575. saying he had lied to her and beguiled her—and besides, they used a condom.

576. God made earth and heaven, man and woman, our foreparents.

577. Sleeping together is a consolation and recovery from the Fall.

578. Clergy now sanction the union of Adam of Sorrows and Eve of Rivers.

579. The Fall resulted from love and sex, but God's curses were the inheritance.

580. So God sentenced all animals and mankind to death but left the Serpent immortal;

581. and Adam and Eve's descendants are ashamed and hide their sex in apology for the Fall.

582. Yet God created us—curse, sex, and all—and we are stuck with each other.

583. As in ancient myths, man and woman still have intercourse in varying

584. positions, making love from night to dawn, saved from God's curse

585. of multiple sorrows and conceptions (Gen. 3.16) by contraception. Cleaved together (Gen. 2.24),

586. they knew they were naked (Gen. 3.7). Contraception keeps God from knowing the sin.

587. Joyce, Wilde, and Beardsley also dared to defy sexual prohibition. In the Joyce version

588. Eve was sorry, Adam said all trees look alike, and God should remember Christ was killed too.

589. But God kept on destroying mankind with flood and flaming sword in spite of the evangelists and the Trinity.

590. There is no insurance against God's false colors and welshing promises except woman's blissful union with her husband.

Book IV: The New Conscience

593. A new dawn has come. The poet of *Finnegans Wake* carries the new word of Shem and Shaun [Adam].

594. Death by the vengeful, cursing God shall be overcome by having children and God's bad dream will be washed away.

595. A new world is being discovered. Let the old God sleep.

596. Here comes the new savior and father of the Irish race. His is the new religion.

597. *Finnegans Wake* tells the story. Humans were created naked and not ashamed (Gen. 2.25). What does "eat the fruit" mean?

598. This new day brings a joyous religion which celebrates husband, wife, and family.

599. The old religion was in error. The new faith is: opposites combine. Creation occurred somewhere

600. near a river (Liffey or Nile). Good trees grew (Gen. 2.9). Man and woman were naked and not ashamed,

601. but even then the Irish priest St. Kevin rejected girls as pretty as flowers. People have since left Ireland

602. seeking beauty. St. Kevin was a do-gooder with the voice of doom.

603. Shem is a great improvement and a relief from doom. Not loving women is a Catholic fault.

604. Following St. Kevin's teachings of doom and prohibition is an Irish fault.

605. Following priestly conventions, St. Kevin preached celibacy, baptism,

606. and controlling sex by a cold bath. God made man and woman, his helpmeet, but allowed the Serpent to interfere.

607. The first man, Finn, may have sinned, but he had lots of fun with the first woman.

608. The Trinity promoted the fraudulent nightmare of death from which man and woman awake.

609. The new Adam/Juva longs for the memory of past pleasures. He hears God's threatening voice when God/Muta calls to him (Gen. 3.9):

610. "You sinned and I'll kill you like Buckley." Adam/Juva: "I kissed and ate [Gen. 3.12] and lost the paradise gamble."

611. Then St. Patrick showed the Druid the world was not an illusion of God by turning everything green

612. then by restoring the sun and colors of the rainbow as God's promise.

613. Thus the Garden of Eden was replaced by Ireland, and Eve and Adam accepted their fate of death to be woman and man.

614. Their descendants can make a clean start. Discard the old Bible and rework it into *Finnegans Wake.*

615. Eve/ALP's letter: "Dear God, Thanks for sex. We look back with pleasure on the dream of Eden. The Serpent wasn't necessary. What was the harm or shame of sex between man and wife?

616. So forgive the Serpent. You got a picayune fee for inflicting death. Man has great possibilities. Adam did only what was evident as natural and right."

617. God interrupts: "ALP, kiss my ass. You ought to bless me. I can't remember all my creations, particularly a stinker like man. The saints will keep him in line. His death is certain."

618. Eve/ALP continues: "The Serpents should run the churches. If Lilith tempted St. Patrick, he'd find out about love. Exile was not nice, and the clergy can kiss my ass. God and His disciples sent us to death.

619. Whoever likes women should thank Adam. The best answer is to be deaf to the church. ALP." The river-woman ALP wakes man in resurrection and dresses him for a new day.

620. She is proud of him and their children, who will grow up like their parents.

621. They take an early morning walk to catch a fish to *eat* for breakfast, holding hands as when they were young and innocent.

622. They walk slowly while ALP takes man back to the garden where they ate the fruit.

623. It's no good to ask God's forgiveness. They have chosen. A new conscience will come in *Finnegans Wake.*

624. They will start a new life and live respectably as man and wife,

625. pretending grandeur although in the poverty of Dublin.

626. The creation of woman and her meeting and cleaving to man as one flesh, unashamed (Gen. 2.20–25), is made like an epiphany as ALP, the river meeting Dublin,

627. then going forth from the Garden of Eden

628. to their death with promise of everlasting life through procreation.

Chapter Five

Multiple Personalities

It has been well documented that Joyce used *The Dissociation of a Personality* by Morton Prince in *Finnegans Wake*. Adaline Glasheen discovered very early that Christine Beauchamp is "a model for Issy" and "that Issy was indeed meant to be a multiple personality" ("Girls from Boston, Mass.," 90). Prince's work was one of the first to record publicly a case of multiple personality and its psychiatric resolution, which have subsequently become the subject of many popular reports as well as works of fiction and movies. It concerns a young woman given the pseudonym Christine L. Beauchamp, who was sexually attacked and who subsequently developed a mischievous personality called Sally as well as a contrary, obstreperous one referred to as B IV. Prince's resolution was to extinguish Sally and integrate B IV with the original Miss B.

Episodes of interaction among these three personalities provided Joyce with a number of opportunities. Sally was conscious of the other two personalities but could communicate with them only by writing letters, which she did often. After she consented to her elimination, she wrote a "last will and testament" in the form of a series of autobiographical letters, which she refused to show to Prince but instead buried them in a box in a secret place in the woods. Glasheen suggests, probably correctly, that Joyce used this to create the mystery of the letter from Boston, Mass. (Morton Prince was a physician practicing in the Boston City Hospital, where Miss B. was a student nurse). Glasheen suggests that Issy practiced writing early letters (see **ALP's letter**) which were buried in a dump and which finally became the mature expression of ALP. (Joyce may have transformed CLB's initials into ALP.)

Another thing that Sally did was to make Miss B. stutter and have hallucinations. Although it is HCE who stutters in the *Wake,* I propose that this is a sign of his split personality. As for his hallucinations, they are ubiquitous.

Atherton (40–41) also discusses Joyce's use of Prince's book. He suggests that Joyce tended to split all of his characters into two parts so as to oppose Bruno's fusion of opposites. I submit that Joyce's purpose in using the concept of split personality was literary. This is a device he used that permitted him to integrate all of the stories and literary sources he assembled into the Genesis story of the Fall; he unified his own narrative by condensing essentially all of the characters into the four of Genesis 3.

Joyce tells us of his debt at 617.22: "Pens picture at Manchem House Horsegardens shown in Morning Post as from Boston transcripped" [Shem the Penman {who is the exiled Adam} has his picture, taken at a Dublin horse show Garden of Eden, in the newspaper as a multiple personality].

"Who are those component partners of our societate . . . ?" he asks at 142.08. Even though the answer to the riddle is "The Morphios" (142.29) [Morpheus = Murphies = sleeping Irishmen], the "partners" are categorized by identities that can be classified as

Adam	doorboy, lounger, christymansboxer
Eve	cleaner, squeezer, bleakablue tramp
God	sojer [soldier], curman, funpowtherplother [gun-powder plotter]
Serpent	crook, tourabout, mussroomsniffer

"howmulty plurators made eachone in person?" asks the washwoman of Adam and Eve (215.25). Joyce answers that in *Finnegans Wake* "the continually more and less intermisunderstanding minds of the anticollaborators" will be "variously inflected, differently pronounced, otherwise spelled, changeably meaning vocable scriptsigns" (118.24–28). The "variously intermisunderstanding minds" of his vast array of characters are all absorbed into just four active hosts. An "inspection of the *bordereau* [inventory or case history] would reveal a multiplicity of personalities inflicted on the documents. . . . In fact . . . the traits featuring the *chiaroscuro* coalesce, their contrarieties eliminated, in one stable somebody" [An inspection of the inventory of people in *Finnegans Wake* reveals that they are multiple personalities inflicted on the documents of Genesis. In fact, their traits coalesce into one of the stable characters in Genesis 3] (107.24–30).

He is also careful to call our attention to specific personality combinations. For example, "it was this overspoiled priest Mr. Browne . . . in his secondary personality as a Nolan" (38.25–28) indicates that HCE/God as priest Brown incorporated Nolan because, just as Bruno of Nola contended that opposites merge, so God created woman and then contrarily forbade her mission. Issy tells Adam "don't forget, in your extensions to my personality" (144.23) that he must succumb to her seduction before she can change into Eve. Issy has some difficulty in understanding what seems to be a masculine component of her nature: "to conceal her own more mascular personality" (166.24) and "extend my personnalitey to the latents, I'll boy me for myself" (461.04) show she is aware that she is sexually aggressive, and perhaps she lacks the caution of feminine genes, having been formed from Adam's rib. At least twice Shaun behaves oddly because another personality is dominant. At 484.05 he says, "what I (the person whomin I now am) did not do," complaining that as Yawn/Shaun he did not commit the sin of the Fall but that Shem did. Earlier he was tempted by the woman but "control number thrice [Trinity] was operating the subliminal of his invaded personality" (247.08–09).

It is evident that Joyce was well aware of the multiple personality phenomenon and used it uniquely and effectively.

The following sections of this chapter catalog in some detail the multitude of characters and rationalize their subsumption into just four personalities.

Personalities of HCE

The Initials

Most readers assume that HCE are the initials of Humphrey Chimpden Earwicker but this full name is never given in the *Wake*. H. C. Earwicker is mentioned at 33.30 and 36.12, but this is a name for Adam, as is H. C. Enderson (138.16). Another occurrence of what might be an authentic name is *Hermyn C. Entwhistle* (342.20), but he is merely the owner of a race horse. All other groups of words beginning with the capitals HCE are epithets, not cognomens.

In fact, even the initials H. C. E. occur only twice. The statement at 32.12–14—"The great fact emerges that . . . all holographs so far exhumed . . . bear the sigla H. C. E."—suggests a direct parallel to YHWH in the Masoretic Bible text and also connotates the necessity never to reveal His name. The discussion which precedes on pages 31 and 32 relates to God's treatment of Adam, and at 32.04–05 we are warned "Bear in mind . . . this man is mountain"—that is, we are talking about God (the "man that means a mountain," 309.04). The other occurrence at 198.08—"H. C. E. has a codfisck ee"—means "God sees all" [a camera fisheye lens sees 180°].

Right after the initials are given, we are told (32.18–21) they stand not for a name but only for "the nickname Here Comes Everybody," who is "An imposing everybody he always indeed looked, constantly the same as and equal to himself and magnificently well worthy of any and all such universalisation"—which definitely sets up the repetitive use of HCE's initials as the primary "connundurumchuff" in the book. HCE is the unmentionable God, the "most unmentionablest of men" (320.12).

Even in lowercase the initials occur only six times, including three permutations at 284.01 ("ceh" and "ehc" do not occur); other variations are "hec" (once), "Hec" (once), "hek" (twice) and "Hek" (four times). (For those interested in such esoterica, Jack Dalton wrote a musical accompaniment that was published in the *Old Series A Wake Newslitter,* Sept. 1963.)

God's omnipresence is, however, signaled thousands of times with the initials embedded in three-word phrases, in various orders and both uppercase and lowercase, sometimes sequential and sometimes not; for example, at 310.22–23, "*H*ouse of *c*all is all their *e*venbreads though its *c*artomance *h*allucinate like an *e*rection."

Very often they occur as epithets which may or may not be nicknames, such as "He'll Cheat E'erawan" (46.01), *"He Can Explain"* (105.14), *"Hatches Cocks' Eggs"* (71.27), "Hocus Crocus, Esquilocus" (254.20), "Helpless Corpses Enactment" (423.31), "Haveth Childers Everywhere" (535.34), and so on. Occasionally these may refer to God directly, but most often they encompass Adam and imply God's presence by the initials.

Another source of confusion in the *Wake* is the fact that speakers are not identified. This problem is compounded when God/HCE sometimes speaks three times in succession as His Trinity—as he does, for example, at 314.10–12 and 360.17–23. Book II, Chapter 3, is especially rich in Trinity references (see Chapter 7).

God the Tailor

One of the most ubiquitous of HCE's personalities is God the tailor. This comes about because Gen. 3.21 reads "Unto Adam also and to his wife did the LORD God make coats of skins and clothed them." Until Gen. 3.7 they did not even know they were naked. When Adam said, "I was afraid because I was naked" (Gen. 3.10), God said, "Who told thee that thou wast naked?" (Gen. 3.11), and Adam confessed. Therefore God made them clothes and became the first tailor. The personality is most prominent in the *Wake* episode on pages 309–29 (see **Norwegian captain**), where He is combined with the tailor who could not fit the Norwegian captain of Joyce's father's story and the actual Dublin tailor named Kerse. This third component allows the character to develop into the revengeful God who forces Adam and his descendants to be ashamed because their nakedness reminds them of Adam's Original Sin. Throughout the *Wake* whenever clothing is mentioned, it is a reminder that the cursing God prepared Adam and Eve for exile by equipping them with coats. The following are some of these segments:

172.05–10
and 181.27–33   These paragraphs in the form of advertisements show that the "different butcher" is God as a source of skins; Shem feels the lamb and sheep skins and is excommunicated. The next few lines (172.11–16) reinforce the statement of his exile to death ("among morticians" and "he fell heavily"). In the second ad Joyce identifies himself with Shem as a wearer of cast-off clothing.

247.18   "Highly momourning he see the before him." [God sadly sees Adam and Eve.

.19   Their innocence maligned, they stand naked.

.22   Their nakedness displays their sin.

.23   Should he wash their sins away or exile them?

.25   He does not want their shame to be apparent.]

.29   "all skirtaskortas must change her tunics." [Those who skirt the law must have clothes, then be exiled and struggle for life.

.31   May they be clothed by splitting hides.]

292.11–12   [Adam and Eve take warning from their past behavior. Why? Because cowhides made man a shirt and the woman a movable skirt. Therefore as good Catholics they won't do it.]

344.15–17   [Adam sees God bringing his skins to make the clothing {"lugging up and laiding down his livepelts"} just like that crazy King Nebuchadnezzar and promoting Himself as a skillful tailor with skins.]

453.15   "Ole Clo goes through the wood with Shep. . . ." [God the tailor goes with the shepherd to get his skins.

.24 Eve says you'll see her clothes spread out while she
.25 is singing and why should they have trimmings?]
455.03–06 [God says: You will hardly recognize Eve in her new clothes or the former sinner Adam. They belong in a waxwork museum after bailing out from My horrible curses.]
459.07 [Issy divulges the boots, stockings, and bargain
.08 clothes she will wear when she becomes Eve,
.13 including a dress {"ithel"}
.16 and shoes.]
508.12 [The day they fell, were their behinds covered? asks HCE/God.
.14 He continues: Neither knew the necessity of under-garments.
.15 One is reminded that a shirt killed Hercules.
.16 St. Patrick comments, "Ay, another good button gone wrong," implying that God's clothing was part of His sentence of death on Adam and Eve.]
529.12 [Issy and Eve are the two draper's assistants.]

Cod and Cad

Besides the tailor, HCE/God appears under two frequent epithets which are derived from the letter mutations God = Cod = Cad. These are the explanations for Cod:

46.21–24 "Thok" [Thor] is the Norwegian "cod" and "old cod. He is [be] god."
54.20 In what seems to be a television program (starting at 52.18) describing *Finnegans Wake* the commentator says, "And, God [note capitalized Cod], . . . Would you care to know the prise [also price] of a liard [liar-Lord]?"
102.34 In this little poem, which is ALP's equivalent to Hosty/HCE's ballad, ALP asks "[Who] *was the C. O. D.?* Bum!" The capital initials with periods equate C. O. D. = H. C. E. ALP answers her own question with a typical *Finnegans Wake* opinion.
121.34 Here Cod/God is doubly disguised. First, as food to be eaten as the Eucharist, and second as bell-ringing notations for the "muffinbell." Elsewhere in *Finnegans Wake* the sound of bells signals the Holy Ghost of the Trinity.

313.08   The phrase "piece Cod" refers to a piece of the Trinity (as well as "please God").

427.20   Shem laments Shaun's loss of innocence "beyond cod's [God's] cradle."

587.2   This can be read as: Do not listen to the wind in the trees; it is God luring you to death.

577.09   The phrase "cod and coney" occurs in a long list of characteristics of Adam and Eve, "our forced payrents" (576.27). Since *cod* is in lowercase, it here represents Adam/Michael, who looks like God. Coney signals ALP/Issy, who couples like a rabbit.

579.21   "No cods before Me" is plainly the "Thou shalt have no other gods before me" of Exod. 20.3.

The encounter with "a cad with a pipe" is usually thought to have occurred in Phoenix Park and is considered to be a crucial episode. It is but one of the many repetitions of Gen. 3.10 which are explicated the "Encounters" section of Chapter 6. The following discusses each case where "cad" appears:

35.11   The "cad with a pipe" is HCE/God, whom Adam met in Eden and feared (35.24) would hurl him into eternity by plugging him with a soft-nosed bullet (God kills in many ways in the *Wake*). In this episode God also asks Adam what time it is, thereby starting time (see **Time: 1132**). Note also that this scene is repeated at 153.35–154.16.

88.13   In Gen. 9.15–21 God makes a covenant with mankind never again to destroy all living creatures by flood. In this passage Noah wonders whether he could trust God to keep his word: "As cad could be. Be lying!"

127.06–07   The first riddle of Book I, Chapter 6, is one of the longest and most difficult because so many of the aphorisms could apply to God as well as Adam. This phrase containing "cad" is one clue which helps the deciphering: "has a quadrant in his tile to tell Toler cad a'clog it is." It can be paraphrased: has a bearing on his escutcheon to tell the mortality-sentencing God what time it is. Thus Finn MacCool's [Adam's] heraldic shield acknowledged God's time.

178.02   The "bad cad dad fad sad mad" means, among other things: the bad God-the-Father is only a sad, mad fad.

270.07 The phrase "that perfect little cad" seems to refer to Shaun, the brother most closely reflecting Cad/God's image, who has no helpmeet [Gen 2.20]. In the marginal note Shem agrees with Shaun's desires as long as he can have "that small polly" [Issy], and Shaun preserves his innocence by drinking lemonade.

332.23–26 Before Adam was exiled ("his loudship was converted to a landshop" and "amudst the fiounaregal [funereal] gaames"), he collided with God the cad, as at Gen. 3.19.

511.32 [St. Patrick, in nursery rhyme cadence, asks: So this was the dope {probably Serpent} that worried the cat {cad/God} who objected to the intercourse and tried Adam, who hugged the woman?]

588.10 The phrase "after the cad came back" refers to Gen. 3.8, when Adam and the woman were hiding in the trees and heard God searching for them.

618.03 In ALP's letter (see Chapter 8), she links cad/God with Lilith.

101.21 "caddishly" is an example of several other occurrences of "cad" buried in associated words. This includes such names as Cabury, Caddy, Cadwalloner, and so on.

Willingdone and Nap

The "Museyroom" episode, at 8.09–10.23, provides the opportunity for Joyce to confuse the identities of "Willingdone" and "Lipoleum," who on the surface appear to be Wellington and Napoleon at the battle of Waterloo. Since Wellington was the victor and Napoleon the defeated and exiled, Willingdone must be HCE/God, and Lipoleum Adam. "Willingdone" indicates that God's sentencing Adam to exile and death was willingly done. "Lipoleum" is from the Greek *lipo,* meaning "without" and the Latin *oleum,* "oil"; "without oil" means "unannointed," or theologically without grace, which is Adam's state. There is another battle going on here simultaneously, that of the Gnostic Sophia against the wicked Yahweh. Sophia's troops are the "jinnies"—not *jinnies* = mares, but *jinniyeh* = female jinnies or genies, the pagan deities who control magic. They are probably also the collective Issy (see **ALP: personalities of**). At any rate they are her soldiers attempting to thrust God back into His darkness; this foreshadows ALP's ultimate victory over HCE. "This is the jinnies with their legahorns feinting [pretending to fight] to read in their handmade's [Sophia/ALP] book of stralegy [astrology + knowledge of god and evil] while making their war undisides [undermining] the Willingdone [God]" (8.31–33). "This is the jinnies' hastings dispatch [hastening to dispatch] for to irrigate [by flushing out the loo with water] the Willingdone" (9.02–03). "That was the tictacs [tactics] of the jinnies for to fontannoy [to annoy] the Willingdone" (9.06). The fact that "The jinnies is jillous agincourting [jealously courting again] all the lipoleums [men like Adam]" (9.07–08) confirms they are representatives of ALP/Issy trying to save Adam. True to form with "This is the Willingdone's hurold dispitchback [hurried return thrust]" (9.11–12), God vituperates them as He does in ALP's letter; "Cherry jinnies. Figtreeyou! Damn fairy ann, Voutre. Willingdone." [Virgin jinnies, I curse you to be barren {Matt.21.19}. Damn and fuck Anna/ALP, who doesn't matter. Yours, HCE] (9.13–14). In the middle of this scrimmage we have a strange line, 9.05: "Leaper Orthor. Fear siecken! Fieldgaze thy tiny frow. Hugacting. Nap." From this, another divine threat can be extracted: [God-or-Thor is the Highest. Fear His conquering. How insignificant is your woman. Act like Huguenots fleeing the Catholic God. Signed, God.] This reading requires "Nap" to be God where we already have Napoleon/Lipoleum/Adam; therefore Nap is not Napoleon. Indeed there are seven more occurrences of "nap" which establish it as another HCE/God personality. This is a good example of Joyce's rummaging the world's literature looking for klang words to build ambiguity. Petr Skrabanek reports (75) that a Joyce notebook contains the entry of an Elamite (Median) word, "na-ap (Nap)," which means God and ties in with "cunniform letters" (198.25) and "Meades and Porsons" (18.22). The other citations reinforcing the God reading for Nap are:

131.30–31   "nods a nap for the nonce but crows cheerio when they get ecunemical" [Adam bows to God for the moment but cheers when they get united in the Trinity].

176.11   "*Nap*" is in the list of games Shem/Adam used to play. It means God in the context of "*Habberdasherisher*" [tailor] and "*What's the time?*" [God started time].

202.3   "Grandfarthring nap and Messamisery and the knave of all knaves and the joker" [Grandfather God, Mass misery, betrayer and player of practical jokes on Adam].

313.08   "nap" occurs in the context of Kersse, Cod, and godfather.

478.21   The phrase "sham nap" embedded in St. Patrick's sham French is the sham God.

516.31   "Nap" with "The Wearing of the Green" medley makes

Him God the tailor, who started the Fall with the curse
which follows at 516.32–36.

550.27   Here, "nap" may be a game, but if so, it is a cruel game
played by God causing distress ("withers"), crying and
pounding ("bray, and slapbang") by God the tailor
("drapier-cut-dean"); compare 176.11.

Avenging Personalities

Critics have usually identified the three soldiers as anonymous characters
having something to do with whatever happened in the Park. Glasheen's
Second Census (253) finds a multitude of allusions to "three soldiers," but
they are actually mentioned (in the plural) only twice in *Finnegans Wake:* at
58.24, where "three tommix [not Tom Mix but to mix in one Trinity],
soldiers" blame "the first woman" for the Fall; and at 338.4, where "Citizen
soldiers" appears to describe the speaker of the next line, who is TAFF/
God. These occurrences present the Trinity as a military authority figure.
When Issy (366.07) and ALP (619.17) refer to soldier (singular), they mean
Adam as the Son in the Trinity. The concept of three soldiers and two
temptresses in the park has been perpetuated since Campbell and Robinson's
A Skeleton Key. God as Trinity and the two first people were, of course, in
the Eden of Genesis, but only one was a temptress. The three soldiers
constitute the enforcers of the vengeful Trinity.

There are several allusions to Tommy Atkins, a slang reference to a
British soldier, although the actual name does not occur. In the Buckley
and the Russian general episode, BUTT/Adam uses the term "troupkers
tomiatskyns" (350.27) to plead his presence in Eden as being merely that of
a peaceful, innocent soldier of God. But other usages identify a rapacious,
vengeful God. At 241.22–25 the "queerest man in the benighted queendom
[HCE/God] . . . purely simply tammy ratkins" is called a Loch Neagh
monster who "found the kids" and gave them gonorrhea. At 534.33 God's
horrible curses on Adam are related to a stuttering "atkinscum," and at
588.18 God is "Mr Black Atkins." Adam is "Wanted for millinary servance"
by "the Totty Atkinses" (125.11), and the marginal note at 281L identifies
"Threes Totty Askins" as the Trinity, who caused war. Atherton (196) has
pointed out that using the name "Tom" for God may come from the *Book
of the Dead:* the consonants for *god* were T and M, producing Egyptian
names like Atem, Tema, Tem, and so on. Thus we have at 176.01 "*Thom
Thom the Thonderman.*"

"Sully is a thug," says ALP in her letter—and also, "The thicks [thugs] off Bully's Acre was got up by Sully" (618.08, 29). She is accusing Sully/ God as if He were the Gnostic God of Darkness ordering His angel thugs to attack Adam. At 558.12 and 14 we find that for Sully the remedy for contravention of legislation is corporal amputation [for God the remedy for disobeying is death]. "Sully the Thug" (212.03), "Sully van vultures" (435.29), and "Sully, a barracker" [like the soldiers He lives in a barracks] (495.01) associate with Druids and Serpents. His alter ego is "constable Sistersen . . . the parochial watch, big the dog . . ." [a parochial watch dog, a big (reversed) God, keeping order in Eden parish] (186.20). ALP also thinks God is a clown: "Cloon's fired him [Adam] through guff" (616.21), and "the senior king of all, Pegger Festy" threw stones and killed Adam (91.01). The song "Do Ye Ken John Peel?"—which echoes throughout the *Wake*, starting at 31.28—should recall God the killer, since John Peel leads the fox hunt in which the fox is dragged from his lair and killed by being thrown to the dogs.

Lally seems to be the personality by which the four evangelists (or Masters) know HCE/God in connection with His sentencing Adam and Eve. At 94.26 the four are sitting as judges, with Lally to issue the charges. At 387.19 they remember the dismal day when the woman (Fair Margrate) and Adam (Swede Villem) met Lally/God. Adam answers Marcus's question about the Fall (389.21–30) by pointing out that Lally "lost part of his half a hat" (389.34) by condemning God's first son to death. The logic here is that before the Fall, the Trinity was only two-thirds complete—that is, only the Father and the Son (Adam). When the Father expelled the Son, He retained only one half of his divinity, whose authority is signified by the hat. Lally's identity is reproachfully confirmed at 390.03 by indicating that His action contradicts the behavior of "Lally, the ballest master [greatest God] of Gosterstown [heaven]." The condemnation continues at 394.18, where "Lally of the cleftoft bagoderts" may be either a left-off bag of dirt or an often-split bag of Gods (the Trinity). At any event, here God is again with the Four. Although offered in lowercase at 396.25, "a lally [God] a lolly [Issy] a dither [Adam] a duther [Serpent]" form the 1132 combination connected with the "four dother" (see **Time:1132**). "Long Lally Tobkids, the special" (67.11) does not seem to be associated with the four, but since He is "a conscientious scripturereader" and swears like a Norwegian tailor, He is indeed God.

Attributes: Thunderer, Stutterer, Smoker

Atherton (31) makes a strong case for God's being the stutterer. Joyce takes this attribute from Vico, who claims that language derives from the stutter of God's thunder. Thus not only do the thunder words denote the presence of HCE/God, but so do the stutters. Accordingly, Hosty stutters in HCE's ballad at 45.13; and at 119.18, there is a stuttering enunciation of HCE's initials. In keeping with the planned confusion, Adam appears to stutter in some places. For example Yawn/Shaun/Adam imitates HCE/God out of courtesy (480.30–32), and Jaun defends his stutter by calling it "his unpeppeppediment" (463.11). Adam does not normally stutter but does mock God at 339.30. Also "Scutterer of guld" (said by God of Adam at 340.01) means "scatterer," not "stutterer," and at 171.10 is Shem's hiccup ("his glottal stop"). On one occasion (532) Adam stutters quite a bit, perhaps to persuade St. Patrick that he is God's image and Son; likewise St. Patrick stutters back at as he defends HCE/God (534). Even ALP seems to stutter at 530.36–531.26. She may be imitating HCE or sharing His guilt or exhibiting Vico's primitive language.

The planned confusion also extends to the hundred-letter words, all of which are uttered by God, except the one at 424.20–22. This one is different in that it has 101 letters, is obscene, and is mouthed by Shaun.

Starting with "a cad with a pipe" (35.11), whenever smoking or tobacco is mentioned we may be sure that HCE/God is present. For example at 347.36 TAFF/God is "*smolkinq his fulvurite turfkish.*" He smokes like a volcano erupting at 386–87. At 609.24 we find "What now is that smoke rolling out of the Lord?" and the ensuing passage suggests that the smoke is God's spirit or voice, as in Gen. 3.8. More examples are given in the Generic Paraphrases **Encounters, Time:1132,** and **Ondt and the Grace-hoper.** Joyce apparently felt the smoking was descriptive of the Old Testament, vengeful God, noting in *Scribbledehoble* that "tobacco is like a soul in sin, fair without and foul within," a quote apparently from Samuel Lover's *Handy Andy.*

Miscellaneous Names

The ubiquitous but unnamed HCE/God presents Himself disguised throughout the *Wake*. Some, but by no means all, of His other personalities are listed below. Many of them are further explicated in Chapters 7 and 8.

Ashe	Mark the Wans (-Twy, -Tris)
boss	Mengarments
Grand Precursor	Muta
Gripes	Mutt
Honuphrius	mutter

Hosty	Ondt
I AM	Puropeas Pious
Jarl van Hoother	Sulla
Kersse	TAFF
Laraseny	tailor
lopp	Taler
Loud	tayloren
mabby	Thor
	Twelve-eyed man

Personalities of Adam

H. C. Earwicker

The constant confusion in the *Wake* between HCE/God and Earwicker/ Adam is one of the most difficult ambiguities to overcome. As Jaun/Adam says at 439.20–25 "Whoo? What I'm wondering to myselfwhose . . . I feel spirts of itchery outching out from all over me and only . . . the darkens alone knows what'll who'll be saying of next. However." This planned confusion results from Adam's being made in God's image (Gen. 1.26). It is appropriate to have them be mistaken for one another, but fortunately they do not talk or act alike. Once the reader realizes the distinction, much of the narrative starts to make sense.

Clive Hart uncovered the source of the "Earwicker" name and reported it in the *Old Series A Wake Newsletter* (o.s.) in July 1962. In the summer of 1923, when Joyce was writing the original "Here Comes Everybody," he was vacationing in Bognor, a small southern seaside town between Brighton and Portsmouth, England. The churchyard at Sidlesham, which is only a few miles away, has many headstones of the Earwicker family. Sidlesham is in the "Manhood" district of the "Hundred" (county division) of Sussex. It seems likely that Joyce visited it and appropriated the name.

It is introduced in *Finnegans Wake* at 30.02–16:

> concerning the genesis of Harold or Humphrey Chimpden's occupa-
> tional agnomen (we are back in the presurnames . . . period) . . . and
> discarding once for all those theories from older sources which would
> link him back with such pivotal ancestors as the . . . Earwickers of
> Sidlesham in the Hundred of Manhood or proclaim him offsprout of
> vikings . . . the best authenticated version, the Dumlat [right to left,
> Hebrew Talmud] . . . has it that it was this way. We are told how in

the beginning . . . the grand old gardener was saving daylight . . . in prefall paradise peace . . . in the rere garden.

The passage makes it clear that "Harold or Humphrey Chimpden's" occupation was a gardener (Gen. 2.15: "and the LORD God took the man and put him into the garden of Eden to dress it and keep it.") His "agnomen" [gardener name] did not derive from the ancient Earwickers or Vikings as representatives of the first men in England but goes back even earlier to the biblical account of the peaceful paradise of the Garden of Eden before the Fall and before the first man had a surname and was called simply Adam (or sometimes Harold or Humphrey in the *Wake*). (A further explication of this passage is given in **Encounters, Exile, and Time:1132.**)

As has already been pointed out, the full name of Humphrey Chimpden Earwicker does not occur in the *Wake*. H. C. Earwicker does occur, however, and at 33.30 he is described as Christ-like and clean-minded, and it is asserted that "the mere suggestion of him as a lust-sleuth nosing for trouble in a boobytrap rings particularly preposterous," thus defending Adam against God's indictment and distinguishing him from HCE/God. We are also told that he is a "good and great and no ordinary . . . Earwicker," a "homogenius [generating mankind] man" (34.14–15) who is "unwishful" of dying (35.24). At 73.03–07 HCE/God curses Mr. and Mrs. Earwicker, Adam and Eve (Gen. 3.16–19): "after exhorting Earwicker or . . . Messrs or Missrs Earwicker . . . to cocoa [stutter] come outside to Mockerloo [leave Eden for their mock Waterloo of defeat] . . . Gog's curse to thim, so he could brianslog [strike his brain] and burst him all dizzy." This is not enough: at 70.34–35 HCE/God orders him "to come out, you jewbeggar [compare Bloom in *Ulysses*], to be Executed Amen. Earwicker, that patternmind [his capability of thinking for himself is the image of God's], that paradigmatic ear [he listens to God and tries to obey] . . . longsuffering," then sits in a corner and compiles a page and a half of additional "abusive names" (71–72). These passages epitomize the eternal Wakean struggle between HCE/God and Earwicker/Adam but also serve to distinguish them from one another. In the end though, ALP says in her letter (619.12) that whether God likes it or not, "herewaker" [Earwicker/Adam, resurrected and awake] is God's real namesake.

In a paragraph of encouragement to his readers (108.08–25) Joyce starts out by advising patience in trying to understand who is being discussed and ends by asking: where in hell is the author going to tell us what it means? In the middle at 108.20–22 he says, "our great ascendant [Adam whose descendants we are] was properly speaking three syllables less than his own surname" [the syllables are *H, C,* and *E,* which Adam hereby disclaims], thus telling the reader that HCE and Earwicker are not the same character.

Another equivocation is the similarity of the word *Earwicker* to *ear-wig*—something that leads to endless opportunities for confusion. (The distinction is explained in **Serpent: personalities of.**) Needless to say, Earwicker/Adam is not the same character as earwig/Serpent. To further distinguish them, at 326.06 the Serpent baptized Adam as Earwicker, first man of Irish Vikings.

Shaun and Shem

As early as 1941 Harry Levin (161–63) decided that Shem and Shaun take after "their father Earwicker" and "If all men are brothers, then their natural state is fratricidal warfare." The *Skeleton Key* (Campbell and Robinson 217) extended this misreading to conclude "the brother battle becomes magnified to gigantic terms in the imperial conflict" and included all pairs such as BUTT and TAFF and Mutt and Jute as being brothers equivalent to Shaun and Shem. These assumptions have been followed by virtually every critic since, a practice which has prevented any clear understanding of the underlying narrative.

Shaun and Shem are two personalities but only one character: Adam. Shaun is the innocent, naive first man before the Fall; Shem is the guilt-ridden, cursed, and condemned Adam after the Fall. At 306.02–07 we find: "when Heavysciusgardaddy, parent who offers sweetmeats [omniscient God offering the woman but guarding against the fruit of sex], will gift uns his Noblett's surprize [Nobel's dynamite explodes to cause death] . . . let us be singulfied . . . mizpah ends [the Fall, like a bar mitzvah, ends childhood, and Shaun and Shem are joined as Adam to be exiled]." Adam's father is indeed HCE, but God is not "Earwicker," which is one of Adam's names. The repeated battles in the *Wake* are not fraternal but paternal. Joyce's view is that God is responsible for all the battles because He imposed the penalty of death on mankind. The Napoleonic Wars, the Crimean War, and all other wars and calamities are grafted onto the original Genesis conflict in *Finnegans Wake.* This is the theme of the Buckley and the Russian general narrative. Therefore TAFF and Mutt are HCE/God, and BUTT and Jute are Adam—as is explained later in the Generic Paraphrases. Shaun and Shem do have different outlooks and sometimes they quarrel, but they never fight to the death.

Shaun

Book III, Chapter 1, identifies Shaun and discusses his origin and attributes. The first seventeen lines of 403 indicate that time has not yet
started (see **Time: 1132**), but there is a vague dream hinting that a man and
a woman will commit a sin which will cause Adam's Fall. Then at line 18
someone starts talking in the first person—continuing the dream of time's
being about to start ("at zero hour") in Ireland/Eden—and, at 404.07,
calling "Shaun! Shaun! Post the post!"

First let us demystify Shaun the Post, which seems to be the identity
most critics consider quintessential. Nearly all such discussion arises from
the information in *The Books at the Wake*, in which Atherton describes the
great lengths to which he went to track down Boucicault's play *Arrah-na-
Pogue*, where the character Shaun the Post appears. While Joyce does
utilize that "Shaun" and the play, as Atherton points out (157–61), one of
the principal usages is the symbol of the woman passing a key to the man
with a kiss. "The keys to. Given!" says ALP at the end of the book; and in
her letter (615.28) she explains "That was the prick of the spindle to me
that gave me the keys to dreamland" (which I have interpreted: That was
the start of sex which gave me the keys to heaven; see **ALP's letter** for the
context). Such a connection reinforces Shaun's identity as Adam. The first
chapter of book III does suggest that Shaun the Post carried or delivered
either ALP's letter or *Finnegans Wake* itself, but where and to whom is not
clear. It does become evident that Shem (not here named "the Penman")
wrote the book and that innocent, Christ-like Shaun does not approve.

One of the other Shaun sources identified by Atherton (99) quotes
William Carleton describing "Shaun Buie McGaveran to be the cleanest
best conducted and most industrious boy . . . fine, well built handsome
young man . . ."—a description which adequately fits Joyce's Shaun, "good
boy, to begin with" (409.09) as well as the Adam of Genesis 1 and 2.

"What a picture primitive!" says our *Wake* commentator (405.03),
confirming the presence of the first man; then three lines later he identifies
himself, "I, poor ass," as Christ and connects Himself to the four evangelists as their "dunkey" (the key to their resounding [dun = Old Norse
thunder] message). The identity of the ass as Christ has been suspected ever
since the *Skeleton Key*, where a footnote states: "The Ass of the Four
Gospelers slowly reveals itself to be Christ himself" (295). Following the
prohibition of naming God, Joyce must also refuse to name Christ, the
Son of the Trinity, as Jesus. From the Vulgate Bible as well as from the
Catholic INRI, he would have known that the Latin spelling in Roman

times was *Iesus*. Concealing this name as the Masoretic rabbis would have done by omitting the vowels would result simply in one's writing "ss"; then the pun is completed by the use of the simple vowel *a*. At 256.21, in a discussion of similarities between *Finnegans Wake* and the Bible, we find: "Four Massores, Mattatius, Marusias, Lucanias, Jokinias," where the four evangelists are named in pseudo-Latin, and *Massores* may include the Four Masters but also refers to the Masora, the Hebrew tradition of Bible text, thus relating Latin spelling to Masoretic. Then at 609.09 is "Ah ess, dapple ass!" which confirms that the sound of *a* combined with double *s* produces *ass*. The preceding lines (609.06–08) name the four evangelists again with whom the ass (and Christ) is usually found, thus reinforcing the name "ass."

Throughout Book I, Chapter 3, the ass acts as the God-the-Son part of the Trinity in the dialogue with Shaun, being considerably more sympathetic than God-the-Father, and eliciting information (to help the four evangelist-historians) about the cause of Shaun/Adam's Fall. Likewise Shaun/Adam identifies with Christ, both being HCE/God's sons and both being sentenced to death by him. Shaun says, "It should have been my other [Christ, not Shaun] with his leickname [nickname: corpse] for he's the head [God-the-Son] and I'm an everdevoting fiend of his" (408.17–18). "Yet I cannot . . . recollect ever having done of anything of the kind [as Christ did] to deserve of such. . . . I just didn't have the time to" (409.04–07), Shaun continues; "I wants to do a strike of work but it was condemned on me premitially by" HCE/God (409.34). This is why Joyce includes the Stations of the Cross, showing that Shaun/Adam also suffered at the hands of HCE/God. It is also why "Lipoleum" is the unannointed Adam (see **Willingdone and Nap**).

Although there are fourteen questions asked by God-the-Son on pages 409–25, they neither follow the order of the Stations of the Cross, nor are they directly concerned with Christ's walk to Calvary. Instead some are concerned with Adam's encounter with, and subsequent curses by, God in Gen. 3.8–24. For example, the first question—"who out of symphony gave you the permit?" (409.09–10)—is Christ's sympathetic version of HCE/God's hostile Gen. 3.11, "Who told thee that thou wast naked? Hast thou eaten of the tree, whereof I commanded thee that thou shouldest not eat?" Question two—"Then . . . you possibly might be so by order?" (409.31)—prompts Shaun's reply, "it was condemned on me," which reflects Gen. 3.12, "The woman thou gavest to be with me, she gave me of the tree, and I did eat." Question four— "where mostly are you able to work" (410.29)—shows that God-the-Son knew HCE/God's curse at Gen. 3.17–19, "cursed is the ground for thy sake. . . . Thorns also and thistles shall it bring forth to thee. . . . In the sweat of thy face shalt thou eat bread till thou return unto the ground."

On the other hand, many of the questions are concerned with *Finnegans Wake,* its purpose and authorship. Question five asks Shaun: "how you have . . . painted our town a wearing greenridinghued" [how have you transferred the location of the story from Eden to Ireland?] (411.23). Shaun replies: "only by a scripchewer in whofoundland who finds he is a relative. And it was my extravert davy" [it was done by my brother Shem/Joyce] (412.03–05). In question seven, God-the-Son, apparently worried that He will not be able to learn Shaun's story, asks: "how shall we complete that white paper" (413.28), whereupon Shaun/Adam composes the Ondt and the Gracehoper, explaining how HCE/God unjustly tricked him and exiled him from Eden. Question nine asks, "But could you . . . read the strangewrote anaglyptics of those shemletters patent. . . ?" (419.17–20), to which Shaun replies: "it is not a nice production. It is a pinch of scribble, not wortha bottle of cabbis. Overdrawn! Puffedly offal tosh!" (419.32–33)—followed by five pages of additional disapprobation. This is not the first time Shaun criticizes Shem. As early as 95.19 he says: "I sniffed that lad long before anyone. It was when I was in my farfather [when I was part of the Trinity as God-the-Son]." Finally, in question fourteen, God-the-Son asks Shaun why he doesn't write *Finnegans Wake,* to which Shaun replies: "I would never for anything take so much trouble of such doing" (425.33).

In the last paragraph of the chapter, Shem's comments on "mine bruder [my brother], able Shaun" are kinder and more appreciative: "for all your deeds of goodness you were soo ooft and for ever doing . . . you were the walking saint . . . may the tussocks grow quickly under your trampthickets and the daisies trip lightly over your battercops" (427–28). Shaun is pious and more clearly related to the Christ figure than Shem because he still displays God's image, not yet having been tempted and fallen. He is Bruno of Nola when Shaun/Justius says, "Brawn is my name" (187.24).

Shem also observes that Shaun is changing his persona: "it is to bedowern [regrettable] that thou art passing hence" (427.18); "we miss your smile" (427.36); " 'Tis well we know you were loth to leave us" (428.14). Shaun will assume the personality of Jaun in the *Wake's* next chapter.

Jaun

In Chapter 2 of Book III, Adam becomes "Jaun," appropriately suggesting the amorous Don Juan, since the story being told is the seduction in Gen. 3.1–6. Jaun/Adam appears to be resisting temptation by trying to preserve

Shaun's saintly character of the previous chapter. He preaches to the twenty-nine girls of St. Berched's, advising them of the correct antemeridian behavior even though they are in night school (430.02–04). His advice sounds as though it were scripted by Shem, however, and leads to some of the most hilarious comedy of the *Wake*.

He singles out "his fond sister Izzy . . . since he was brotherbesides her benedict godfather" [since the woman was made from Adam's flesh, he was her brother as well as her father] (431.15–18) and addresses his remarks directly to her (431.21). He also recalls "This is the gross proceeds of your teachings in which we were raised" (431.28), thus tying Issy/woman with ALP (see **Prankquean**).

"First thou shalt not smile. Twice thou shalt not love" (433.22–23), he says, reminding her of God's command in Gen. 2.17: "But of the tree of the knowledge of good and evil, thou shalt not eat of it." "Look on a boa [Serpent] in his beauty and you'll never more wear your strawberry leaves" (435.20–21 [God replaced the fig leaves with coats in Gen. 3.21]) and, he continues, "Don't on any account acquire a . . . habit of . . . wriggling with lowcusses and cockchafers [relatives of the earwig/Serpent] . . . with the end to commit acts of interstipital indecency" (435.32–436.01). Thus he warns her of the Serpent's wiles as related in Gen. 3.4–6. Nor does the Serpent himself escape Jaun's castigation eleborated from 441.24 to 445.25.

He struggles with the Don Juan impulse of his ethos, imagining the joys but mindful of the consequences of succumbing to temptation (445.26–455.30), and finally eats not only the forbidden fruit but such a hearty meal that it becomes the sacrament of the Last Supper and the end of his Mass (and life). Issy commiserates with his fate but also glories in their Fall and calls him "Juan" (457.25–461.32).

Jaun/Adam says Amen (461.32–33) to Issy's views, convinced that God's prank of sex is really salvation and that he must mutate to another personality. "So gullaby, me poor Isley! . . . I'm leaving my darling proxy behind for your consoleing" (462.15–17), he says, and then gives several pages of instruction to his successor. The narrator "I"—God-the-Son of Book III, Chapter 1, from whom we have not heard since the first line of this second chapter of Book III—now makes His reappearance (470.24). He records Jaun/Adam's departure: "making a brandnew start for himself" (471.10–11), "he was quickly lost to sight" (471.27–28). He assesses Shaun/Adam's character: "may the good people speed you, rural Haun, export stout fellow [to be exiled] that you are" (471.35–36); "Good by nature and natural by design" (472.10–11; a reference to Gen. 1.27); "For you had . . .

the nucleus of a glow of a zeal of soul of service such as rarely, if ever, have I met with single men" (472.25–27). Christ calls him "Haun," not really as a personality change, but as an honorific for "dearest Haun of all . . ." (472.20)—that is, dearest one [Juan] of all, God's other son, Adam.

Yawn

In Book III, Chapter 3, the four evangelists are searching for the history of Christ when they discover the Adam of Gen. 2.21: "And the LORD God caused a deep sleep to fall upon Adam, and he slept." Sleeping and snoring, he is appropriately called "Yawn" (475), and they confuse him with Christ. But on page 477 they see the continuation of Gen. 2.21–22: "and He took one of his ribs, and closed up the flesh instead thereof; And the rib, which the LORD God had taken from man, made he a woman." Matthew says that Adam is giving birth, that he has lived (477.03–04). Mark asks what that thing (the woman) is. The four ask, "—Y?" [Why did you give birth to a woman?] (477.31), and Yawn/Adam answers, "—Before You!" [To provide your ancestors] (477.32). St. Patrick also appears to try to persuade Yawn not to fall for the woman, but the events of Genesis 3 occur in a new version which is *Finnegans Wake* and which defends Yawn/Adam and Issy/ALP/woman.

Yawn confirms his identity to St. Patrick at 532.06—"Amtsadam, sir, to you [I am Adam, sir, to you]"—which he preserves through the rest of the chapter.

Christ/Adam/Finnegan

The comparison of Adam with Christ, which is prominent in Book III, Chapter 3, is a dominant theological theme of the whole book. Although St. Patrick objects to the comparison, he recognizes the validity: "And mine it was, Barktholed von Hunarig [a snide remark suggesting Adam thought he was the father of Swift's "Vanessa," Hester Vanhomrigh], Soesown of Furrows (hourspringlike his joussture, immitiate my chry! as urs now, so yous then!)" [It was my Man of Sorrows (you imitate Christ with your gesture. As you are about to die now, He will then!)] (535.01–04). The gesture is explained when Adam/Kevin is a "limb of the Lord, with his lifted in blessing, his buchel Iosa" [Adam, a part of the Trinity, lifted the staff of Jesus] (562.24–25). And at 408.05–07 Shaun bears the burden of Jesus, who fell at the third Station of the Cross. St. Patrick continues to be critical but also predictive as he asks Yawn, "did it ever ocur to you . . . that you might . . . be very largely substituted in potential succession from your next life by a complementary character" [Did you ever think you might be replaced as God's Son by Christ?] (486.35–487.04).

The fusion of Adam the sinner with Christ the Redeemer, both being sons whom God killed, is Joyce's revision of Genesis. The fusion is made specifically evident in the Buckley and the Russian general episode (see the Generic Paraphrase) and especially when the killed BUTT/Adam merges into the Trinity (354.08). It is also suggested at 533.11–13 when Adam says "olso haddock's fumb, in that Upper Room can speak loud to you some quite complimentary things about my clean charactering." The fish in the Upper Room implies that Christ at the Last Supper speaks favorably about Adam as his killed brother; "olso haddock's fumb" further suggests the fish (in this case an Irish salmon) which Finn MacCool touched with his thumb to get wisdom, thus tying to Adam Finn MacCool plus all the other Finns Joyce could reconnoiter, including Tim Finnegan.

Among the multitude of hidden meanings contained in the first mention of Finnegan at 3.19, we can deduce that the "great" story of the Fall in the Bible "entailed . . . the pftjschute [fall] of Finnegan, erse solid man" [first real man and therefore Adam]. The next mention, at 4.18, combines elements from freemasonry and Ibsen, but then at 4.24–25 "all the guennesses had met their exodus so that ought to show you what a pentschanjeuchy [Pentateuch] chap he was!" [Adam, Eve and the Serpent of Genesis had been exiled from Eden, and that ought to show you that he was the Biblical Adam.]. His identity is confirmed at 5.05 [Adam was the first to bear arms, according to *Hamlet*], and Finnegan is tied into mythical giants and the Russian general; but in lines 10–12 of the same paragraph, it is predicted that the mythical Finn will be Finnegan again [Tim Finnegan, among other aliases] and, as wine turns to vinegar, he will be "fined" by God's curse and death sentence.

Adam's identity as the Tim Finnegan personality is established at 24.03–15: "He dug in and dug out by the skill of his tilth . . ." [dressing and keeping the garden of Eden as God commanded in Gen. 2.15]; "our ancestor most worshipful, till he thought of a better one [his helpmeet, the woman, Gen. 2.22] . . . with that blushmantle upon him [blushing with shame (Gen. 3.7) after succumbing to temptation] from earsend to earsend" [to the end of his life]. Adam asks: "will you whoop for my deading is a? Wake?" [will you celebrate the death sentence that God imposed on me at a wake?]. Tim Finnegan answers in Irish Gaelic, "Anam muck an dhoul!" [Soul of the Devil]—then in English, "Did ye drink me doornail?" [Do you think I'm dead as a doornail?]. This line derives from "The Ballad of

Finnegan's Wake," a song long ago established as the source of the book's title; the drunken Tim had fallen from a ladder and was thought to be dead, but he revived when whiskey was splashed on him at his wake. As a whimsical dead Irishman who was resurrected, he is an appropriate personality for the fused Adam-Christ hero of *Finnegans Wake.* The song title itself is given at 607.16, and the ballad echoes more than forty times; but Finnegan's specific name occurs only three more times (at 221.27, 531.28, and 580.19).

Under the general designation "Finn" and its many modifications, there is a multitude of repetitions (see Glasheen, *Second Census*) of which Finn MacCool is of primary importance. MacCool was a hero of Irish legend, an ancient ancestor figure, and another appropriate personality for the Adam of *Finnegans Wake,* where Eden is in Ireland. The first riddle, on pages 126–39, asks a nearly four-hundred-part question whose answer is given as Finn MacCool; most of the phrases have little or nothing to do with MacCool, but they do concern Adam. The chapter starts with a question to the reader: "Who do you no [know]? . . . The echo is where in the back of the wodes" [We know it is Adam, who in Gen. 3.8 heard God's voice while hiding under the trees]. To make sure that the reader knows, Joyce also parenthetically includes Shaun (already established as Adam) with the surname Mac Irewick to emphasize the Irish Adam. A few of the semicoloned phrases more obviously pertaining to Adam are:

126.10	"myther rector" [erector {initiator} of religious myth]
126.13–14	"went nudiboots with trouters into a liffeyette" [was nude {Gen. 3.7} and had intercourse with the woman {Gen. 3.6}]
127.12	"was evacuated at the mere appearance of three germhuns" [was exiled by God the Trinity]
128.17	"shot two queans and shook three caskles" [had intercourse with Issy and Eve and annoyed the Trinity]
128.29	"makes a delicious *entrée* and finishes off the course" [ate food = forbidden fruit, and died]
129.19–20	"eats with doors open and ruts with gates closed" [after Adam ate the fruit with the woman, God closed the gates of Eden]
139.05–07	"is a farfar and morefar and a hoar father Nakedbucker in villas old as new" [Adam, originally naked, is our forefather]

Besides Adam, his *Finnegans Wake* co-brother Christ is included:

127.30   "commands to dinner and calls the bluff" [Christ's Last Supper]
128.34   "forbids us our trespassers as we forgate him" [Lord's Prayer]

Other phrases refer to *Finnegans Wake:*

135.33–34   "can be built with glue and clippings, scrawled or voided on a buttress" [Joyce said he was a "cut and paste man"]
137.10   "who guesse his title grabs his deeds" [he who knows Adam knows what he did; and also, he who knows what *Finnegans Wake* means will understand the contents]

And still other phrases connect with prominent episodes in the book:

127.02   "is too funny for a fish and has too much outside for an insect" [compares Christ and Adam/Gracehoper]
128.06–07   "shipshaped phrase of buglooking words with a form like the easing moments of a graminivorous [grass eater]" [refers to the Gracehoper as well as *Finnegans Wake*]
138.13–14   "was waylaid of a parker and beschotten by a buckeley"
127.17   "Dook Hookbackcrook" [the Norwegian captain, who is also Adam]
129.06   "tells the tailor to his tout" [Kersse the tailor is HCE/God, who conspired with the Serpent in the Norwegian captain episode]

Why is this vast catalog of misfit appellations listed for the legendary Irish hero? Because in Wakean logic all is one and one is all; Adam is our legendary ancestor, and therefore all legendary heroes are contained in Adam. Finn MacCool relates all of the other Finns as well as the Macs in *Finnegans Wake* to Adam through himself; "in fact, the sameold gamebold adomic structure of our Finnius the old One . . . may be there for you, Cockalooralooraloomenos," says ALP to her Irish descendants (615.06–08). She also advises in her letter: "While for whoever likes that urogynal pan of cakes one apiece it is thanks, beloved, to Adam, our former first Finnlatter" [Whoever likes women, or her genitals, should thank Adam, the first Finn] (619.02–03). It has already been shown that the statement at 108.21 indicates that Earwicker is not HCE; but in addition by calling him

"Fionn Earwicker" the conclusion is reinforced that all mentions of Finn as well as Earwicker refer to Adam.

Shem

The last riddle of Book I, Chapter 6—a brief two lines in Latin—has been the subject of considerable critical discussion, partly because it appears not to follow the Latin rules of grammar, which Joyce knew well. The controversy is discussed by E. L. Epstein in "The Turning Point" (64–67). Most of the questions raised are answered by this interpretation:

> 168.13 "*Sacer esto?*" [Who will be accursed?]
>   .14 "Answer: *Semus summus!*" [Like Shem, all of us!]

Since all of the questions in Book I, Chapter 6, of *Finnegans Wake* refer to Genesis, we may infer that the last one refers to God's curse and death sentence on Adam and on us as his descendants. By naming Shem as the Adam personality, this question establishes that Shem is Adam after the Fall and distinguishes him from Shaun prior to the Fall. The question also leads into the next chapter, which is about Shem the Penman.

Like God's curses in Gen. 3.14–24, the language of Chapter 7 of Book I is harsh and derogatory of Shem, the fallen Adam. Unlike Shaun, whose ancestor was the heroic Finn MacCool, Shem is descended from rapacious and plundering Vikings and Norwegians (169.04), as was the Norwegian captain personality of Adam when the Serpent baptized him: "Erievikkingr . . . furst of gielgaulgalls and hero chief explunderer of the clansakiltic" (326.07–09).

Another riddle (170.05) causing much consternation among Joyceans is the renowned "when is a man not a man?" The thirteen answers proposed, which Shem says are all wrong, are concerned with doubting the story of the Fall in Genesis. The true answer— "when he is a . . . Sham" (170.23)— may be interpreted as follows: God made man in His own image (Gen. 1.27), including His immortality, but when God exiled man to prevent him from eating of the tree of life (Gen. 3.22) and thus imposed death upon him, He transformed man into a mere sham—that is, a being who looked like God but who lacked His powers. Thus Shem is a Sham, the fallen Adam.

As Shaun is the Post, so Shem is the Penman; but while the Post has a clear literary antecedent, the best suggestion for an external source for Shem the Penman (sole mention at 125.23) was a real-life forger (see

McHugh, *Annotations*). Shaun the Post has many echoes, while "Penman" is parodied hardly at all (Shun the Punman [93.13] and Sheames de la Plume [177.30] [suggesting "nom de plume"]). It seems clear that when Shem is the Penman, he is Joyce himself, writing *Finnegans Wake.*

The rest of Book I, Chapter 7, is painfully autobiographical, with Joyce in the confessional saying *mea culpa*. Having exiled himself (and Nora, his wife) from Ireland, he compares himself with Shem, exiled from Eden. His relatively cautious (but equally anticlerical) brother, Stanislaus, plays the part of the pious Shaun dragged into exile with him. One must read Stanislaus Joyce's *My Brother's Keeper* to understand JUSTIUS's (as Brawn/ Shaun, 187.24ff.) complaint about his brother's ways and apparently insane effort—"You are mad!" (193.28)—in writing *Finnegans Wake;* and also to understand the pathetic apology of MERCIUS (Shem/Joyce), "the days of youyouth are evermixed mimine" (194.04).

Later Shaun/Yawn has a change of heart and says, "Oremus poor fraternibus" [Pray for my brother] (489.6) and "He feels he ought to be asamed of me [not ashamed, but as innocent as Shaun] as me to be ashunned of him [Shaun feels Shem shunned him]" (489.18).

The JUSTIUS/MERCIUS pair, however, is not typical of many similar pairs of names in the *Wake.*

Brothers and Twins

While it is useful in sorting out the vagaries of the *Wake* to consider Shem and Shaun as brothers, it should always be kept in mind that they are actually two personalities of Adam. Their relationship is peculiarly defined at 420.17–19, where Shaun is the son of Hek (read HCE/God) and Hek is the father of Shaun (in accordance with Gen. 2.7); but while Shem is the brother of Shaun, ALP is the mother of Shem (but not Shaun), and Hek is not stated to be Shem's father. HCE is Shaun/Adam's before-the-Fall father but not after he became transformed into Shem/Adam after the Fall. Likewise ALP is not the mother of Shaun/Adam because he is the pious, unfallen Adam (not yet knowing her), whereas she created the knowledge-able Shem by giving him the fruit, thereby transforming Shaun into Shem—as is explained in the **Prankquean** Generic Paraphrase. Similarly, the last two paragraphs of ALP's "mamafesta" (*Wake* 123–25) are a Wakean hodgepodge of *Finnegans Wake* and *Ulysses*, ALP and Molly Bloom, Christ and Adam, Shaun and Shem. She finally says, "thus he was at every time, that son, and the other time . . . passing out of one desire into its fellow. . . . one's half hypothesis . . . was hotly dropped and his room taken up by

. . . Shem the Penman" (125.05–23). Thus Shaun becomes Shem. At 306.05 –06 the brothers unite: "With this laudable purpose in loud ability let us be singulfied"; and at 462.16 Shaun/Jaun tells Issy: "I'm leaving my darling proxy behind" when he is transformed into Dave/Shem the Dancekerl.

References to the "twins" do not necessarily mean Shaun and Shem; as is pointed out in the **Prankquean** Generic Paraphrase, the "jiminies" Tristopher and Hilary are Adam and the Genesis woman because the woman, being created from Adam's flesh, is equivalent to their originating from the same fetal matter, and they are therefore twins. At 223.09 Issy explains her choral appearance as the rainbow girls, saying, "I am (twintomine) all thees [thee = you] thing." The "samuraised twimbs" (354.24) is explained by the sentence in which it is contained: When the old World was the Garden of Eden, ALP/Aphrodite introduced sex with the "same raised twins." At 330.30–31 we find "War's where! Which war? The Twwinns . . . Woos without! Without what? An apple." If we take "war" to mean "were," this question becomes: where were the twins who wooed without an apple? (The apple is not mentioned as the fruit in the Bible.) "*These twain are the twins that tick* Homo Vulgaris," says the Gracehoper (418.26), meaning that the twins of Eden generated human-kind. In all these cases the twins are Adam and Issy. However, Issy clearly refers to Shaun/Dolph and Shem/Kev at 286F4, when she notes these are "Singlebarrelled names for doubleparalleled twixtytwins," and the question "could anybroddy . . . have looked twinsomer than the kerl he left behind him?" is asked at 234.06 as Shaun leaves Shem behind with Issy. But either or both sets of twins can be meant by the washwoman who says at 215.25–29: "howmulty plurators made eachone in person . . . Twins of his bosom. Lord save us!"

Sometimes Shaun and Shem appear together under different pairs of names like JUSTIUS and MERCIUS and Dolph and Kev, already men-tioned. A case in point is Burrus and Caseous (161.12), who "have seemaultaneously sysentangled themselves." "Burrus . . . is a genuine prime [Adam] . . . full of natural greace [grace like Shaun and grease like butter], the mildest of milkstoffs," while "Caseous is obversely the revise [revision, not reverse] of him" (161.15–18). Caseous is also "Cheesugh!" (163.10). It should not be forgotten that both butter and cheese are derived from milk. This passage (161–68) is full of food and eating references, which recall the fruit eaten in Gen. 3.6; it is in fact an elaborate revision of the biblical Temptation story, with the woman present as Marge and Margareena, and the Serpent as Antonius. Toward the last of the book,

ALP is describing Finn/Adam's resurrection and anticipating their life in exile. She sees their life as a repetition of Eden, with their children as Shaun and Shem: "Them boys is so contrairy. . . . Galliver and Gellover. Unless they change by mistake. . . . Som. So oft. Sim. Time after time. The sehm asnuh" (620.12–16). The last mentioned pair are anticipated by "sammy and sonny" (335.08), named to set up the stage for Buckley and the Russian general.

More often than not, the pairs named are not the equivalent of Shem and Shaun but rather of God and Adam acting out the encounter of Gen. 3.8–13 or the exile of Gen. 3.22–24. The controversy and antipathy of these episodes has lead many critics who have misidentified the pairs to the conclusion that Shem and Shaun are at war. It has been shown above that this is not the case and that generally Shem and Shaun appreciate and acknowledge their identity. Most of the personalities in the following list are explicated in the Generic Paraphrases:

When Adam is:	HCE/God is:	at page and ff.
Jute	Mutt	16
Persse O'Reilly	Hosty	44
Mookse	Gripes	152
GLUGG	CHUFF	219
Norwegian captain	Kersse the tailor	311
BUTT, Buckley, and Russian general	TAFF	338
Gracehoper	Ondt	414
Eugenius, Jeremias Mauritius, Barnabas, and Michael	Honuphrius and Sulla	572
Juva	Muta	609
Tristan, Tristy, Trustan, and so on.	Mark	383

Additional Adam Personalities

Before "the rann that Hosty made" (44.07) Hosty/God runs through a list of seventeen names for Adam before selecting "Persse O'Reilly." None of these names is used again except "Mike," which together with Mick and Michael occurs frequently. This is because Michael means "Who is like God" in Hebrew; and since God made Adam in His own image (Gen. 1.27), Michael is Adam's name eighteen times. One example is the "funferall of poor Father Michael" (111.15). (Note that the Wakean Michael has no connection with the biblical Michael, archangel or king, other than his name.) The Mick in "*The Mime of Mick, Nick and the Maggies*" (219.19), "the mime mumming the mick" (48.10), and "*Mick, Nick the Maggot*" (399.26) is Adam.

An important personality is "Porter," so-called because he is Adam outside the gate of Eden after God's exile; a porter is one who stands at a portal expecting some kind of consideration. Joyce has been careful to conceal the identity of the Porter family. He wonders with us at 558.33: "Where are we at all? and whenabouts in the name of space? I don't understand. I fail to say. I dearsee you too." Then he proceeds to drop clues detectable to the diligent. We are in the bedroom of a "dwelling on outskirts of city [Dublin]" (558.36). It has contemporary Irish furnishings including "Adam's mantel" (559.02–03) and "Over mantelpiece picture of Michael" (559.11). Then comes the notorious passage describing the Porters having intercourse (559.14–29)—which was the very first thing that Adam and Eve did after their exile, according to Gen. 4.1, and they continued until Eve had two children (Gen. 4.2). Like the Porters "For them whom he have fordone make we newly thankful" (560.20–21), "Eve . . . said, I have gotten a man from the LORD" (Gen. 4.1).

"The Porters . . . are very nice people" and 560.22–36 tells us who they are: "Mr Porter . . . is an excellent forefather and Mrs Porter . . . is a most kind hearted messmother. A so united family pateramater." This means they are our ancestors, Adam and Eve in the personalities of a modern family living in Dublin. Since the Genesis story does not provide for the birth of a girl to perpetuate our race (Cain had to go to the land of Nod to get a wife, Gen. 4.16), Joyce digresses to repeat on page 561 God's creation of woman as in Gen. 2.22: in one of the "rooms on the upstairs . . . sleeps in now number one . . . the noveletta and she is named Buttercup [Issy] . . . to grasp the myth inmid the air . . . I will show herword in flesh. . . . It is dormition [the myth says she was made from Adam's flesh as he slept]" (561). After this digression, the story returns to Genesis 4: "who doez in sleeproom number twobis? The twobirds" (562.17). Although they might be Cain and Abel, one "Kevin is on heartsleeveside . . . with his lifted in blessing, his buchel Iosa [staff of Jesus]" (562.23–25) is Shaun; "The other . . . . making sharpshape his inscissors on some first choice sweets fished out of the muck. . . . How his book of craven images!" (563.01–04) is Shem/ Joyce. They are also Jacob and Esau, puck and prig, Formio and Cigalette (563.24–28)—in fact, anybody to throw the reader off by "passings sembles quick with quelled . . . kerryjevin [naming resemblances, alive and dead, to Adam]" (563.35–36).

In the catalog of Earwicker/Adam names he is called "*Sublime Porter*" (72.02), and in the attributes of Finn MacCool/Adam, "porter" is listed three times (135.07, 136.04, and 138.32). The concealment of the Porters' identification begins in the prankquean riddle. Sometimes the evident reference is to "porter" as a beverage—as when St. Patrick and St. Luke are trying to determine what happened in Eden and Luke says, "I've a big suggestion it was about the pint of porter" (511.19). Similar meanings occur at 510.24, 530.12, and 553.27 ("lindub" = lionn dubh = porter). In all cases, there is at least a veiled implication of Adam's presence.

There remain a few miscellaneous names, perhaps not fully activated personalities, but certainly references to Adam:

39.16   "Treacle Tom" seems to be Tom the piper's son, who stole a pig. Pig, pork, ham, or indeed anything to eat is equivalent in *Finnegans Wake* to the forbidden fruit; and therefore, especially since Tom's pig was stolen [forbidden], he is Adam. (Glasheen's *Census* gives additional citations.)

49.02   "His husband": since Adam kept and dressed God's garden (Gen. 2.15), he is HCE/Hosty's husbandman.

117.16   "Highho Harry" is Henry VIII, who married an Anne (Boleyn) as Adam did A[nna]LP.

255.28   "Father of Truants": the Gaelic etymology of *truant* refers to a poor, distressed, or wretched creature, here meaning Adam and Eve cursed.

307.14   "Parnellites": although Parnell is never named exactly, Glasheen and others have found a number of allusions; he was an acceptable surrogate for Adam, having been sacrificed and effectively exiled for a sexual involvement.

336.21–22   "Publius Manilus, fuderal private" and "old gartener" involve Adam's service as gardener and peaceful, innocent soldier of God.

619.17   "Soldier Rollo" also refers to Adam's service to HCE/God. Buckley and the Russian general are also both Adam as soldiers (see Chapter 7).

Personalities of ALP

Anna Livia Plurabelle exists as three principal personalities:

1. Issy, the Genesis woman (Gen. 2.22) before the Fall;
2. Eve, the wife and mother (Gen. 3.20) after the Fall; and
3. ALP, the Mother Goddess.

She has many sub-personalities, making her a plural belle indeed.

We are told that "her name is A.L.P." (102.23). This really doesn't tell us who she is, "But there's a little lady waiting" introduces the next chapter, about her "mamafesta," which develops aspects of the Mother Goddess. Issy is uggested by "her holden heirheaps" [golden hair heaps + descendants] (102.24) and the "rainbow" girls (.27) with colored names, while Kate/Eve is "who but Crippled-with-Children would speak up for Dropping-with-Sweat" (102.29). As a composite ALP, "she made up all her myriads of drifting minds in one" (159.07).

Issy

Isha, which is the Hebrew word for "woman," was the name used in the original, ancient Masoretic text of Gen. 2.22 for the first woman. That name at 140.27 is the direct confirmation of her identity, although over fifty homophones announce her presence elsewhere. At 146.15–17 she says, "I'll teach him when to wear what women callours. On account of the gloss of the gleison Hasaboobrawbees isabeaubul." This might be paraphrased: I'll teach him to like the woman so-called because the word requiring explanation is derived from the sacred Hebrew song "Isha the Beautiful."

The name "Issy" is used only once at 459.06, but readers of *Finnegans Wake* have come to use the diminutive to refer to the young, naive temptress personality. One of the first attempts to render the Bible into English is an Old English song written about A.D. 1250 titled "The Story of Genesis and Exodus" (edited from the Cambridge text by Richard Morris in 1865 and reprinted in America by Greenwood Press), where the section on Adam and Eve says "Issa was her first name." Our modern Bibles translate *Isha* as "woman," and as such she is called until Adam names her Eve in Gen. 3.20. She is depicted as a delightful, innocent, sexy young girl in those parts of the *Wake* relating activities before and during the Temptation and seduction (Gen. 3.1–6). Here is how she looked as she was created at 255.27–36 (and in Gen. 2.21–22):

> For the producer (Mr. John Baptister Vickar) [HCE/God] caused a deep abuliousness [sleep] to descend on the Father of Truants [Adam] and, at a side issue [God "took one of his ribs, and closed up the flesh instead thereof"], pluterpromptly brought on the scene the cutletsized [rib] consort ["made he a woman"], foundling filly of fortyshilling fostertailor [HCE/Tailor] and shipman's shopahoyden [see **Norwegian captain**], weighing ten pebble ten [little stones, probably ten

pounds], scaling five footsy five [five feet, five inches tall] and span-
ning thirtyseven inchettes round the good companions [breasts],
twentynine ditties round the wishful waistress [waist], thirtyseven
alsos round the answer to everything [hips], twentythree of the same
round each of the quis separabits [thighs], fourteen round the beginning of happiness [calf] and nicely nine round her shoed for slender
[size 9A shoe].

Her character and history also incorporate Lilith, the female demon probably of Sumerian origin, from the Jewish Pseudepigrapha. Various versions
have Lilith coupling with Satan and other demons and also with Adam.
Lilith occurs as Hilary in the prankquean episode (which see) and is clearly
joined with Issy at 513.25: "And whit what was Lillabil Issabil maideve [the
virgin maid or woman], maid at?" Among other related names are lilady,
lilyth, Lillytrilly, and Lil. Sometimes (for example, at 306F4) Lily refers to
Issy/Lilith, but usually Lily is more directly connected with the flower or
vegetation goddess aspect of ALP. In the only occurrence of Lilith as such
(205.11), she seems to be still Satan's wife and not yet absorbed into Issy.

As Nuvoletta at 157.08 and following, she seems to be the Issy which
had been reabsorbed into the ALP persona after the appearance of Eve.
Here she reemerges briefly, perhaps as a mother-goddess nymph, to ob-
serve the encounter between Mookse/Adam and Gripes/God. At 159.06–18
she reflects sadly that she could not prevent or settle their quarrel although
she was created to be a helpmeet. Finally she retires to Elysium to join
ALP's godhead.

Atherton (197) has identified Issy with the Egyptian goddess Isis in his
discussion on *The Book of the Dead* and cites "Is, is" at 570.30 as an
example. That Isis recovered Osiris's body parts, which were scattered by
Set, is referred to at 26.10; the recovery of all except the penis, which was
replaced by Isis, makes her character appropriate for Issy.

Isolde is also appropriate in the Issy personality because of her Irish
origin, her seduction of Tristan, and his saving her from King Mark. She
appears under such names as Iseut, Isod, Izod, Ysold, Liselle, Izzy, and
Tizzy. Soldi, Sally, and Criss come from the *The Dissociation of a Personality,* the multiple personality work by Morton Prince.

The aspect of an attractive young virgin also incorporates Jonathan
Swift's two Esthers, in the names Isther, Estarr, Essie, Yssia, Stilla, and
Vanissy, as well as Pipette.

Two groups of girls appear in Book II, Chapter 1, which are collectives representing Issy as a sort of Greek chorus. The first are the Maggies named at 219.19 (as well as at 48.11) along with Mick (Adam) and Nick (Serpent). Maggy is a sub-personality of Issy/ALP from the very beginning at 7.32, where "our maggy seen all, with her sisterin shawl"; and ALP's letter "proceded to mention Maggy" (111.11) and was "a letter to last a lifetime for Maggi" (211.22). We learn at 234.34–36 that the Maggies are "Hymnumber twentynine. . . . Happy little girlycums. . . . They've come to chant en chor," and at 249.36 that they are "Twentynines of bloomers gegging een man." They seem to be the same girls that Jaun meets at St. Berched's, where "there were as many as twentynine hedge daughters out of Benent Saint Berched's national nightschool" (430.01–02). Notice, however, that Jaun/Adam converses only with his (singular) sister, Issy (for example, at 431.21, 439.26, 441.18, 448.34, and 452.08), until she answers him at 457.25ff. "Marge" (at 165.14, 22, and 166.05)—"she is *so* like the sister" (165.14), "that demilitery young female" 166.04)—is just another version of "Maggy," who is associated with the brother personalities of Adam (Burrus and Caseous) as Margareen (at 164.14–20, and 166.30).

The other collective Issy is what we have come to refer to as the "Rainbow Girls," although that appellation does not occur in the *Wake*. They seem to be a subdivision of the Maggies at 223.06, and Issy says, "Well, Maggy, I got your castoff devils all right and fits lovely" (273F6). This may refer to the seven devils cast out of Mary Magdalene (Mark 16.9) or to the demons Lilith bred. In any event they are named in the "Mick, Nick, and the Maggies" chapter (at 223.06–07, and again at 572–73) and are called the "Seven Sisters" at 248.35. They are also known as the "seven hores" (379.14), "seven honeymeads" (558.19), and "rainbow huemoures" (102.27). None of these names are actually colors, although they probably have the rainbow colors hidden in their content, as has been discussed frequently by critics. In any event the girls do not seem to be around when God's rainbow promise to Noah is mentioned.

The "jinnies" in the "Museyroom" (8–9) are probably not representative of Issy, although they behave like her; they are probably Sophia's aids in the Gnostic war with the evil God.

Eve

Eve received her name in Gen. 3.20, after being cursed by God, when "Adam called his wife's name Eve; because she was the mother of all living." In the Masoretic text the name is *Hwwh,* or *Hawwah,* supposedly meaning "life" in Hebrew. The Latin is *Heva,* which occurs at 494.26:

"Three cheers and a heva heva for the name of Dan Magraw [Serpent]," thus connecting her with the Temptation; and at 38.30 we find "the writress of Havvah-ban-Annah" where the "writress" is ALP, who wrote the letter as "Annah."

Giving "woman" a name establishes a change in personality; this is accomplished on pages 457–59, when Issy is transformed into Eve. After Juan/Adam performs the sacrament of the Last Supper (from 455.30 to 457.04), as Christ did when preparing to die, he bids good-byes to the girls at St. Berched's (457.05). Issy responds in the following Generic Paraphrase, perhaps in a "Tizzy," knowing she will be transformed into Eve:

457.25	We were too happy, I knew something would happen . . .
.30	but listen, I want [anticipating Adam's death, like the girls in the Maronite ritual of Christ's burial; see Atherton 189 and Joyce's letter of August 8, 1928] to whisper my whish [departure].
.32	Of course engine [penis] dear, I'm ashamed
.34	[Gen. 3.7] . . . over this lost moment's of memento nosepaper [knows paper is ALP's letter imparting the knowledge from the tree]
.36	which . . . is all at home [with ALP] . . . but accept this
458.01	teeny witween piece . . . in place of [the original with
.03	much left to learn. Kisses] . . .
.09	when (n)ever you make use of it . . . think galways [always of Nora] again and again, never forget . . . sister Maggy.
.12	. . . since levret bounds [she is soon to marry her husband's {Shaun's} brother {Shem} as Eve, following the Hebrew custom of levirate] . . .
.17	. . . but it doesn't do her [Eve] justice . . . in the magginbottle [the body which contains the collection of Issy/ Maggy personalities].
.35	I will pack my comb and mirror [to see her mirror image Eve] to practice oval owes and artless awes [girls in the Maronite ritual; see above reference].
459.02	. . . I will say for you the Allmichael [Our Father + all
.04	Michael/Adam] with nurse Madge [cunt], my linking class
.05	girl [Eve, her mirror image, links her through Adam/Shem to Shaun] . . . in her sleeptalking when I paint measles on
.06	her and mudtuskers [mustaches] to make her a man [refers

to Sally, one of Morton Prince's "Christine Beauchamp's" personalities, who so annoyed her person-mates].

.10   I call her Sosy [double] . . .

.18   . . . she's terribly nice really, my sister . . .

.30   And, of course, dear professor [ALP], I understand [why

.31   she has to change personalities]. You can trust me

.32   though I change thy name [from Issy to Eve] though not the letter [letters: ALP].

The paragraph at 226.04–20 also describes Issy's transformation: "Poor Isa sits a glooming. . . . She is fading out. . . . And among the shades that Eve's now wearing she'll meet anew fiancy . . . Mammy [ALP] was, Mimmy [Issy] is, Minuscoline's [minus colleen {maiden} = Eve {no virgin}] to be. . . . The same renew."

"Lo, lo, lives love! Eve takes a fall" (293.21) indicates that Issy (as Lola) lived the life of love with Adam but let Eve take the punishment. Also "to make plain Nanny Ni Sheere a full Dinamarqueza" (328.14) is to convert Issy into Eve/Kate since Kate is a servant like Dickens's "Marchioness" (see **Norwegian captain**).

"Eve" is the first name to occur in *Finnegans Wake,* even preceding Adam's in the first line, where it is linked to ALP by "riverrun." It occurs twenty more times in both uppercase and lowercase, such as "haloed be her eve" [not only the Lord's Prayer's "hallowed be thy name" but also implying that by "eve" replacing "name" it is ALP's halo or shadowy subpersonality] (104.02). "Die eve, little eve, die!" (215.04) announces the Liffey's fate as it flows into the sea near the Poolbeg Lighthouse, as it does at the book's end.

Eve is combined with Pandora to give the presents listed in detail on pages 210–12 to "her furzeborn sons and dribblederry daughters." They seem to be a combination of God's curses and Pandora's ills alleviated by the hope that was also contained in her "box" [vagina]. Joyce's letter of March 7, 1924, indicates he included Pandora with ALP. "Nanette" (117.16) also links "little Anna" with Eve. Nevertheless, in keeping with Joyce's style, her presence is never overtly connected with the action.

Eve as Kate

After the exile from Eden, Eve most often appears as the sub-personality Kate (or Kathe, Kavya, Katy, katey, and so on), while the names "Kateclean,"

"Kothereen the Slop," and "swabsister Katya" identify her role as cleaning woman. It may be that, like the washwomen, she is trying to eradicate the stain of the Fall; it is more likely that "Kate the Cleaner" (211.19) emphasizes the state imposed on woman by God's curses (Gen. 3.16) and certainly, as Joyce saw it, on Irish women.

79.27   "Kate Strong, a widow. . . ." This Dublin garbage collector is thoroughly described in 79.27–80.06. Her presence is required in the creation of Dublin perhaps as the first city after the Fall or as the original creation

.33   of Eden. She is a widow, "as her weaker [husband, Adam] had turned him to the wall [fell and died]." But she is also one of those "Ladies [who] did not disdain those pagan ironed times" (79.14) as well as one of the "Venuses [who] were gigglibly temptatrix" (79.18). Thus she is an ALP personality, most probably as soon-to-be widowed Eve whose husband has been sentenced to death.

211.19   "Kate the Cleaner" gets a muck rake and brush from the Varians Factory as an appropriate gift. Adaline Glasheen (136) says "Kate" is derived from the Greek *kathairein*, "to clean."

380.01–04   "Variants' Katey" links Kate with drudgery as a result of her curse of sorrow (Gen. 3.16). Here "at the end of this age" she "tells of all befells" [that is, the story of the Fall in Genesis 3].

221.12–16   "KATE . . . kook-and-dishdrudge" is the fallen Eve who believes "the show must go on."

556.32   "Kothereen the Slop" is the woman about to become Eve after being tempted by the Serpent.

566.10   "The swabsister Katya to have duntalking [at Gen. 3.2–3 Eve talks to the Serpent] and to keep shakenin dowan her droghedars [take down her drawers—that is, ate the fruit. {Gen. 3.6}].

334.28   This identification of "katey" as Eve requires some explication of the context. At 334.06–16 God in His Trinity recites Gen. 3.22, giving His reasons why Adam must be cast out of Eden. He then recapitulates at 334.20–23: "it is the chomicalest thing how it pickles up the punchey and the jude ["Behold, the man is become as one of us"]. If you'll gimmy your thing to me I will gamey a sing to thee ["to know good and evil"]. Stay where you're dummy! To get her to go ther ["lest he put forth his hand"]. He banged the scoop and she bagged the sugar ["and take also of the tree of life and eat"]." (The rest of the paragraph—to 334.27— relates HCE/God's death sentence to the Tavern scene and the Buckley episode.) Gen. 3.23 is contained in 334.28–30: "So the katey's came [Eve has come] and the katey's game [Eve is willing to go with Adam]. And so gangs [went] sludgenose [the Serpent]. And that henchwench what hopped it [wench Eve went hence] dunneth there duft the. Duras [and shut the door of Eden]."

116.22   The phrase "waiting kates" combines wedding cakes with Kate to defend her being considered a prostitute (116.16) by "the curate [HCE/God] one who brings strong waters (gingin! gingin!)" (116.18) because "the beautiful presence of waiting kates [Eve] will unto life's (!) [! = violent end] be more than enough to make any milkmike [young Michael/ Adam] . . . hate into his twin nicky [Nick = Serpent] and that Maggy's tea [Adam's seduction], or your majesty [HCE/ God]" (116.21–24).

40.11   In the phrase "he [Adam as Tom the piper's son, who stole a pig to eat, which in Wakean logic, is the same as eating the forbidden fruit] having beham [been eating] with katya ["widow" Kate]," the word *beham* also ties together Behan/ Serpent (27.31) with the Dublin ham merchant at 39.17 and 379.36.

27.31   The phrase "old Kate" occurs within the context of HCE/ God's having been consoling dead Finnegan at his wake (since line 24.16). He promises he'll keep "an eye on queer Behan [Serpent] and old Kate [Eve exiled] and the butter" [food equal to the forbidden fruit. In other words He will keep them apart].

335.19   "Katu." Preparing for the Crimean War in the Buckley episode which follows, a Maori war chant is distorted to say: Kate-ty is his! Kate-ty wants to! [in other words, Eve belongs to Adam and wants to be his wife {Gen. 3.16}].

333.07   The character called "katekattershin" is the same Kate who conducts the tour of the "Museyroom" (8.08). Here, she is present near the Crimea, getting ready for Buckley and the Russian general.

8.08   The character "mistress Kathe" knows the story of the exhibits in the "Museyroom." Embedded in that story of the battle between Wellington and Napoleon is Genesis 3, with Willingdone as HCE/God defeating Lipoleum as Adam. Kate was there as a "jinnie" [camp follower]. (See **HCE: personalities of.**)

530.32   "Kitty." The Four Old Masters call for Kate/Eve as a Dublin dweller as well as the figure on the coat of arms to tell them the history of what happened in Eden, which she does from 530.36 to 531.26. At 531.15 she identifies herself as Kate Lanner, the Dublin soubrette (see Glasheen, 144).

394.28   "parkside pranks of quality queens [prankquean and the woman/Issy/ALP], katte efter kinne [Kate ever after related to them]."

239.21   The word "catholeens" involves Yeats's Countess Cathleen (not loved by Irish Roman Catholics) as Kate/ALP/Maggies, who want "all us romance catholeens shall have ones [once and] for all amanseprated [a separate man {Adam} and emancipated]."

448.10   The phrase "Cowtends Kateclean" also includes Yeats's Countess Cathleen in Joyce's Kate.

93.22   The name "Kavya," which is the Sanskrit word for "poet," also includes Kate as the ALP personality since we are instructed to ask her for "the kay" [the key, which is sex, according to ALP's letter].

421.04   In the phrase "Key at Kate's," as with "Kavya" at 93.22, the key is a reference to sex in the letter.

113.21   Continuing a discussion of ALP's letter, it is supposed to tell "why Kate takes charge of the waxworks"—in other words, why ALP as Mother Goddess takes over creation from HCE/God.

141.29   Although not even named here, Kate is certainly in the kitchen with "the Housesweep Dinah." [In Gen. 34.1–29 Dinah was raped by a Hivite prince and was avenged by her brothers, who at first agreed the Hivites could marry Israeli women if they submitted to circumcision. The Hivites agreed, but two days later, while the Hivites were still in great pain, the brothers boldly entered the city and killed every male.]

Personalities of the Serpent

The Earwig as Serpent

Readers have long conjectured about the significance (if any) of the earwig in *Finnegans Wake*. Most have been content to consider such references as merely a variation on "Earwicker," who in turn is believed to be HCE. Both assumptions are wrong. Only variants containing a *g*, such as *earwigger, earwugs, ladwigs,* or *eeriewhig* are equivalent to *earwig* itself, a word which occurs only five times, including plurals. There are numerous other references to earwig/Serpent which do not incorporate the "earwig" spelling, such as variants on the French *perce-oreille*, lobsters and worms. All of these are listed below, explicating the Serpent inclusion.

Words containing a *k*, such as *Earwicker, earwicked, earwanker, Eyrewaker,* and *Eelwick* do not refer to the Serpent of Genesis 3, although they serve Joyce's purpose of producing ambiguity and confusion.

Adaline Glasheen's *Census* has reference to a Jacob Earwig, who is a character in an 1842 play, *The Boots at the Swan,* by Charles Selby. Jacob Earwig does not appear as such in *Finnegans Wake,* but there are several references to the play's title and to other characters in the play, as Marion Cumpiano explains in *The Boots at the Swan* (517). There is one possible reference that might include the Serpent: at 145.22, Issy is attempting to tempt Adam and says she would risk attention by a "policeman" or "boots at the Post." In the play Jacob Earwig is known as "the boots" and dresses as a policeman, so he is here by inference, but it is doubtful that the Serpent is included. All other citations refer to Shem and Shaun, as mentioned by Cumpiano. These are therefore *generically* related to Adam.

Earwigs are brown to black insects about one-half to three- quarters of an inch long and less than one-quarter wide. They resemble beetles, although technically they are not. The abdomen comprises about one-half of the body length and terminates in a pincer-like appendage that is used defensively. Since the legs are all positioned in front, this rather large abdominal segment tends to wiggle from side to side as it is dragged forward when the insect walks. They are geographically widespread and sometimes occur in such large numbers that they can become a nuisance. The insects are otherwise harmless and are, in fact, beneficial because they are scavengers, eating garbage and accumulated grass and garden litter. They are nocturnal, hiding during the day under stones, boards, wood-piles, shrubbery, and steps. The superstition that they crawl into the ears of sleeping persons is unfounded, but they do tend to crawl into confined places. An easy way to trap them is to lay down a short length of pipe closed at one end; during the day they hide inside and may be captured by closing the open end of the pipe.

Why does the earwig of *Finnegans Wake* disguise the Serpent in the Garden of Eden? There are several reasons.

First, the garden in *Finnegans Wake* is in Ireland, specifically Phoenix Park, Dublin. But there are no snakes in Ireland because, as legend has it,

St. Patrick drove them out. Consequently some other creature must take the Serpent's place in the retelling of the story of the Fall of Man. Since earwigs wiggle their abdomens from side to side, thus resembling the locomotion of a snake, Joyce substitutes the earwig but credits St. Patrick for doing, so as will be shown below.

Second, in Gen. 3.14–15, God cursed the Serpent: "upon thy belly shalt thou go, and dust shalt thou eat all the days of thy life: And I will put enmity between thee and the woman, and between thy seed and her seed; it shall bruise thy head, and thou shall bruise his heel." Now not only does an earwig crawl on its belly in the dust but also we descendants of "her seed" are inclined to "bruise the heads" of earwigs by stepping on them.

Third, earwigs are supposed (incorrectly) to crawl into the ears of sleeping persons. This extends the analogy of snake for penis by including the idea of penetration of a body cavity.

Fourth, a slang use of "earwig" is as a metaphor for a private and malicious prompter; that is, it carries a message into the ear as did the Serpent when he tempted the woman in Gen. 3.1–5.

Clive Hart's *Concordance* lists only two actual occurrences of "earwig," but there are eight closely related words (plurals, vowel change, and so forth) and seventy-one "overtones." The following citations and Generic Paraphrases substantiate the presence of the Serpent in *Finnegans Wake* wherever "earwig" is referred to:

> 19.12–18   In this passage snakes were swarming over Ireland but St. Patrick caught ("cotched") them. "Sss! See the snake wurrums everyside! Our durlbin is sworming in sneaks. They came to our island from the triangular Toucheaterre [touch Eve's pubic area] beyond the wet prairie rared up in the midst of the cargon of prohibitive pomefructs [forbidden fruit] but along landed Paddy [St. Patrick] Wippingham and the his garbagecans cotched [caught] the creeps of them pricker ["quicker," but also St. Patrick is catching "pricks"' to promote chastity] than our whosethere outofman [woman] could quick up her whatsthats."
>
> 287–89.   This passage concerns St. Patrick (288.14, "twiced-hecame") and his banishment of snakes (288F6, "Creeping Crawleys"; 289.07, "ophis"; 289.19, "schlang"; 289.25, "reptile") from Ireland. The presence of the earwig is noted in the entomological terms "pupal," "tailwords," "eggways," and "znigznaks" [humbug].
>
> 20.23   Here Joyce says to the reader: "every busy eerie whig's a bit of a torytale to tell."

17.34   The phrase "alp on earwig" reflects the temptation of the woman by the Serpent.

31.11   The word *earwuggers* occurs as Adam in the guise of "Humphrey or Harold" encounters God ("yer maggers" = your majesty) and in answer to God's challenge (Gen. 3.11) answers: I was just taking the bait of Your bloody earwig/Serpent.

31.25–28   The "earwigger," "our red brother" [the Devil], "would audibly fume" if he knew he was to be an earwig in *Finnegans Wake.*

47.17   "Big earwigs on the green / The largest ever you seen." This implies that the Serpent will be an earwig in green Ireland, but they could also be lobsters.

79.16   In "carry, as earwigs do their dead, their soil to the earthball," Joyce confuses (probably intentionally) the earwig with the dung beetle, the prototype of the Egyptian scarab.

164.25–29   The use of a bowl as a guide to cut hair "might be usefully compared with an earwig on a full bottom"; that is the earwig/Serpent is a guide to the woman's bottom.

173.09–15   Here it is suggested that the earwig/Serpent would crawl into the woman's ear and prattle his proposal like Adam used his penis in her orifice and Joyce would insert heresies in his reader's ear.

243.14–17   The woman nourishes ("noutre him") the young lad Adam with her apple ("elmer") while trying to keep "the ladwigs out of his lugwags"—the earwig/Serpent's message from his ears. The presence of the Serpent on this page is reinforced by "devlin" at .22 and "Pursy Orelli" at .34

354.32–33   The insect products carmine dye, silk, and honey relate "lucifug" [Lucifer + bug] to the "bettle" [earwigs resemble beetles].

360.32–33   This reference to earwig implies that the enormous Serpent is indeed a little bug in Ireland.

467.28–36   The earwig/Serpent is also an "Illstarred punster" sent by God in the form of His Trinity or the four evangelists, to whisper temptations in Irish ears. Meanwhile God/HCE is far away spreading his false gospel.

579.25   In what seems to be a list of proverbs, "Let earwigger's wivable teach you the dance!" seems to recommend the Serpent's activities.

512.23–27   The French name *perce-oreille* for earwig which means literally "pierce ear" is referred to in "So lent she him ear to burrow his manhood (or so it appierce)" and in the Latin for "You first earpierced me." [Of course Adam was the first to pierce her other body cavity—or was he?]

491.23–36   St. Patrick asks: [Is the story being told again with the woman {"sallies"}? Yawn answers: "Perce" O'Reilly {earwig}, Quick. Now Eve/ALP says, "And he said he was only taking the average grass temperature" in the Irish Garden of Eden. She continues: Many felicitations to the earwig who was just waiting for the poor Irish person, but he stepped into the breach {absence of snakes} and put on his recruiting trousers {recruiting sinners for God}.]

390.04–07   The statement "his old fellow . . . earing his wick with a pierce of railing, and . . . the old croniony, Skelly, with the lether belly" connects earwig and *perce-oreille* with the Serpent cursed to crawl on his belly (Gen. 3.14)

496.14   The earwig/Persse O'Reilly/Serpent was cursed (Gen. 3.14).

482.03–04   Yawn/Adam and St. Patrick are discussing who caused the Fall of Man. What's his name, asks Yawn. *Perce-oreille*, answers St. Patrick.

378.09–12   "P.R.C.R.L.L. Royloy" means *perce-oreille* the "unnamed nonirishblooder" [Serpent] who becomes Irish ("Greenislender"). "But we're molting superstituettes out of his fulse thortin guts" [But we're making a substitute by molting the earwig into a Serpent].

There are other references to *perce-oreille* as earwig in the Generic Paraphrase **Buckley and the Russian general;** they do not always have earwig as the dominant element as they do for example in the **Ballad.**

Another foreign-language equivalent for *earwig* is the Irish *geille,* usually transliterated "gill":

36.35   "Gaping Gill, swift to mate errthors . . . (diagnosing through eustacetube that it was to make with a markedly postpuberal . . . ethics)" [The watching Serpent, swift to mate erring immortals, overhears the stuttering HCE/God, Who in the previous paragraph is instructing Adam as in Gen. 2.16–17 about the ethics of not eating the fruit of the tree of knowledge].

227.30   "Gillie" is probably the Serpent here with whom Adam is having a hurried communion of food or fruit.

244.23   The Serpent "Gill" has not yet appeared in the retelling of Genesis 3.

354.13　The phrase *"Goll's gillie"* is a reference to God's devil, the Serpent. (See **Buckley**.)

617.19　"Gilly in the gap" says that the Serpent will help. (See **ALP's letter**.)

In some places the Serpent may be a lobster, perhaps because earwigs vaguely resemble small lobsters, although they have their claws on the wrong end. Many of the lobster usages are not so intended, or else are so obscure as to be doubtful. The following references seem to be pertinent:

31.03–11　In a confrontation (Gen. 3.9) God asks Adam if he was flyfishing for lobsters. Adam answers: [No your majesty, I was just catching earwigs].

138.03–04　The statement "the lobster pot that crabbed our keel, the garden pet that spoiled our squeezed peas" refers to the Serpent and his part in the Temptation.

249.03　Reflecting on her temptation, Issy/Eve/ALP says, "he'd be the grand old greeneyed lobster."

351.09–10　"Homard [lobster] Kayenne was always jiggilyjugging about . . . when our woos with the wenches went wined for a song" [Although Omar Khayyam is present, so is the lobster/Serpent who was wiggling about when the woman was tempted].

Similarly, because worms crawl and wiggle on the ground, there are a few places where they substitute for earwig/Serpent:

37.13　Adam says to God: "I have met with you . . . too late" (Gen. 3.10), already having met with the worm/Serpent. Page 37 is filled with fruit and food references, suggesting the forbidden fruit and the consuming of it.

509.26–29　[It is a lie that the woman was the cause of the Fall, so "puff the earthworm outer my ear" and denounce the myth of the Serpent.]

539.33–540.03　The statement "the twotoothed dragon worms with allsort serpents" may refer to the Serpent. Since it occurs where Adam is "here where my tenenure of office and my toils of domestication first began," it refers to Adam's charge to "dress and keep" the Garden of Eden (Gen. 2.15) and to name the animals (Gen. 2.19). It indicates that even before God made woman, snakes had completely vanished from

Ireland and the "notorious naughty livers are not found on our rolls."

Other Personalities

Joyce uses the word *serpent* only three times in *Finnegans Wake*. At 89.31–32 "a head in thighs under a bush . . . would bait a serpent" certainly refers to the biblical animal; at 494.10 and 540.01 the relationship is more obscure but definitely present, as in the Latin *coluber* at 157.01. There are also four inclusions of "serpentine" which vaguely include temptation and sin.

There are twelve verbatim uses of snake and at least seven derivative words including:

19.12 [Snakes swarmed in Dublin and St. Patrick caught them.]
36.07 "triplehydrad snake"—implies that the Serpent was related to the Trinity
132.16 "hissed a snake charmer off her stays"—says that Adam kissed Issy
494.15 "Holy snakes"
435.20 "boa"

Book II, Chapter 1 was published separately in 1934 as "The Mime of Mick, Nick and the Maggies," and here Nick is the Serpent. The folk title "Old Nick" for the Devil is derived from the German *nickel,* meaning "demon" or "devil." The word *Nick* or *nick* is used nine times, four associated with "maggies" (a collective personality of ALP/Eve) and always referring to the biblical Serpent. At 296.17 he is called directly by his German name, "Nickel," and occasionally by "nickelname," "Nickekellous," and "Nickil."

There are at least ten occurrences of "Coppinger," or "Carpenger," "Cabbanger," or "Coppercheap," all of which seem to refer to condoms, especially 574.13 and 22, 55.18, 280L, and 341.35. Joyce equates condoms with Satanic temptation.

The Serpent is also "Magraw." At 511.07 he is "in search of a stammer" (that is, HCE), and at 494.26 a stuttering HCE/God gives him "three cheers." As Magraw he is the "wedding beast[best]-man" for Adam/Norwegian captain (511.02).

"Magrath" seems to be another name: he is ALP's "pegger" at 584.06, and at 495.03 HCE/Sully is called "Magrath's thug." The connection here is conveniently obscure, but the "ballets in Parsee Franch" is HCE's "Ballad of Persse O'Reilly" (see Chapter 7), wherein the Serpent is designated as

HCE/God's "sheriff Clancy." All this refers to the idea of the Serpent's seducing the woman as God's agent. The three occurrences of "Kinsella" also appear to refer to the Serpent, although this is far from clear; it may mean "kin of Sully."

Another vague name is "Mr. Fry," perhaps invoking "hot as hell." At 43.09 he is present in Dublin as "Paul Fry," and at 342.10, he is at the racetrack. Shaun/Adam makes conversation with HCE/God at 413.35 by asking: By the way, how is Mr. Fry?— apparently meaning the Serpent.

Some miscellaneous cognomens for the Serpent include:

27.31	queer Behan	313.15	Rechnar Jarl
38.26	Mr Browne	313.15	Roguenor
65.05	old geeser	315.04	Shufflebotham
65.17	Mr Hunker	315.09	Burniface
69.32	Herr Betreffender	325.26	Gophar
75.20	Nash of Girahash	353.11	Cocksnark of Killtork
144.30	Mr Polkingstone	390.07	Skelly, with the lether belly
145.32	Brimstoker	436.11	Temptation Tom
167.01	Antonius	516.05	MacSmashall Swingy
221.06	Saunderson	572.30	Magravius
241.15	Aasdocktor Talop	606.29	Old Toffler
241.22	Master Milchku	618.01	MacCrawls
311.21	ship's Husband	618.05	Mr Sneakers

Other sobriquets include:

38.19	director	335.08	varlet de shambles
38.31	Crookedribs	351.36	stumblebum
75.21	kreeponskneed	416.13	sexton
145.16	meddlar	442.18	insister
146.06	old somebooby	467.29	Illstared punster
241.01	Big dumm crumm	491.26	sharepusher
271.26	glider	561.34	strifestirrer
315.01	butcheler	615.29	Sneakers in the grass
316.11	good mothers gossip	617.31	dumb tyke
317.06	shop's housebound		

Atherton and Glasheen both suggest that "hog" citations refer to devils. For example, "oggog hogs" (366.26) may be false gods, devils, or evil spirits which may infect humans, but this is not the biblical Serpent nor are any other "hogs." All occurrences of "pig," "pork," "ham," "lard," and so forth refer to food, which is equivalent to the fruit of seduction, not to the Serpent. These words are frequently associated with Tom the piper's son, who, like Adam, ate forbidden (or stolen) food. Likewise the name "Lili Coninghams" (58.30) contains Lilith of the Cunning Hams [buttocks] plus the woman's fruit.

Chapter Six

Generic Paraphrases of Bible Segments

The Fall Story

The segments of the third chapter of Genesis are ordinarily used as the basis of separate *Finnegans Wake* episodes; normally it is not followed in its entirety. One instance where the complete saga is used is in the conversation between St. Patrick and St. Luke. This version starts at 515.23, with St. Patrick's asking Luke "how these funeral games . . . massacreedoed as the holiname rally round took place" [how God came to bring about the Fall of Man and massacre his creations]. Luke begins with Gen. 3.1–5 in this Generic Paraphrase:

> 516.03 Luke:—Well then, Master Chairman, first he came along, a conceited young fellow from the west [Gen. 3.1, "Now the serpent was more subtle than any beast of the field . . ."], a bachelor and a rake to most people, the
>
> .05 Serpent cursed above all cattle [Gen. 3.14] dressed with a cock [penis-snake correlation] on the Irish side of his vest, in his rattlesnake demon clothes and his horrid contrivance [barbed penis] as seen from above, whistling delicately "The Wearing of the Green," and taking off his plush, stuffed busby hat in his usual free and easy
>
> .10 manner, saying good morrow in an evil way, and dragging on the ground in the usual way, he was ever so terribly nice [he was also a Naassene: a member of the Orphitic snake-worshipping sect], really, telling him to clean his nails and clean himself up, soldier [Adam was God's Christian Soldier], and so on and so forth; and to calm his irritable state

and what caused that sly freakish thing sticking out like hell's fire from his pubic hair; and claiming there was only half a threat of death and he

.15 would want his calico-speckled body back before he risked his life [Gen. 3.4: "And the serpent said unto the woman, Ye shall not surely die"]. Then, by God, counting on the Fall [see **Time:1132**] and death from God's hidden pistol, as I said, one wants one [the woman wants the fruit, and Adam wants the woman], this is my authority [Gen. 3.5: "For God doth know . . ."], he forecast Adam's [whose cup runneth

.20 over] Fall, defeated like an early Irish governor, and forecursed himself as the Devil. For the woman was coaxing the key of love before it was too late (the way Juliet was robbed of Romeo) and was anxious to know all that happened in the heat of passion [Gen. 3.6: "and the woman saw that the tree was good . . . and to be desired to make one wise"]. Perchance you will say, before God would kill all His children, what price a man would have to pay for being false to God's image; the man, Adam,

.25 God's antagonist, risen up from the mud, was raging with a sacred thirst [Gen. 2.24: "Therefore shall a man . . . cleave unto his wife: and they shall be one flesh"] and who, as a matter of fact, so far as he was concerned, was only standing there nonplussed, perplexing about whether to urinate or prepare to ejaculate, wanting to know what the woman had in her mind that she wanted from him that he

.30 knew nothing about [Gen. 3.6: "she took the fruit thereof, and did eat, and gave also to her husband with her"].

St. Patrick:—A stone crusher like that Irish music hall song? In other words, in the usual course of things, as an effort to help and after the manner of men

.35 which I must say seems extraordinary, was that how their heavenly warfare with a photoplay finish started?

517.01 Luke:—Truly.

St. Patrick:—Did one player in the melodrama, the deaf one [who was God, since Adam and the woman "heard the voice of the LORD God" {Gen. 3.8}, and therefore it was not Adam who was deaf] after some clever play in the mud ["LORD God walking in the garden" {Gen. 3.8, cont.}], mention to the other undesirable, a dumm [Adam, who

had not yet spoken] during diverse intentional instants
["Adam and his wife hid themselves from the presence of
the LORD God amongst the trees of the garden" {Gen.
3.8, concluded}]; did God mention after the summary of
the angry conversation [Gen. 3.9–13] how, for

.05 Adam's actions, he was a pigheaded Swede and to find
himself a doctor? [God's curses, Gen. 3.14–19]
Luke:—To be sure He did, the Juggernaut. He said Adam
was a turnip-headed dunce, I'm sorry to say, and He would
for a joke blow Adam from the green Garden of Eden
[Gen. 3.17–18: "cursed is the ground for thy sake. . . .
Thorns and thistles shall it bring forth"].

.10 St. Patrick:—Sublime was the warning!
Luke:—Adam, in fact, was murdered.
St. Patrick:—Did He, the first one to kill a man [God] do
anything to him, the last one to plead for mankind [Adam],
when after quarreling some more [Gen. 3.19] they joined
together in knowledge [Gen. 3.22: "And the LORD God
said, Behold, the man is become one of us, to know

.15 good and evil"]? Was that the last wall of defense?
Luke:—No, He had eyes in the back of His head so that
He could see the future [Gen. 3.22 continued "and now
lest he put forth his hand and take also of the tree of life,
and eat, and live forever"].
St. Patrick:—Did God then try to preserve Shaun [who
was Adam before the Fall]? [Gen. 3.23]
Luke:—No, but Adam did become Shem [Adam fallen].
St. Patrick:—Was that the worst cry for him never to look
on heaven's home again and the last outcry of a

.20 felon who might never see sunlight again? [Gen. 3.23:
"Therefore the LORD God sent him forth from the gar-
den of Eden."]
Luke:—Truly. He could never resist the flaming sword.
[Gen. 3.24]

.22 St. Patrick:—That final loud touch of fortification to protect the gate of Eden was the straw that broke the camel's
back.

The following four groups of Generic Paraphrases illustrate how the
successive segments of Genesis 3 are used as the basis for many of the
Finnegans Wake narrative episodes.

Temptations (Based on Gen. 3.1–7)

The sin in the park throughout *Finnegans Wake*, whether in Phoenix Park or elsewhere, is actually the Temptation in Eden. The principals are not the two girls and three men as has been supposed by some previous critics, but the woman in the duality of Issy/Eve and God's omnipresence as the Trinity. References to three in the park are to Adam, Eve, and the Serpent. Whenever food of any sort is mentioned—including "bacon," "ham," "pork," "Pig," "Swine," and "Sow" (sometimes connected with Sir Francis Bacon)—it is to be understood that the forbidden fruit is incorporated.

38.09–39.27

.09	The "cad's bit of strife" was the woman whom God created and who caused
.10	Him so much trouble. She was "glaned up" with desire for
.11	her "dumbestic husband" Adam.
.12	She spoke "of the matter"
.18	"to her particular reverend, the director,"
.17	who was the Serpent or Satan "because he appeared a funny colour"
.25	and "was this overspoiled priest"
.27	and "in his secondary personality as" Bruno of Nola
.28	and was "underreared," i.e. crawled on the ground like a snake.
.30	He recommends ("outpuffs") to Eve [Hebrew *Hawah*] that she have a banana [eat the fruit].
.31	In a soft-pedaled version ("pianissime . . . version") of Mohammed's claim that women were created out of Adam's crooked rib,
.33	he "in fealty sworn" that eating the fruit
39.01	was "for safe and sane bets," that is, it is well worth the gamble that she would not die.
.02–13	The woman saw that eating the fruit was as good as winning a horse race.
.14–27	Like Tom the pipers's son, who stole a pig to eat, Adam also ate the fruit.

65.05–33

.05–06	The "old geeser who calls on his skirt" is Daddy Browning and also the Serpent in Gen. 3.1,
.07–11	who says, "Shall ye not eat of every tree in the garden?" like "Creampuffs."

.14 But the woman (who is also Peaches) knows that "God hath said, Ye shall not eat of it" [Gen. 3.3], and "She wants her wardrobe to hear from above."

.17 She remembers, "so tollol Mr Hunker you're too dada for me to dance" ["lest ye die].

.23 Like Daddy Browning, the Serpent is fond of girls and would like to tempt [Swedish *canoodle* = fuck] both the innocent woman and the fallen Eve she

.26 is to become [there is also an implication that Browning "ate" Peaches]

.28 as well as "their cherrybum chappy," who is Adam.

143.29–147.06

.29 "What bitter's love but yurning?" asks the woman, who desired to eat the forbidden fruit. The answer seems to be in the form of a love letter by Adam/Swift/Joyce to Eve/Stella/Nora with replies.

144.02 Here Adam indicates she was fond of food such as

.15 cream, egg, seed, and chocolate,

.25 "but look what the fool bought"

.30 from "the rubberend" [reverend priest] or the "fleshmonger" Serpent.

145.07 "If I did [eat the fruit which caused funerals] I'm not [God]."

.15 "I mean to make you suffer," Adam says to the meddling Serpent.

.23 "The flame" is the Cherubim's sword of Gen. 3.24, which flashed after their

.25 "jaculation from the garden" and was their punishment, so

.31 "Let's root out Brimstoker" [Satan].

146.03 Adam assures Eve that he still loves her: "I'm not so dying to take my rise [erection] out of you, adored."

.05 Eve replies, "I'm only any girl, you lovely fellow of my dreams."

.06 And because the Devil is not around, she continues,

.10 sure that his red gown will make her forget his face,

.12 "I hope they threw away the mould or else we'll have . . . assassiations

.14 all over the place."

.19–26 [Echoes of Nora Joyce and Isolde]

.30 In this passage as in Gen. 3.6, the woman "did eat and gave

unto her husband with her; and he did eat." Then Adam
says, "You know bigtree are all against
.34   gravstone" as they hid among the trees as in Gen. 3.8,
147.01   where they also "heard the voice of the LORD God" as
.06   "Hearhere! Sensation! . . . to commission their noisense in.
. . ."

227.03–11

.03   When "The grocer's bawd she slips her hand in the haricot
[bean] bag, the lady in waiting sips her sup," she is the
woman in Gen. 3.6, who "saw that the tree was good for
food . . . and did eat."

.08   When "the girl . . . kneeled in coldfashion [confession] and
she's told her priest," she is the woman in Gen. 3.13, who
said, "the Serpent beguiled me and I did eat."

232.09–23

This passage is a radio message on heart waves seemingly from Vanessa,
Stella, Astarte, or Isolde but reminiscent of the Genesis woman, who is
about to give her husband the fruit which is "Satanly, lade!"

241.01–33

.01   The crooked Serpent ("Big dumm crumm")
.03   offers apples, blood oranges, and sugar candy
.04   as presents to Lilith, the woman,
.07   knowing that the fruit was forbidden.
.08   God's judgment is a lie [echoing Gen. 3.4, "Ye shall not
surely die"],
.09   said the Serpent, who now looks like an ancient white
caterpillar.
.10   The woman has little determination,
.12   seeing the fruit as golden aureoles [a celestial crown in
Roman Catholic theology, granted to virgins who have
overcome the flesh and to people who have overcome the
Devil].
.13   With inner passion
.14   this shameful Aphrodite
.15   believed the Serpent's ["Aasdocktor Talop" = practitioner
of death who crawls on his belly]
.16   one-legged lecture. God ["mish" sounds like Irish *mise,*

which means "I AM" {emphatic} and which equals the God in Exod. 3.14]

.18   knew the Viking poet or Norwegian captain,

.21   whose primary identification was

.22   Adam [*Michael* means "like God"], "queerest man in the benighted queendom,"

.23   and "found the kids" [Adam and the woman, as in Gen. 3.9–13],

.33   who were "frockenhalted victims" [naked, as in Gen. 3.10].

271.24–29

.24   "Eat early earthapples" shows we are in Gen. 3.1.

.26   The Serpent "glider that gladdened the girl" is also present and

.27   "lifted the leaves" as he invites the woman to eat the

.28   "fruit that hung on the tree that grew in the

.29   garden Gough [God] gave."

315.01–317.21

.01   Don't forget the Devil, the bachelor of arse

.05   as he sidled

.06   through Eden, a place where he was "licensed all at ones"

.09–20   God in His Trinity had threatened to kill, by drowning or otherwise, anyone who disobeyed him.

.21–26   Adam/captain enters the garden/tavern, feeling guilty for having eaten the fruit and asking if anyone had seen the Devil digging for his supper with his tail (or penis) tucked up.

.27–33   For the Serpent had said in Gen. 3.4–5 that the fruit was safe and God knew their "eyes shall be opened and ye shall be as gods."

316.01–02   The Norwegian hunchback captain is Adam in Gen. 3.8. "Puckkelsen . . . told. . . . how their ulstravoliance [violation

.03   of God's charge in Gen. 2.17] led them infroraids" [invisible (infrared) + afraid]. They met their fateful

.06   God ("Kish met. . . . for landlord"). The Serpent, wriggling on his belly, "bobbing his bowing both

.12   ways with the bents and skerries" explains that although banished from Ireland ("hiberniating after seven oak ages,

.16   fearsome where they were he had gone") he

.23   nevertheless offered food for Adam and Eve with a

.25   "fireball feast." With "the sign of the hammer. God's

.26   drought," he belittles God's prohibition [Gen. 3.4].

.33–36   Just some salmagundi and a bit of cheese, said

317.05   Adam/captain. Okey dokey, said the Serpent.

.11   "He made the sign on the feaster. Cloth be laid!" and

.16   supplied oysters, fishballs, ham, and so on [Gen. 3.6].

351.35–352.14

.35   But God, says Adam/BUTT, I never went wrong

.36   until that stumblebum of a Serpent

352.02   went, without your stopping him,

.03   with his foolish story to the woman, who was easily per-suaded to sin,

.05   about how the father provided food like ham and eggs

.06   and scarlet runner beans and how he wanted them to eat of every tree [Gen. 3.1].

.07   He disputed your words of prohibition.

.10   And that's how the Serpent/earwig got me to disobey.

.12   It was a great mistake!

.13   We were wrong including my wife, the woman,

.14   but before I could explain, you doomed us.

361.26–31

This delightfully poetic paragraph depicts Adam and the woman before the Fall ("they were as were they never ere") and the rightful pleasure of eating the forbidden fruit.

396.07–26

.07   The strapping old ancient Irish princess is not only Isolde but also the woman of Gen. 3.1–6.

.13   Given her nature of being made for a wife, "Could you blame her" for being tempted?

.15   Especially with that tiresome old God with his duty re-quirement.

.20   It wouldn't be excessive to offer him a pinch of hen shit.

.21   What God did was the meanest thing ever, especially since Eden was created for man's enjoyment.

.23   No, the whole story must be retold, whoever was culpable and whatever

.24 the purpose was. The man and wife lived together, and given their

.25 passionate nature, what they were doing was sweet and natural.

435.19–21

Adam in the guise of Jaun is advising the girls to ignore temptation. Convert your impulse, he says. Stick wax in your ears when you hear God's voice. Look on the Serpent in his beauty and you'll never more have to wear your fig leaves of shame.

439.27–32

Jaun, even more obviously Adam here as "first of our name," considers the woman his "receptacle . . . free of price." You were tempted "cheekacheek with chipperchapper" by the Serpent, he says, while God "the padre in the pulpbox" was laying down his prohibitions. Don't believe everything is simply black and white.

442.16–27

Adam/Jaun defends the good name of the tempted woman and castigates the Serpent: "He's a markt man from that hour." We will be "breaking his outsider's face for him" [Gen. 3.15: "it shall bruise thy head"] because he tempted the woman "with his bringthee balm of Gaylad and his singthee songs of" Araby. If I were God ("Blonderboss"), I'd curse this imposter.

459.23–30

Eve/woman/Issy gives her version of Gen. 3.6: "she took of the fruit thereof and did eat and gave also to her husband with her; and he did eat":

.23 She says: I must tell the truth. I love my husband and I am sure I did

.24 something with him. I like him a lot because he never curses me.

.26 He's shy, so I love taking his cock out when I unzip his fly.

.27 Oh, he adores me and dotes on me.

The next three lines need no paraphrasing:

.28 "He fell for my lips, for my lisp, for my lewd speaker.

.29 I felt for his strength, his manhood, his do you mind?

.30 There can be no candle to hold to it, can there?"

491.21–32

Up to this point in this chapter St. Patrick, as God's representative, has been conversing with Yawn/Adam. Now they are joined by Issy/woman and maybe ALP:

.21 We are talking about giant Gods in the Garden of Eden? asks St. Patrick.
.22 And the woman, interjects ALP/woman.
.23 The story is beginning all over again about Adam and Eve and God?
.25 Don't forget the Serpent, Yawn points out.
.26 An interloper in the garden, says ALP/woman.
.27 "He was more subtle than any beast of the field" [Gen. 3.1].
.30 With many misquotations of God, Mr. earwig/Serpent
.32 was just lying in wait for the poor innocent woman.

493.03–11

Issy/woman continues her account of the Temptation: I was welcomed with an aperitif from the earwig/Serpent. He never took his eagle or parrot's eyes off my nakedness but looked in my face and at my genitals and put the plum in my mouth like doomsday "morning in the end of time." With the light of hope on his ruddy cheeks, my charming Adam showed me his perpendicular Serpent-like penis, which was then as now displayed, as is every man's way.

523.33–524.26

.33 Suppose, whether fact or fiction, that Adam
.34 took obscene license
.35 with regard to his genitals
.36 and with respect to
524.01 the woman.
.04 And assuming this was against God's edict of Gen. 2.17,
.06 not to eat of the tree in Eden,
.07 the reverend gentleman [God]
.08 acquainted with fire fittings [at the east gate of Eden]
.09 obligingly explained the
.12 merits of creating both man and woman, and cited
.14 the man Adam, who shot his cock and owned the pretty woman

.15 and was the image of God.

.16 But while Adam had his assignation with the woman,

.18 God reckoned

.19 he was a dozen miles

.20 above them

.21 in heaven.

.26 And Adam said to God: my erring was a happy fault. [The "erring" klangword *herring* induces a spate of piscatorial words in the passage.]

561.15–562.02

.15 She is God's daughter and

.16 her brother's sister-bride (Gen. 2.22) [as well as Tristan/ Adam's aunt]

.23–27 Adam named her woman [Gen. 2.23] because she was "flesh of my flesh."

.30 What happened to her the "two dare not utter."

.33 Of course when presented with that "enticer"

.34 and "strifestirrer" [Serpent], she flirted

562.02 and talked.

567.5–23

.05 Are you leering at temptation by that wiggling bellied Serpent?

.07 Yes, because I see a condom in place.

.08 It is for true lovers meeting [Gen. 3.6], and many women

.09 use it in this way. It has long

.10 been standard practice of royalty

.11 and the rich to collect sperm ["come" and "milt"].

.19 Her purpose will be sanctioned and

.20 the use publicized. Progress will be made in *Finnegans Wake*.

.21 Her husband shall come to her aid,

.22 as will intelligent people.

.23 Who can doubt it?

621.04–32

In this recorso Joyce presents his version of what Gen. 3.1–6 should have been:

.04 It is morning. ("Yes. We've light enough.")

.07 Adam and Eve take a walk ("out after you on the hike.")

.12 to catch a fish for breakfast. ("The trout will be so fine at brookfisht.")

.20 They hold hands. ("Give me your great bearspaw . . . fol a miny tiny.")

.24 Eve is tempted by Adam's caresses. ("Reach down. A lil mo. So. Draw back your glave [glove + glans].")

.25 Adam applies a condom ("Here's where the falskin begins"), and the Fall of Man begins.

.29 Eve thinks of the young and innocent Adam. ("I'll close me eyes. . . . Or see only

.30 a youth in his florizel [virginity], a boy in innocence.")

.32 What they did was not a sin. ("All men has done something.")

Encounters (Based on Gen. 3.8–13)

The Genesis segment describing the encounter of Adam and the woman with God is a dominant theme in *Finnegans Wake*. All of the detailed Generic Paraphrases in Chapter 7, are based on it. In addition, some of the incidental episodes using it are given here:

15.29–18.16

15.29–16.03 Adam is like an ancient Jute.

16.04 "Come on, fool porterfull" is Gen. 3.9: "God called unto Adam." In the ensuing conversation Adam is Jute, and God is Mutt.

Adam: Yahweh! [the Old Testament name for God]

God: Pleased to meet you.

Adam: Are you deaf? [Do you answer prayers?]

16.13 God: Sometimes.

Adam: But you do speak?

God explains that when he calls, he stutters because of guilt for allowing people to die, for example in the battles of Irish heros. Adam says: That stinks (17.31). God then explains that because Adam and Eve sinned, He sentenced all mankind to death [Gen. 3.24].

30.12–31.29

Adam is the "grand old gardener . . . under his redwoodtree" in Gen. 3.8, where Adam and Eve "hid themselves . . . amongst the trees of the garden"; "when royalty was announced," God appeared (30.16). Adam "stayed not to yoke or saddle" (30.21), which indicates he was naked, as in Gen. 3.7. At 31.03–05 God calls to Adam, as in Gen. 3.9. The rest of the passage relates to Gen. 3.10–13, where God "indulging that none too genial humor" questions "Sophy" [the Gnostic Sophia plus Parnell's aunt, Sophia Evens, a practical joker] and Adam [*Michael* means "God's image"].

35.10–36.34
Adam's encounter with God as the "cad with a pipe" is explicated in **HCE: personalities of.** The passage also introduces the motif that time started with Adam's exile and death (see **Time:1132**).

186.19–187.01
God is "the parochial watch, big the dog . . . who had been detailed . . . to save him" and Who "wrongcountered" (186.20–24) Adam and Eve as "the tenderfoot . . . with his arch girl . . . under a hideful" (.24–30) in a version of Gen. 3.8 with a drunken Adam/Shem/Joyce.

244.13–246.35
"There is a wish on them not to be doing or anything" (244.16). "Where is our . . . spousefounderess? The foolish one of the family is within. Haha . . . where's he? At house . . ." (.18–20). These passages indicate Gen. 3.8: "Adam and his wife hid themselves from the presence of the LORD God." At 244.34 the "Panther monster" appears, but the pater noster (priest) is now the cruel, monstrous God of Gen. 3.9. "Soon tempt-in-twos will stroll at venture" (245.19) as Adam and the woman meet God. "But meetings mate not as forsehn . . . none iron welcome" (.22–25) reflects Gen. 3.9, and "Housefather calls enthreateningly" (246.06). Adam said (.09, "he work his jaw"), "I was afraid" (.10, "Ansighosa" = anxious) as in Gen. 3.10. But "Whatalose when Adam Leftus and the devil took our hindmost, gegifting her with his painapple" (.27–29)

323.11–12
"Where is that old mutiny, shall I ask?" is Gen. 3.9: "Where art thou?"

393.24–28
The statement that "they used to be getting up from under, in their tape and straw garlands, with all the worries" signifies Gen. 3.7–8, where Adam and the woman knew they were naked and made aprons of fig leaves and hid in the garden. Then, as at Gen. 3.9, God called, "come in, come on, you lazy loafs . . . come out to hell, you lousy louts!" Adam was "so frightened," as in Gen. 3.10.

409.08–419.08

As in Gen. 3.9, "Where art thou?" and Gen. 3.11, "Hast thou eaten of the tree whereof I commanded thee that thou shouldest not eat?" God/HCE asks: "But have we until now ever besought you, dear Shaun . . . who it was . . . gave you the permit?" (409.08–10). God/HCE continues to cross-examine, through eight questions to "So you [Italian *vi*] ate [colloquial *et*]" at 414.14. Shaun/Adam replies as best he can to the other questions, but his explanation of why he ate—"The woman who thou gavest to be with me, she gave me of the tree and I did eat" (Gen. 3.12)—turns out in *Finnegans Wake* to be a "fable one, feeble too . . . of the Ondt and the Gracehoper" (.17–21).

445.01–22

At "If you twos goes to walk . . . behind the bush!" God/HCE knows, as in Gen. 3.8, that Adam and Eve "hid amongst the trees of the garden" and goes on to say to Adam: "I'll be hatsnatching harrier to hiding huries hinder hedge" (445.01–04)—as God calls to Adam in Gen. 3.9, "Where art thou?" Adam hears him (Gen. 3.10) at 445.18: "do you hear me now. . . ?" God knows Adam disobeyed and ate the fruit, saying "failing to give a good account of yourself" (.22).

452.10–14

Adam hides: "I'd like myself to be continued at Hothelizod [Eden]"; hears God: "pricking up ears to my phono"; and is afraid:"'tis tramsported with grief I am."

557.03–06, 16–17

God called to Adam and Eve, "there was a crick up the stirkiss," and they were afraid: "downand she went on her knees to blessersef that were knogging together like milkjuggles" (Gen. 3.10).

565.06–16

This paragraph revises Gen. 3.5–12, where God calls to Adam, who hears his voice and is afraid but answers God: "The woman . . . gave me . . . and I did eat." It can be *Paraphrased* as God's saying: Why do you tremble when I am about to call you? Where are you? You are trembling, you wretched man. Were you naked? Did you eat and drink of the forbidden tree? Why are you trembling? Adam answers: Oh God of Mercy! I am afraid. I heard your voice, but you must have been joking. I must have clothes. Why should I be ashamed? You gave me the woman and she comforted me.

566.28–31

With the "Gauze off heaven! Vision," their eyes were opened as in Gen. 3.7. They were afraid (Gen. 3.10) that the "accident" of God's discovery of their sin and His retribution was about to commence. God's voice said: What have you done? What are you afraid of? Of robbing fruit from the tree?

571.15–33

This revision of Gen. 3.7–13 is told by Issy/woman ("my blanching kissabelle"), hiding amongst the trees ("in the wunder close"). I am Pipette, she says; I must also hide myself in this garden. I would rather be here than in Ireland. What shall I do to appease you, Oh God? And why are you afraid, my precious Adam, of that swollen God? I am not afraid I assure you; I am just sorry about the death sentence for becoming your wife. I hear God again. He sounds like a horse coughing. Our union was legal [Gen. 2.24]. He made me as a helpmeet [Gen. 2.18], not as a wild beast, out of your bones and flesh, to have and to hold [Gen. 2.24].

But God answers: Who told you that you were naked? Have you done what I forbid? Get ready to be sacrificed.

609.24–610.32

In this final encounter, Muta is a mutated God, and Juta is a rejuvenated Adam:

.24 God: Is God's word to be interpreted as so much smoke?

.25 Adam: It is God's voice puffing like a volcano.

.26 God: You should be thoroughly ashamed of yourself for misbehaving.

.28 Adam: God [the Gnostic Ialdabaoth] is the master of sleep and darkness, death and evil.

.30 God: Disaster! Where art thou? [Gen. 3.9]. In *Finnegans Wake?*

.32 Adam: Buddha! He is like a Japanese false god with his priests and followers maneuvering over the battlefield of the slain.

.35 God: I bellow! Where art thou?

610.01 Adam: The killing God: he is fundamentally and theologically disgusting over the whole proceeding.

.03 God: He is supposed to be dead! Horrors! Who the dickens now resurrects himself from underneath his memorial?

.05 Adam: Believe firmly, you are caught out, Lord!

.06 God: It is all over? My lightning cannot defend me!

.07 Adam: Relentlessly! To the tip of your staff. And our submission to our kiss is our happiness.

.09 God: Why does your God smile doubtfully?

.11 Adam: Bitch or botch it up! Everytime! You helped Buckley shoot the Russian general.

.14 God: You hide a lot! Is your self-pity twice cynical?

.16 Adam: That the book may live, let paradise be lost!

.17 God: You gambled against my prohibition.

.18 Adam: It was a ten-to-one outsider.

.19 God: So, why did you indulge?

.20 Adam: I was parched and needed relief.

.21 God: With a woman?

.22 Adam: With wine, woman, and bed.

.23 God: When I have unified into the Trinity, I shall become diverse, and when I have become diverse, I shall have acquired the instinct of combat, and when I have become combative, should I then pass back to the spirit of appeasement?

.28 Adam: That is the light of bright reason which descends to us from on high.

.30 God: May I take that as your confession, you old sinner?

.32 Adam: Here it is, and I hope it is the way to eliminate you, you Irish fraud!

Curses (Based on Gen. 3.14–19)

209.18–212.19

This catalog of gifts is a gentler, kinder version of God's curses. It seems to be influenced by Pandora, the woman Zeus sent down to Epimetheus which is thus analogous to God's creating the woman for Adam. Although Pandora loosed the evils on the world from her jar or box (a metaphor for vagina), Hope alone remained within. This poetic idea blends congruently with Joyce's sympathetic vision of Eve and helps us to understand his conception of ALP. The Genesis God was vicious and unrelenting with his curses of toil, trouble, pain, and death (210.06: "For evil and ever. And kiks the buch"). ALP's gifts are always playful and sometimes helpful. Instead of curses they serve as gentle admonitions for perceived faults. Although they seem to be given to individual characters, they (like God's curses) are inherited by "aisch and iveryone of her childer" (209.27). ALP is the caring, conscientious Supreme Being and the antithesis of "God."

252.11–12

The God of St. Jerome's Bible and of Mount Jerome's Cemetery curses the three participants in the Fall: Adam, Eve, and the Serpent.

282.01–04

God's "*Trick stunts*" [curses] were the "ANTITHESIS" of the pair's "ANTICIPATION." Adam sobs from the thorns, thistles, and sweat (Gen. 3.18–19) God imposed on his toil.

313.04–12

.04   Get on with your curses, shouts the crowd in the tavern.

.07   I will do that with pleasure, said God, and belched out his curse.

.09   The Serpent ("ship's husband") was sober when he heard his fate. Adam,

.11   temporarily satisfied after his good loving, got expelled (out in the cold with pneumonia

.12   and no money) and consistently sentenced to death (blown to atoms).

325.13–26

.13   Come here, says God, I am with you oldest man

.14   adapted to Eden. Listen to your tailor God [Gen. 3.21]

.15   until I have found you guilty.

.18   Then the Serpent admitted the evil story of Adam's seduction,

.20   but added: you sanctioned it by making the woman and giving her to the man.

.23   You're unrelenting and as bad as Adam is

.25   if you want to save mankind, the Serpent continued.

.26   As their savior and tailor, you should swallow your bloody curses.

327.02–28

.02 Praise be to God that Adam has for a spouse

.03 a nice needlewoman and, says God to the Serpent,

.04 the daughter of a tailor [God made woman, Gen. 2.22].

.05 But "I will put enmity between thee and the woman,

.07 and between thy seed and her seed

.09 it shall bruise thy head."

.14 while you go "upon thy belly" (Gen 3.14) [a truckle bed rolls low]

.28 "and dust shalt thou eat" ("you soil me").

328.09–36

God's curse on the woman (Gen. 3.16) includes:

.09 "I will greatly multiply thy sorrow" ("tie up in hates and repeat")

.10 "and thy conception" (predestined to have little tailors);

.15 "in sorrow shalt thou bring forth children" ("all needed for the lay [in the sense of laying eggs] . . . down to forkpiece and bucklecatch" [physician's equipment on the birthing table]. (Also at 328.36 is "blessing the bedpain."

.28 "and thy desire shall be to thy husband" (the "raptist bride is the aptist breed . . .

.30 . . . 'tis no timbertar she'll have then in her armsbrace"),

.33 "and he shall rule over thee" ("oversear of the seize who cometh from the mighty deep").

440.26–27

Gen. 3.19 says: "for dust thou art, and unto dust shalt thou return." *Finnegans Wake* says: "thou dust art powder but . . . thou must return."

444.06–29

.06 God starts his curse with "I hereby admonish you!"

.08 For the woman: to desire her husband and he to rule over her, and

.10 "In sorrow shalt thou bring forth children" [Gen. 3.16]. "And lest there be

.11 no misconception . . . over" whose fault it was

.13 when the stinking baby cries in his cradle,

.14 the dirty old Serpent will be squealing in his coffin.

.21 He will be "cursed above all cattle" [Gen. 3.14]

> .22   and eat dirt ("dust shalt thou eat").
>
> .24–29   You must be true to your husband ("thy desire shall be to thy husband").

455.24

God's statement to the Serpent in Gen. 3.17, "cursed is the ground for thy sake," in *Finnegans Wake* becomes "a humpty daum earth looks our miseryme."

460.11–35

This paragraph gives Issy's view of God's curse on her. Gen. 3.16 starts: "Unto the woman he said . . . ," but Issy observes: How he talks to himself louder and louder, imitating everybody. When God says "thy desire shall be to thy husband," Issy thinks that's fine and goes on to say how much she will enjoy it. God continues, saying "he shall rule over thee," but Issy loves her "prince of the courts who'll beat me to love!"

506.05–08

The curse on the Serpent (Gen. 3.14) is echoed in "the Grand Precurser," who called ("coiled") to the Serpent ("crawler") and cursed ("thundered at him") to crawl on his belly ("flatch down off that erection") all the days of thy life ("for the bellance of hissch leif").

543.02–545.23

God elaborates on the thorns and thistles He cursed the ground with and the toil and sweat He sentenced Adam to (Gen. 3.18–19). This great charity, He says, devalues and curtails mankind (543.02–03); then He goes on to show how it took effect in Dublin by quoting Rowntree in detail for three pages. Finally He extends the curse to all mankind: "Wherefor I will and firmly command . . . that from the farthest of the farther of their fathers to their children's children's children they do inhabit it and hold it for me . . ." (545.14–18).

594.35–36

ALP takes charge, telling God if ever again "you've tippertaps [vengeful ideas] in your head or starting kursses, tailour [God, Gen. 3.21], you're silenced."

615.28–29

ALP reminds the Serpent of God's curse on him: "Sneakers in the grass, keep off!" or else "we were to tick off all that cafflers head."

Exile and Death (Based on Gen. 3.20–24)

5.05–12

    .05   Adam was the first man to have a name, says Gen. 2.19, and *Hamlet* claims he was first to bear arms.

    .10   He is "going to be Mister Finnagain!" [to die and have a wake as well as be the subject of *Finnegans Wake*] and

    .12   "you're going to be fined again!" [found guilty and exiled].

14.06–09

All is "Silent" after exile. Eve the "brazenlockt damsel grieved . . . because" Adam was ravished by God, "the ogre Puropeus Pious."

21.19–20

The obstinate God answered Eve: I've shut the gate of Eden to drive out you and Adam.

24.03–14

    .03   God created Eden and kept it for himself

    .04   but cursed Adam and Eve ("sweated his crew") and

    .06   delivered them to death.

    .12   The sentence continues to all mankind.

    .14   Will you cheer for death at a wake?

31.32

The phrase "the amossive silence of the cladstone allegibelling" implies that the gate of Eden clanged shut like a bell, producing a massive, ancient silence.

47.10–11

"The Ballad of Persse O'Reilly" (see Chapter 7) reviews Adam's activities and his Fall. These two lines suggest Gen. 3.24, wherein God closed the gate of Eden and kept Adam from "the tree of life."

69.05–29

This paragraph contains numerous references to the east gate of the Garden of Eden, where God placed Cherubims (Gen. 3.24) to keep Adam from reentering. There was a "whole of the wall" and "such a wallhole did exist." In *Finnegans Wake* a convenient wall is suggested around the "garthen of Odin," both to keep Adam out and to provide a place from which to fall. Also mentioned are "A stonehinged gate," "an applegate," and "the iron gape" which was "triplepatlockt on him."

98.01–02

The gate of Eden "went . . . bang," and then there was "silence."

181.09, 20

Adam is exiled from Dublin/Eden by being "ordered off the gorgeous premises" and by "shoeing the source of annoyance out of the place altogether."

257.27–31

The thunderword is the sound of the door slamming after Adam's expulsion. "The . . . Game, here endeth."

258.28–34

"Thou hast closed the portals of the habitations of thy children and thou hast set thy guards thereby . . . the cheeryboyum . . ." (Gen. 3.24).

274.03–06

The "flaming sword which turned every way" (Gen. 3.24) "is alruddy with us." It is the lightning which kills Dathi ("Dathy"), with its "Five Positions (the death ray stop him!). . . ."

334.29–31

"Shut the door" in Irish is followed by "Silents."

372.13–16

They wanted to get out of Eden/Dublin by the gateway before they were cast adrift and drowned.

378.17–20

"He's alight there still, by Mike!" shows that Michael = "looks like God" = Adam is present. Then comes "Bung! Bring forth your deed [dead]! Bang! Till [it] is the right time. Bang! . . . The playgue will be soon over." The Old Irish warLORD shoots to kill, and Adam is exiled to death.

454.26–455.12

    .26   With "A word apparting . . . shall the heart's tone be silent" God sent Adam "forth from the garden of Eden" [Gen. 3.23] to

.30   "the suburrs of the heavenly gardens," the suburbs being "the ground from whence he was taken" and

.31–33   to his death: "after surceases . . . to our snug eternal retribution's reward."

.34   If you wanted to be happy, you should have stayed in Eden (or Phoenix Park), says God.

455.07   They might have eaten from the tree of life ("Saffron buns or . . . give it a name"), but

.12   "Postmartem is the goods" [Gen 3.22–23 puts it "lest he . . . take also of the tree of life, and eat, and live for ever: Therefore the LORD God sent him forth . . ."].

469.29–36

Here poor Adam/Jaun meets the flaming sword placed at the east of his heavenly Eden, carried by winged Cherubims (Gen. 3.24).

514.07–08

The "wellfired clay" is Adam being formed from the dust of the ground by God in Gen. 2.7. He was "cast out" through the gate of Eden from God's house.

Chapter Seven

Generic Paraphrases of Six Episodes

As mentioned in Chapter 1, the term *generic paraphrase* has a specialized connotation. It means that the *Wake* narrative revealed has been generated from Genesis. This underlying generic literality of *Finnegans Wake* is the story told in Genesis 3, onto which Joyce grafted the world's literature and the Irish condition as he saw it. The comprehension of this fundamental level of the text when expressed in more colloquial English produces a paraphrase which suffers, as all paraphrases do, from being incomplete and overly simplistic. Nevertheless it does generate an intrinsic English meaning essential to the enjoyment and understanding of *Finnegans Wake* language. Generic Paraphrases provide the "germinal deep structure"; in the words of Clive Hart, "a thread of English meaning . . . a simplistic meaning . . . [which allows us] to pay as much attention as possible to the surface . . . its colour wit and pathos. . . ." Furthermore, making sure the paraphrase is *generic* reduces the excessive possible interpretations down to the most probable ones.

This chapter provides line-for-line Generic Paraphrases of six major episodes. They demonstrate the power and utility of the technique. They also illustrate, even through the generic screening, how Joyce is able to invoke such variety while using the potentially monotonous repetition. They provide the sense of a continually developing narrative and, when considered with those of the next chapter, show how the Joycean theology develops from an evil to a vanquished God, to be replaced by an eminently humane Mother Goddess.

The Prankquean (21–23)

The prankquean episode is crucial to the development and the understanding of *Finnegans Wake*. Coming early in the book, it identifies and lays the foundation for the opposition between HCE and ALP. The language is dense and can be decoded only with great difficulty which poses problems of explication. Intratextual notes would make the Generic Paraphrase which follows almost unreadable, and footnotes would be overwhelming and irksome.

It seems best to present first the cast of characters by collecting the explanatory notes, which are numbered and referenced in the paraphrased text. These can be regarded as explicatory "headnotes."

Like all of *Finnegans Wake,* the basis of this episode is a retelling of Genesis 2 and 3 but with the addition of ancient competitive myths and religions. The scene is the Garden of Eden before the Fall.

[1] Gen. 2.15 reads: "And the LORD God took the man and put him in the garden of Eden to dress it and keep it." The fact that Adam is named establishes that the episode is about him. He is dressing and keeping the garden by "delvin" [delving].

[2] God had "planted the garden eastward in Eden" (Gen. 2.8), so the prankquean/ALP ran into the "westerness" wilderness, the trees of Gen 3.8 where they hid.

The four characters in Genesis—Adam, Eve, God, and the Serpent—are also the characters in the prankquean episode, as these notes will now explain. The action starts with Adam and woman in their infancy before the Fall.

Notes Pertaining to Adam

[3] Adam, one of the "jiminies" = gemini = twins, was created (Gen. 2.7) out of dust. Since the woman was created from Adam's flesh (Gen. 2.21) we can say they were created from the same fetal matter and are therefore twins. Another relationship results from the kidnapping of a twin by the prankquean at 21.21. This may reflect her mythological Goddess aspect, possibly as Leda, who coupled with Zeus as a swan and gave birth to the twins of opposite sex, Helen and Pollux. ALP/hen is instructed at 112.09 "Lead, kindly fowl" who (112.13–14) "knows, she just feels she was kind of born to lay and love eggs (trust her to propagate the species." Later the ass/Christ tells Shaun to "Speak to us of Emailia" (410.23). Emelia is the mother of twins in *The Comedy of Errors.*

[4] Adam has two primary personalities in *Finnegans Wake:* Shaun, the innocent and reverent Adam before the Fall; and Shem, the seduced, persecuted, pugnacious Adam after the Fall and the exile.

[5] "Larryhill" is the opposite of Hilary and therefore the same as twin Tristopher.

[6] The word *porthery* derives from Welsh *porthor,* or "porter." See note [32] for identification as Adam.

Notes Pertaining to Eve/Issy/ALP

The Genesis Eve is here a much more complicated character; she is also the woman/Issy and ALP developed into the prankquean.

[7] The phrase "his madameen" refers to the woman God made for Adam. She is not yet Eve, who received her name from Adam (Gen. 3.20) after the Fall. Genesis refers to her at this stage only as the "woman," so this convention will be adhered to here. Since woman is one of ALP's personalities (see [9]), there is a reference to water at 21.06.

[8] Woman was made from Adam's rib (Gen. 2.21–22), so she is a rib-robber.

[9] As indicated in [7], mention of water is a sign of ALP. Her connection with water, such as rivers, comes from another of her personalities, the Mother Goddess including Aphrodite who was created in the sea from Uranus's castrated genitals. Her name derives from the Greek for "foam." The "oil cloth" floor at 21.13 is waterproof, showing that ALP is not welcome.

[10] The construction "niece-of-his-in-law" implies that ALP is a very distant relative of Jarl/HCE. The prankquean as Mother Goddess personality is related to HCE/God as His mother Sophia and his sister Aphrodite.

[11] The rose (and other flowers) is a signifier of Aphrodite or Demeter as the fertility goddess of vegetation; compare 337.16, 338.21, 354.22.

[12] A flame is another signifier of Aphrodite or Venus. Ovid's story in *The Metamorphoses* goes that Pygmalion made a statue of ivory and fell in love with it. On Venus's feast day he made an offering at her altar and asked Venus for the statue to become his wife. "As an omen to her kindly will a tongue of flame burned bright and flared up in the air."

The goddess was present at the marriage of Pygmalion and Galatea. Demeter may also contribute to the flame, since her celebration at the Eleusian rites included carrying torches.

[13] In Ovid's myth Aphrodite wore a shining gown which glowed like the moon, more brilliant than a gleam of fire, in order to seduce Anchises. (Their son was Aeneas.)

[14] Not only does ALP have rain (water) as her sign (see [9]), but she also reigns like Aphrodite, who was a major goddess reigning in Phoenicia, Cyprus, and Corinth, and also in Assyria as Ishtar, in Babylonia as Tammuz, and in Phrygia as Cybele.

[15] Swans or doves were sacred lovebirds or phallic symbols to Aphrodite. They are usually depicted as drawing her chariot. At 22.03 they are "redcocks."

[16] Pre-biblical pseudoepigrapha relate that Lilith was the wife of the Serpent before she consorted with Adam. This is implied in Gen. 3.1–6, and in the phrase "second infancy" in the *Wake* (22.26).

[17] In the Gnostic text *The Raising of Adam from the Mud by Eve,* God with a committee of six Aeons created Adam out of mud, but he had no spirit because the God of Darkness had no light. After forty days Sophia sent her daughter, Zoë-Eve, to breathe the spirit of life into Adam.

[18] The woman/Issy/Hilary was tough on the tree of knowledge by defying God's order to abstain. "Toughertrees" at 22.24 may also refer to the Gnostic legend where Zoë-Eve, in order to escape rape by God's angels, enters and becomes the tree of knowledge.

[19] The Four Old Master historians of Ireland at 21.29 are probably combined with the four evangelists of the New Testament. This sets up Shaun/Yawn to be accompanied by the evangelists in III, 3. The *four* may be assigned to ALP as the "four heads" of Gen. 2.10 into which the river (ALP's source) divided after it flowed out of Eden. Also included is the Gnostic statement that Zoë-Eve went into and became the tree of knowledge (see [18]).

[20] The "monitrix" are the female counterparts of the Old Masters and probably include the sacred Vestal Virgins or the temple prostitutes who teach love. See [19] for the tree of knowledge relationship.

[21] The word *brannewail* from *Brangwen,* (Isolde's maid who arranged for her to share a bed with Tristan), relates ALP/ Eve with Isolde.

Notes Pertaining to the Serpent

The Serpent is the third character present, deeply disguised as the dummy.

[22] In each of its six occurrences in *Finnegans Wake,* "dummy" refers to the Serpent. A "dummy" is an imitation, a surrogate who takes the place of another. The Serpent, according to Joyce, was acting for God (compare 313.04–13 and 315.01–08), when he tempted the woman. (See **Norwegian captain.**) In the Gnostic *Raising of Adam from the Mud by Eve* the God of Darkness, equated with the Jewish God by the Gnostics, came to Eve as the Beast and tempted her.

[23] In Gen. 3.15 God cursed the Serpent to have his head bruised by the descendants of Adam and Eve, who would kick it with their heels.

Notes Pertaining to HCE/God

The fourth character, of course, is God/HCE.

[24] A "Jarl" is an earl and therefore a ruling lord. The author of Genesis 2 and 3 is referred to as "J" because he used the sacred name of God transcribed into English as "Jehovah." This was actually written in the ancient Hebrew texts as *YHWH,* which was considered too sacred to be pronounced properly as Yaweh and was hence disguised as *Jehovah,* a word meaning "Lord."

[25] The use of HCE's initials indicates He is God.

[26] The word *skirtmisshes* means "skirmishes about skirts" or clothes. Since God made coats for Adam and Eve at Gen. 3.21 he is the tailor in *Finnegans Wake.*

[27] God's clothes (22.34ff.) indicate that he was dressed like a Toff, a British dandy, or TAFF in the Russian general episode. It also emphasizes God's role as tailor in the Norwegian captain episode. In particular His "cumbottes" or gum (rubber) boots not only were waterproof against ALP but also were used for kicking Adam and Eve out of Eden. Compare 323.12, 618.08, 618.11, and 618.30.

[28] Crom Cruach was a Druid god who required a first-born sacrifice. There is an implication that the Jarl/God is no better because He sentenced Adam to death (Gen. 3.22–24).

[29] In Gen. 9.12 God promised with a rainbow not to drown all living things again.

[30] In Gen. 1.28 God told Adam and Eve "be fruitful and multiply and replenish the earth."

[31] When Adam and Eve hid in the trees, God called, "Where art thou?" (Gen. 3.9).

The Prankquean's Riddle

Finally we come to the crucial element, the riddle.

[32] Like all riddles the obvious question the prankquean riddle asks (if any) is not the right one; the true question is buried in puns. Indeed there are at least three questions here, each of which can be answered.

At 21.18 we read: "why do I am alook alike a poss of porterpease?"

The obvious misleading question seems to be something about being like peas in a pod, or about drinking porter. It is not about that.

In order to discover the puns, we will first examine the words individually with regard to their biblical connection; then the logical combination will be rephrased.

"I am" occurs in Exod. 3.13–14, where Moses said to God, "If I go to the Israelites and tell them that the God of their forefathers has sent me to them and they ask me His name, what shall I say?" God answered, "I AM; that is who I am. Tell them that I AM has sent you to them." This sounds appropriately Wakean, so we can substitute "God" for "I AM" where it all makes sense.

The phrase "alook alike" obviously means "look" and "like," taken together or separately. The presence of the initial *a* preserves the iambic feet of the rest of the heptameter. As to what looks like whom, Gen. 1.27 explains: "So God created man in his own image, in the image of God created he him; male and female created he them." Therefore God looks like both Adam and Eve.

The word *poss* has two meanings. The first is the

German for "joke" or "prank." This is a frequently repeated motif in *Finnegans Wake* and refers to God's making a woman for Adam and then exiling him and sentencing him to death because Adam only did what God naturally intended. Joyce regards this as a practical joke. The woman is also the prankquean, not because like Grace O'Malley she perpetrated a prank, but because she herself is the joke God made. In the *Finnegans Wake* episode the prankquean also embraces the additional aspects of ALP, so it is here written "prankquean/ALP." At 468.05 we find: "In the beginning was the gest [jest] he jousstly says, for the end is with woman, flesh-without-word, while the man to be is in a worse case after than before." This refers to Adam's creation as God's joke, as do "What, sir? Poss, myster? Acheve!" (466.30) and "with his ancomartins" [prank] (467.33).

The second meaning of *poss* is "boss"; this meaning is reinforced by the echo of the riddle at 417.07: the "boss of both appease." That echo is further reinforced at 623.04–19, where ALP suggests Adam and Eve (both) might call on the Lord and ask His forgiveness. So in the echo "boss" refers to God. In the riddle, however, "boss" has a different referent, as explained below.

Finally, "porterpease," although one word in the first two repeats of the riddle, conveniently hyphenated at the end of the line 21.18. Its meaning must be considered in two parts, as in the third repeat at 22.30. A porter is one who stands outside an entrance or gate, offering help or service and expecting a consideration. At Gen. 3.24 God drove Adam out of Eden and prevented him from returning. Adam therefore stands at the gate of Eden and is a "porter." This reading is confirmed by "porthery" at 23.10, which derives from the Welsh *porthor,* or "porter." The obsolete spelling "pease" can mean either Adam's peace or Adam's piece. The latter requires additional explication: since Eve was made from Adam's rib, she is a piece of Adam. There is also the sexual connotation of "piece" for Adam. If "boss" is combined with "Adam's piece," we have "boss of Eve." That clearly means Adam because in Gen. 3.16 God sentenced her to "thy desire shall be to thy husband, and he shall rule over thee."

We can now reconstruct some meaningful questions out of this intentionally obscure riddle. All are asked by the prankquean/ALP. The first version can be framed:

(a) Why does God look like the boss of Adam's piece?

or (b) Why does God look like the boss of Eve?

or (c) Why does God look like Adam?

Answer: Because Adam was made in God's image (Gen. 1.27).

The second version of the riddle is:

Why do I look like Adam?

Answer: Because I was made from his rib (Gen. 2.21). I am the flesh of his flesh and technically his daughter as well as his wife (says ALP/Eve).

The third version of the riddle is:

Why does God like the joke on Adam's peace?

Answer: Because He is the unreasonable, unrelenting, unforgiving God of the Old Testament and of *Finnegans Wake.*

The prankquean/ALP asks the riddle three times because she is addressing God in His Trinity. That is why she says: "Mark the Wans," "Mark the Twy," and "Mark the Tris."

It seems likely that ALP asks these questions as the fallen Eve to accuse God and ask for forgiveness because He exiled them from Eden and sentenced them to death (Gen. 3.22–24). The Jarl/God's behavior sets up the constant theme in the *Wake* of the evil Old Testament God, who killed His own children, a theme developed thoroughly in the episodes of the Norwegian captain, Buckley and the Russian general, and others.

There is also a strong probability that she asks the questions because the Gnostic Zoë-Eve asks a similar question. After she breathed life into Adam and entered the tree of knowledge (as mentioned in notes [17] and [18]), she left her likeness as the "woman" with Adam. God's angels, thinking the likeness was the true Eve, raped her. The chapter of the Gnostic tract *On the Origin of the World* titled "The Rape of Eve by the Prime Ruler (God) and His Angels" states: "They did it with a lot of tricks, not only defiling her naturally but abominably, defiling the seal of her first voice, which before spoke with them, saying,

`What is it that exists before you?'" This question frightened them because it reminded them that Sophia and the Father of Light existed before them and were therefore above them and their God of Darkness. This would explain the antipathy between ALP and HCE, as expressed in ALP's letter (which see).

The preceding notes are part of the following Generic Paraphrase.

The Prankquean Story

21.05 It was late at night a long time ago in the old stone age, when Adam was keeping the Garden of Eden [1] and the woman [7] was spinning ALP's watered silk, when that Irish man was the only man and the first little rib-robber [8] that ever had her own way with everybody with love-seeking eyes and everybody lived above in heaven or Eden with everybody else and the Lord God [24]

.10 of Ireland had His hot head high up in His tower, creating without female help by masturbating. And His two little twins [3], our ancestors, Tristopher/sadness/Adam and Hilary/joy/woman were heel-kicking [23] the Serpent [22] on the waterproof [9] floor of God's home [25]. And be damned, who comes to the stronghold of His castle, only

.15 His relative [10], the prankquean. And the prankquean/ ALP announced her presence with a rose [11] and made her sign [9] of water over the door. And she showed her flame [12] and Ireland was ablaze. And she spoke through the door to the dour God in her caressing language: God the Father, why does God look like Adam [32]? And that was how the skirmish about the clothes began [26]. But God

.20 answered her in anger: The door remains shut! Instead of God's grace she got His malice, so she kidnapped the twin Tristopher/Adam and into the wilderness [2] she ran [9]. And God called after her, denouncing her sacred dove bird sign [15]: Stop thief stop; come back to My hearing [31]. But she answered: Not likely. And there was the

.25 seduction [21] that same night after the confrontation somewhere in Eden/Ireland. And the prankquean/ALP went for her forty [17] years' walk around the world, and she washed the sin of love making off Adam with soap suds, and she had her four old masters [19] to teach him

the good knowledge, and she converted him to the innocent angel and

.30 he became the Lutheran game player Adam/Shaun [4]. So
then she started to run and to reign [14] and, by Dermot,
she was back again at the Lord God of Howth-Ireland's
with the same quest and Adam/Shaun with her as her
night-time lover at another time. And where did she come
but to the barred gate of God's domain. And God, with
His heels bruised from stamping on the Serpent's head [23]
and drunk from whiskey, was congratulating Himself; and
the

22.01 twin Hilary/Lilith/woman and the Serpent in their first
[16] affair were below on the weeping sheet coupling and
talking like brother and sister. And the prankquean/ALP
plucked a rose [11] and glowed again [13] and displayed her
phallic symbols [15]. And she made her water sign

.05 before the wicked God's wicket saying: God the Son, why
do I look like Adam [32]? The door stays shut! said the
wicked God signing with His hands through the door to
the angry ALP. So her majesty ALP set down Adam/Shaun
as she had planned but picked him up again and ran, like
Lilith, all the way back to Woman's Land. And the God of
Ireland

.10 bleated after her with a loud breath: Stop Mrs Stop; come
back with My erring child, stop. But the prankquean/ALP
answered: I like it this way. And there was a wild, old,
grand, brand-new cry that St. Laurence night of shooting
stars somewhere in Ireland. And the prankquean/ALP went
for her forty [17] years' walk around herself, and she forced
the curses of Crom Cruach [28] into the twin,

.15 and she had her four joyful instructresses [20] to teach him
his tears, and she perverted him to the one certain all
secure belief and he became Adam/Shem, condemned to
be a sad lover like Tristan. So then she started running
again, and in a pair of time changes, be damned to her, she
was back again to the God of Ireland's, carrying Adam/
Shem/Tristopher [5] with her under her apron. And why
would

.20 she halt at all if not by the vicinity of God's home another
night late for the third try? And the God of Ireland had
His farting hips up to his pantry-box, digesting in His

oversized stomach (like a ruminant), and the child Hilary/
Tough-on-trees [18] and the Serpent in

.25   their second affair [16] were below on the weeping sheet
kissing and coupling like St. Patrick and St. Bridgit in their
second childhood. And the prankquean/ALP picked a white
rose [11] and glowed [13] and the valleys lay twinkling. And
she made her sign in front of the entrance to the Trinity,
asking God the Holy Ghost: Why does God like the joke
on Adam's peace [32]? But that

.30   was how the confrontations ended up. For like the
Campbells acoming with a stroke of forked lightning, God
son-of-thunder Himself, the old warrior terror, came hopping out through the open gateway of His three-shuttered
castle, in His hat of authority and His civic collar and His
all-above shirt and His Saxon gloves and His snake-proof
pants and His ammunition belt and His far-

23.01   famed warrior gum boots [27] like a rainbow [29] of
indignation to the whole length and strength of His strong-
bow. And He clapped His rude hand to drop His pants,
and He shit, and His thick speech spoke for her to

.05   shut up shop, ALP. And God/HCE shot the bolt closed
[28] with a thunder word! And they parted. For one armed
man will always subdue any girl under an apron. And that
was the first prank against peace for the repeatedly

.10   suffering Adam/Porter [6] in all the created world. It was
how Kersse the tailor made a suit of clothes for the exiled
Norwegian captain [27]. So in the future shalt thou drown.
That was the covenant between man and God [29]. Eve/
ALP was to be held responsible for the Fall, and Adam and
Eve were to start the human race [30] and the God of
Ireland was to get everything in the end.

.15   That is how the obedience of the people makes the whole
of Dublin happy.

"The Ballad of Persse O'Reilly" and the Sequel (44–47)

"The Ballad of Persse O'Reilly" and its sequel outline the plot of *Finnegans
Wake* and establish its tie with Genesis. The Ballad is spoken by God as
Hosty [44.07: ". . . this is the rann that Hosty made. Spoken."] "Hosty" is
the hostile God. He is also a host in each of the word's multifarious
definitions:

1. An army [Latin *hostis* = enemy]
2. One from whom another receives food, lodging, or entertainment; a landlord
3. A living thing affording subsistence to a parasite
4. A sacrifice
5. A eucharistic wafer, bread, or food.

The rann is about the Fall of the man Adam, who is given many names at 44.10–14 including Vike for the viking Humphrey Chimpden Earwicker [46.02, 46.30, 47.15] as well as those at 46.21; and Mike for Michael (God's image). Hosty/God also says at 44.14: "I Parse him Persse O'Reilly," which is not to be confused with the earwig/Serpent, although the French *pierce-oreille* is probably supposed to suggest earwig = Earwicker. The title is more directly connected with Pearse and O'Rahilly, who were leaders of, and died in, the Easter Uprising. The Ballad makes it clear that, like them, Adam rebelled and was sentenced to death.

The Ballad

44.20–21	It begins appropriately with God's thunderword for Fall.
45.01	The first stanza compares Adam's Fall with Humpty Dumpty's but in death like Oliver Cromwell's. Throughout *Finnegans Wake* references to "wall" recall Adam's Fall [Gen. 3.24] but also establish a barrier around the Garden of Eden, the site of the Fall. The angel chorus singing "Hump" relates him to Humpty Dumpty, Humphrey Chimpden Earwicker, and the Norwegian captain.
.07	The second stanza notes that Adam was one time the lord and keeper of the garden [Gen. 2.15] but now "from Green street [Eden] he'll be sent by order of His Worship [note Deity caps in the text] to the penal jail" [exile; Gen. 3.23–24].
.13	Hosty/God stutters "fafafather," referring to Adam, the father of us all, and accuses him of rebellions [Gen. 3.6] unacceptable in Ireland, including free love, the use of contraceptives, and Sabbath Prohibition; and lastly the religious reform of *Finnegans Wake*.
.19	In the fourth stanza God's angels ask Him why Adam didn't succeed in his rebellion. God replies: That was like Adam, fighting a real bull with horns made only of butter.
.25	The angel chorus cheers Hosty/God and urges Him to

change His clothes [as He did for Adam and Eve, Gen. 3.21] and to continue the Ballad.

.28   Stuttering, Hosty/God goes on: In My image he'll cheat everyone when he starts living on earth.

46.05   Adam was snug in Eden but, says Hosty God: We'll soon expel him. Shortly the Serpent acting as My sheriff will be winding up his helpmeet and there will be Cherubims with a bonfire at Eden's gate [Gen. 3.24].

.12   It was bad luck for Ireland/Eden when that hooker, the woman, arrived with the first man.

.18   Where did she come from? I cooked her up cheaply from Finn/Adam when I was Thor, My old Norwegian name as Norwegian god.

.25   The angel chorus chants: Sing the rann, you Devil God.

.27   It was while Adam was keeping the garden and naming the animals [Gen. 2.20] that Adam could not find a helpmeet.

47.01   He ought to be ashamed [Gen. 3.7] to have intercourse with the woman. He's the main offender among the animals I created.

.05   Chorus: They made love, and Noah saved all.

.07   He was exercising his penis, the begging pope's ass, when he was sentenced to death [Gen. 3.22] like the Russian general.

.13   It's too bad for the human race, but look out for his wife, Eve, and ALP. There is plenty of spunk left in her.

.20   ALP will bring about a revolution in Ireland, and Adam will be recognized as the brave hero.

.26   But his body will not be resurrected, for there is no magic that's able to raise the dead.

The Sequel to the Ballad

The stanza on page 175 is spoken by Shem/Adam after "his departure . . . attended by a heavy downpour . . . some thousand rains ago he was therefore treated with . . . parsonal violence"—in other words, after his being exiled by God. It is Adam's reply to God's Ballad, as shown by the last line, which is here transposed to the beginning of the verse:

175.27   The Ballad of Persse O'Reilly [now spelled like the French *earwig*] chirps Hurrah for the Missed Understandings between God and man.

.07 Before the Fall [the language harks back to the first page of *FW*] no one in the whole world had taken a wife (even one made from his rib);

.09 Nowhere have the world's parents been sentenced to death, blood, and God's curses for life;

.11 Not yet has Napoleon forced Wellington out of England;

.12 Not yet have the invaders of Ireland made war;

.14 Not yet has the witchery of the woman struck the passions of man;

.16 Not yet has God's rainbow promised peace.

.17 The Serpent must tumble from heaven and blameful Adam is bound to fall;

.19 Humpty Dumpty's fall will follow eating the forbidden fruit, for where they had desire, God had His prohibition;

.21 But God still frowns on Eve/ALP while their sons celebrate death at a *Wake*.

.23 And woman's charms still flaunt God's prohibition, and all ALP's daughters laugh with delight

.25 Till the beaches of Ireland let the deaf and dumb Irish people unite in resistance.

The Mookse and the Gripes (152–59)

Just how this story incorporates the fable of the Fox and the Grapes is obscure. Combining it with Adam's encounter with God in Gen. 3.8–13 allows us to understand the connection. By applying some Wakean logic, we can decipher the two names. Since "Mookse" sounds something like "fox," and "Gripes" sounds something like "grapes," we can assume that those are the intended identities. The Mookse is also a personality of Adam as the Gripes is of God/HCE, as will presently be shown. Since Adam was the first man and he mocks the Fox, we might combine Man with Fox to make his name "Mox"; but a more dominant personality is also present, namely "Bragspear" (152.33), whose real name was Nicholas Breakspear. He was elected pope in 1154, the only English-born person ever to hold the office. He left England as a youth, became a monk in Paris, and eventually became Pope Adrian IV. In order to secure his papacy he enlisted the help of the German King Frederick I, whom he crowned Holy Roman Emperor six months later. He was therefore more of a German fox than an English one and should be named for the German *fuchs* to become *Muchs,* which is pronounced "Mookse." As pope, he is the dominant personality in this fable. His being pope establishes the identity of the Gripes as God because the Mookse/pope seeks to become God, which is an unattainable goal, like getting the grapes. Also the Gripes gripes like God, complaining and accusing Adam in Genesis.

There is a possibility that Joyce intended the fable of "The Mouse and the Frog" to be embodied in this episode. It is not well known, but Dante associates it in the beginning of Canto XXIII of the *Inferno* with the procession of hypocritical religious brothers. Such usage establishes both its religious connection and the probability that Joyce knew it. "Mouse" sounds a little more like "Mookse" than does "fox," even if Gripes does not sound like frog. Like the Mookse at 153.03, the mouse came to a river he could not cross. A frog offered to carry him across, but the mouse was afraid he would fall off, so the frog tied the mouse to his leg [perhaps as the pope is tied to God]. When they reached the deepest part of the water, the frog dived, intending to drown the mouse. A hawk watching from above saw the mouse struggling and, swooping down to catch it, he also carried off the attached frog. Joyce's tale also ends with both Mookse and Gripes being carried aloft.

At any rate, here is the Generic Paraphrase:

152.18 Once upon a weary time and space there dwelled a Mookse. He was all alone and lonely [Gen. 2.18: "It is not

.20 good that man should be alone"] and wanted to go for a walk (his monk's hood did not quell his romantic desires). [Adam was chaste like a monk and, presumably, the pope, before the Fall.] So one evening after a great

.25 day he prepared himself like a pope, stepped out of the Vatican (which was equipped to resemble heaven and the garden of Eden) and set off to discover the difference between good and evil. [Gen. 2.17: "But of the tree of knowledge of good and evil, thou shalt not eat of it."]

.30 Although he had originally set off from England with his father's surname Breakspear, he now had his own body-guard and wore the triple crown of the pope, and he bragged he was as immortal as God. [Adam was taking a walk in Eden carrying his incapacitated spear between his legs.]

.35 He had not walked far from his refuge when near a

153.01 church [Adam at the point of turning from Shaun into Shem at the Fall], he came upon a river. ALP was there for

Adam as what he perceived as an off-color, perfumed, girlish courtesan; and Issy, like a dribbling brook tempted him.

.10 And there on yonder bank of the river, out on the limb of a tree, was the Gripes. And no doubt He was angry for He was displeased [with Adam's behavior].

The signs of His displeasure were evident. He was forgetting the tailor's design of the fly on the front

.15 [God the tailor {Gen. 3.21}, ignoring the purposes of a penis, forgot to put the necessary fly on the front of the trousers]; and His pompous bowels were in an uproar. In all His false heaven [Vatican], where He was the Best and the Greatest, the Mookse had never seen his Dublin brother so near a pickle.

.20 Pope Adrian IV (that was the name the Mookse assumed) was stuck face-to-face with Gripes/God in an excess of indignation. But as Mohammed must go to the mountain, so the pope must roam through Rome. This was

.25 where he saw the stone on which the church was founded by a preposterous pun on Peter's name. Whereupon with his infallible encyclical to the anointable, god-patriarch of the Western church and the illicit pederast of an early pope he imitated, cheek to cheek with another invested pope, the insatiable beast; every way adding to his

.30 collection for his wallet; for the longer he lived, the more he thought of it; in the name of the Trinity it was a fat sum from holocaust sacrifices; he looked mighty like all the other popes.

.35 —Good hap betide us, sir Mookse/pope! How do you do it?, cheeped the Gripes/God in a very marauding maudlin voice [Gen. 3.9: "And the LORD God called unto Adam and said

154.01 unto him, Where art thou?"], and the nearby jackass attendants laughed and prayed for his intentions, for they knew the sly fox now.—I am of all things blessed to see you, my dear primitive master [the pope as an imitation of God and of Adam as the first man]. Will you please tell me everything, your holiness? All about tree and stone [the tree of knowledge and the stone of God's prohibition in Gen. 3.11: "Hast thou eaten of the tree, whereof I commanded thee that thou shouldest not eat?"] and also

.05 everything about the barbs on the Serpent's penis ["awn"]
and freedom from pain? No?

Think of it! A most wretched repeating tempter! A
God!

—Rats!, bellowed the pope most productively, the dema-
gogue; and all the other popes from their ancient

.10 cultures quailed to hear his tardy noise, for you cannot
make a silk purse from a sow's ear.

—Blast you and your curses to hell! [Adam opposes God
in a similar vein in the Norwegian captain and the Buckley
episodes.] No, hang you for a rustic Beast of Darkness. I
am the superbly supreme high priest! You are abased, you
shadow over the altar! Get thee behind me, you subordinate! Rot!

—I am obliged to have you until infinity, bowed God,

.15 his whining having gone to his paltry praying head. I am
still always having a desire on all my extremities. By the
way, what is the time, please?

Figure that out! The pining griper! To a Mookse/pope/
Adam!

—Ask my permission, be careful of my vulnerableness,
swell my collection, worship my Jewish-Christian origin,
answered the pope, rapidly turning mild, civil, well-born,

.20 and heavenly like other popes in handsome good humor.

—What is the time? That is why I came with laudable
intentions to settle with you and also with Frederick I
[who was called "Barbarossa" by the Romans; Adrian settled
with him by crowning him the Holy Roman emperor]. Let
the gods start the clock. [See **Time: 1132.**] Let there be
peace between the branches of the church. Let you be
beaten, and let me swallow up your angels. Now measure

.25 your size against mine. Well, sour grapes? Is this time of
our meeting too much for you? Will you comply? Will you
give up your godhead? What do you say? It may have
been?

Holy patience! You should have heard the voice that
answered him! A little voice.

.30 —I was just thinking a little about that, sweet little
pope, but for all rhyme or reason, if I cannot make my
submission, I cannot humbly give you up, Gripes/God
whispered from the depth of His despair. I shall be bound

as Christ if you say so. My temple, issuer of lousy bulls, is my own. My felicity is to fit in with hesitation. And my specialty in the highest is

.35 bellowing from above on things below [Gen.3. 14–19, the curses].

155.01 But I will never be able to tell your holiness (here He nearly lost His footing), though my Irish Father was but an impersonation whose clothes you wear [Gen. 3.21].

Incredible! Well, hear the inevitable.

—Your temple; you cast your seed in a sieve!

.05 always excommunicating around. Dividing the church between Europe and Asia. "New Rome," believed to last forever, is now Constantinople. My building space in my Leonine City is always let to lion-like men, the pope concluded with most consistory elocution, pompously and with the immediate jurisdiction of a Roman emperor (what

.10 lying to the shipwrecked Gripes/God!). And I regret to proclaim that it is out of my time to help you from being slowly killed, as we did not meet each other early enough. (Poor little scattered, clown-squashed Gripes/God! I begin to feel contempt for Him!) My side, thanks to my

.15 decrees, is as safe as an abbess's convent, he continued, and I can see from holy sanctuary what it is to be wholly sane. Joining Ireland to Britain is to be joined to a yoke! [refers to Adrian's awarding Ireland to English King Henry II]. Praises belong to him who praises himself. And there I must leave you, Grapes to be Pressed. I can prove that against you; wait a moment, my good enemy [said in part German, showing Adrian's German leanings]! or

.20 gospel is not our major asset. I bet you this dozen odd, this thunder-and-lightning dozen odd. But first—but 'tis better to preserve my sweet knowledge of papal teachings.

Elevating, to give a point to his glance [more German], his jewelled votive pedestal to the mysterious

.25 sky, he luckily struck fire from a few sparks, a cluster of stars from over Dublin, a firefly in the street and a stop sign before the foundress of the congregation of Sacred Heart; he gathered together the odd dozen of his teachings, in Greek, Latin and Rosicrucian, on the lapse of his prologue into a composite bull with one overflow outlet and sat about on his raincoat. He proved it well

.30   a hundred and thirty-three times [more German] the ex-
tinction of his birth name altogether (Nicholas the Fox
having once been God's proper follower) by all the

.35   authorities and church documents; and after that, with
glue hardened with formalin, he proved it again

156.01   altogether, not in that order but in some different order
altering the hundred and thirty-three times by the Bino-
mial Theorem and the penis walls and its end [the walls
around Eden and the Fall], and the roar of spurious leg-
ends, and the roll of the wheel and the hard lessons

.05   of expedience, and the judging of Pontius Pilate, and the
manuscripts in the Pope Sixtus books junkroom, and *The
Book of the Dead,* and the rules of the fox hunt [where the
fox is always caught and killed, the same as in God's hunt
for Adam, Gen. 3.9].

    While the Mookse/pope was assembling with double

.10   duplicity his arguments and contradicting the rascally
Gripes/God, he had all but succeeded in abandoning his
cathedral to heresy. But as often as he had caught his
semen-producing supporters naked, he still proclaimed
the Immaculate Conception; and after he had originated
his own Holy Ghost

.15   to comply with the Eastern Greek church protocol, his
own dignitaries were found in variance with the ecclesiastical council proclaiming his papal infallibility, which caused
the schism between the Greek Orthodox and Roman
Catholic churches.

    —After a thousand years, O God of my edicts, you

.20   will be ignored by the world, said the pope.

    —After a thousand years, answered God the Vigilant,
by the God of Mohammed they will still be ignored, O
Pope the Deaf-Eared.

    —We shall be chosen as the first of the last by

.25   the Valkyrie of Valhalla, observed the pope nobly, for by
the unparalleled Act of Supremacy, I am firmly established
and the pope's blessing is what the people fall for, bless
them. The numerous prescriptions, the

.30   incense, the vestments as British as Bond Street will still
stand when St. Paul's lies in ruins.

    —I, confessed God in a small voice, shall not even be
the last of the first, I hope, when you are visited by Death.

And, He added, I am relying entirely—see *The Book of the Dead*—on the mere weight of breath. [God controlled mortality by giving or removing the breath of life: in Gen. 2.7, he "breathed into his nostrils the breath of life," bringing Adam to life, and as in Ps. 104.29, "when Thou takest away their breath they die."] Puff, you're gone!

.35 Unsightly pursing of the lips, a relentless foe to social and business occasions! (But not pursing for an erotic kiss.) It might have been a happy evening but. . . .

157.01 And they berated each other vituperously, God and pope [*canis* is Latin for "dog," which in English is *God* spelled backward, and *coluber* is Latin for "snake," the Serpent who was cursed by God like the pope], with the wildest fight since before the Old Testament [tar and asphalt are sometimes classed as gums; *Targum* is the name of the Aramaic paraphrase of the Old Testament, preceding the Hebrew Masoretic text by several hundred years].

Pope—Fuck you, you eunuch!

God—Hoofed and horned devil!

.05 Pope—Shaped like a grape!

God—I need whiskey!

And the folly of the papal bulls answered God's word.

[The remainder of the fable introduces ALP the Mother Goddess as the controlling deity in the *Finnegans Wake* theology. This early in the book she is still Issy, which allows the Genesis Temptation incident to enter the story.] Issy, as the little cloud, in her nightdress, a lass of sixteen summers, was looking down on them, leaning

.10 over the bannistars and listening all she childishly could. How she brightened when Shouldrups [Adam should have erupted against God instead of weakly submitting to the Fall] in his belief, raised high his piece of heaven, and how she darkened when Kneesknobs [God had knobs on his knees from praying so much] in His doubtful seat was withholding His help! She was alone. All her young companions [the leap-year girls] were asleep. Their

.15 mother, the Moon Goddess [ALP] was off in the first quarter scrubbing the back steps [like Kate] of Number 28 [where the leap-year girls lived, Issy being Number 29]. Father, that Scandinavian, was up in the north woods

Sokol room eating Viking's pudding. Issy listened as the little cloud, though God and His prohibitions stood between her and Adam; and she tried, Oh how she tried, to make the Mookse/Adam look up at her [Gen. 3.6, the Temptation] (but he was remembering God's threat); and to make God hear how coy she could be (though He was too busy making His own confession about the church splitting to hear her); but it was love's labor lost. Not even her feigned

.25 reflection as a cloud could distract their thoughts, for their minds with intrepid faith and bungled curiosity were plotting with the Holy Roman emperors [Roman emperors + HCE/God] and whatever they did, as the smoke from burning ballot papers and letters issuing from the Vatican indicated [refers to Adrian's election as pope]. As if that smoke were their breath of life! As if their actions could duplicate or set aside ALP's queendom. As if she

.30 would be a party to such proceedings! She tried all the winsome ways her four monotrixes [ALP's instructresses; see **Prankquean,** note 20] had taught her. She tossed her hazy starlike hair like Isolde, and she rounded her dainty arms like Mrs. Patrick Campbell, the actress, and she smiled over herself like the beauty of the image of the

.35 pose of the daughters of the queen of the emperor of Ireland, and she sighed to herself as though she were born

158.01 to wed sad Tristan [Adam]. But sweet Madonna, she might as well have carried her daisy's worth to Florida, a land full of flowers and beautiful girls. For the pope/Adam, a dogmatic mad dog, was not amused, and the Gripes/God, a drunken Dublin ox of a Catholic, was piningly oblivious.

.05 —I see, she sighed. They are stupid men.
The whisper of the soft air sighing through the large reeds repeated the thought; and the shade began to glide along the banks of the river, creeping, griping God's edict of death: dust unto dust; and it was as gloomy as dusk could be in this waste of the peaceable

.10 world. The land beyond the river was soon a uniform brown; a Roman province, watery, unwooded, and deserted. The Mookse/pope had sound eyes but he could not hear. Gripes/God had far-reaching ears but He saw poorly. He stopped. And the other stopped, both heavy and tired,

.15 and the dusk was ever so dark to both of them. But still the pope thought about the depth and profundity of his tomorrow's pronouncements, and God still felt the scrapes He would escape by grace had He luck enough.

Oh how dark it was. From the Vale of Mary to the
.20 grassy plain, everyone was asleep after prayers. Good night! Oh God! It was so dark that the tears of night began to fall, first by ones and twos, then by threes and fours, at last by fives and sixes and sevens, for the tired ones were waking, as we weep now with them. O! O! O! Through the rain!

.25 Then there came down to the farther bank a woman who was invisible (I believe she was comely but reticent), and she gathered up the Mookse, who had metamorphosed into Adam, from where he lay and carried him away to her invisible dwelling that was high and pious, for he was the holy sacred solemn and handsome soiler of her
.30 chastity apron. So you see, the Mookse he was right, as I knew and you knew and he knew all along. And there came down to the closer bank a woman important to all [ALP] (though they say she was comely in spite of her caution) and, for He was like a hangman, she plucked down the Gripes/HCE/God, the panic-stricken self-thunderer, in death from His perch [He was out on the limb of a tree at the start of the story at 153.10] and carried away His beatitudes with her to her unseen hut called *The Dew of*

159.01 *Heaven.* And so the poor Gripes was wrong; for that is how God is, always was, and always will be. And there was left now only an elm tree [ALP] and but a stone [HCE/God].
.05 Tree with stone, stone but tree. O! Yes! And Issy, a lass.

The little cloud, Issy, reflected for the last time in her little lone life and she made up all her myriads of drifting minds [see **ALP: personalities of**] in one. She cancelled all her engagements. She climbed over the banished stars; she gave a childish cloud-like cry: Rain
.10 cloud! A light dress fluttered. She was gone. And into the river that had been a stream (for a thousand years had gone before her and after her, and she was naughty and stuck on dancing, and her dear dirty name was Mrs. Liffey) there fell a tear, a single tear, the loveliest of all tears (I mean for

those cry-love fable fans who are "keen" on the pretty-pretty commonplace

.15 sort of thing you meet in romance novels) for it was a leaptear. But the river tripped on, and by and by, lapping as though her heart was broken, like a brook, she said: *Why, why, why! Woe is me! I'm so silly to be flowing but I cannot stay!*

The Norwegian Captain (309–29)

The humpbacked Norwegian captain was a character in a story told by Joyce's father. The captain ordered a suit from a Dublin tailor named Kerse, but the suit did not fit and he accused the tailor of not being able to sew. Kerse retorted that the captain was impossible to fit. The actual existence of a Dublin tailor named Kerse allowed Joyce to doubly identify him with the cursing God of the Old Testament, who was the first tailor (Gen. 3.21). (This is further explicated in Chapter 5.) The establishment of Kersse as God logically casts Adam as the Norwegian captain.

The episode seems to have a large number of confusing characters, but with the multiple-personality technique, they can be reduced to the four in Genesis 3:

God appears as the tailor, Kersse, Cod, Taif, Alif, the Trinity, Mengarments, Ashe, Taler, tayloren, aleconner, and ninth part of a man, and is called by other foreign words meaning "tailor."

Adam is identified as captain, Pukkelsen, Skibbereen, second suitor, and waging cappon.

Eve is usually unidentified, anonymous, or the tailor's daughter, although Ana, eve (lowercase), and Dickens's "Marchioness" occur once each.

The Serpent is very active as the ship's husband, Recknar Jarl, Roguenor, Shufflebotham, Burniface, Gophar, shop's housebound, ship's gospfather, wife's husband, wife's lairdship, lairdship, shipshanks, earpicker, and earwig.

The speakers can be identified by Joyce's spelling of the word *said:* God "sazd"' or "szed," Adam "sagd" or "swaradeed," and the Serpent "sayd."

The logic of calling the Serpent the ship's husband is consistent with the meaning as an agent who handles the land portion of a ship's business. Joyce involves the Serpent as an agent of God who acts for him by beguiling Eve and persuading her to tempt Adam. There is also the implication that the Serpent did more than merely "beguile" the woman; according to non-biblical mythical versions, the first woman was Lilith, who was also Satan's wife. That is why Adam is also known as the "second suitor." This allows the pun of the Norwegian captain's wearing a second suit.

309.01–10   This might be the story of the sailor Odysseus, or it might happen in a tavern, but it concerns Genesis. The origin actually goes back to the tribal lore when God ("a man that means a mountain") made a woman for Adam, "while the scheme is like your rumba round me garden" of Eden with the prompting of the Serpent. The other characters are in dispute.

.11–12   Why had the Irish designated the one who sentenced mankind to work in sweat [Gen. 3.19: "In the sweat of thy face shalt thou eat bread, till thou return unto the ground"] as their God ("mysterbolder")?

.13   Because Adam and Eve's descendants,

310.01   with their electric appliances,

.21   they listened to that God.

.22–34   This fortune-telling God in a bottle, a dim lamp, or merely a drink, is indeed a wicked tailor who, like Finn, destroyed the land [Gen. 3.17–18: "cursed is the ground. . . . Thorns also and thistles shall it bring forth . . ."].

.35   When God issued his curses,

311.01   Adam shit in his pants so he needed new clothes.

.04   Afterwards Adam and Eve got expelled.

.05–09   Long afterward there was a tailor in Dublin named Kerse who was a model for the Kersse/God who cursed Adam the Norwegian captain.

.10–20   So Adam sought the advice of the earwig/Serpent as well as the woman ("Ana"), with whom he ate and drank.

.21–27   Then Adam said to the ship's husband/Serpent: Where can I get a suit of clothes and a mistress? I know of a tailor shop for your suit, said the Serpent. Then he connived with God to deceive Adam and have him killed.

.28–35   Posing as a tailor ("Mengarments"), with his trousers under a priest's cassock, God described his sewing procedure as though He was making the Garden of Eden.

.36   The Serpent, anticipating God's curse, hailed Adam: Stop. You will stumble and fall. Come back to

312.01 Ireland/Eden. But Adam answered: It will be all happiness! Believing the tailor, he thought he was in heaven, but his voyage was to be on broken waters when he heard the voice of God [Gen. 3.8]. Anyway, for a week or so,

.12 he enjoyed himself and reigned like a king.

.13–16 Prepare to fit his hump, said God's cohorts in heaven [Gen. 3.22: "God said, Behold, the man is become as one of *us*" {italics added}, indicating that God had companions]. "I will do that," said God/Kersse, meaning he would set up a scheme with the Serpent.

.17–24 But Adam feared nothing. He did not yet know the story ("their telling tabled") of God as the Lord of Howth and the prankquean, when he enjoyed his sweetheart.

313.04–13 Start immediately, God is advised. "I will do that," said Kersse, a piece of the Trinity, and He instructed the Serpent to blow the man to atoms.

.14–28 Whereupon the Serpent whispered that the fruit was good in as well as out, after which Adam ejaculated enough to make orphans for the balance of his life. The die [pun including death] was cast. Mankind was thus started in large numbers.

.29 Bolstered by "liquid courage," one of God's entourage or someone in the tavern, fearful he might get the same

314.01 treatment, asked "who caused the scaffolding to be first removed" so that man fell, and who took the planks

.06 away from Dublin?

.08–14 God's thunderword appears to say: All the characters go around again in another summary of the Fall, and the poor fool turns up. His Trinity also answers: He dived, fell like a barometer, or slid.

.15–29 And furthermore in the legend of that mortal scene, Adam did as God commanded; but that clothier retorted that Adam was a bad sinner. Their intercourse was hilarious but the safest love in the world. Paradoxically, to save the man is to expose his wife, Eve, for her sins and to give the Devil his due.

.30–36 That's all mighty pretty, but what about his wife/daughter, Eve? asked God's angels, sympathetic to the pair's wedding. Where is the sign of God the Savior? [In Judg. 6.29–40 God brought down dew on a fleece as a sign to save Gideon's life.] No wonder she tumbled for Adam.

315.01–08   Don't forget the Serpent, who was prompted by the Trinity. Isn't it true he drank to Adam's fate? And, they added, the Serpent (Shufflebottom) played his tricks, overlooking the curse he himself got.

.09–20   The Serpent shortly after babbled to the woman [Gen. 3.1–5], contradicting God's orders ["shot the three tailors" = Trinity] and saying the fruit was as good as Irish fish. Then Adam came, disregarding God's prohibition, and joined the woman. The Serpent gave the apprentices instructions, implying God's directions were wrong [Gen. 3.4: "Ye shall surely not die"].

.21–36   Good morning, lady and boasting bastard, said Adam as he came into the garden and made straight for the sound of them talking. He asked the Devil how or in what church he had met God and how he knew what God had in store for them.

    The Skipper [Adam] is taken in and will be as sad as the raven evermore, said the Serpent softly in what sounded like French but was really in Irish.

316.01–10   The story of Pukkelsen/Adam told again: Trying to be invisible, Adam and Eve hid to await their fate.

.11–32   Good morning to you both, said the Serpent, crawling on his belly [Gen. 3.14], to Adam and Eve in the Irish garden, where they were hiding ("laying low") in the trees, afraid of death by drowning. God, your foe, thinks you should be fit for clothes and drowning, continued the Serpent, and after an interval, here you are back in Dublin. I thought you were drowned before as dead as a mackerel. Hell's Bells! here's a gift for you.

.33–36   So tell me, said Adam with a condom on and with a dead expression, shall I shoot God? Where is that slob?

317.01   I need a bite of cheese and potatoes and a drink for dinner, or my religion is out of temper. When I'm satisfied you

.04   can think me dead and I can be pulled out of hell.

.05–09   All right, said the Serpent, an Irish welcome to you. Amen.

.10–21   He made the sign of the cross for a hungry man's welcome, laid the cloth, and put out a dish of oysters and a fishball for Adam. Wait on him or this angry man will attack us, said he, while the new Adam was getting seasick from the food.

.22–33　　The Trinity of God/tailor now said (as first pantsmaker), Nohow did he like the suit; (as second cutter) Dump him in the sea; (as third tailor) An eye for an eye and no mistake; and They knew why too. Everyman for himself but God for all, and the Trinity is for that union. Place the scars you wear on your coming-home bill, God apologized, oblivious of the Head of Howth that rose before Him with its semblance to mortal man.

.34–36　　This was Dear Dirty Dublin with its cold sea fog stuck in clusters on it with memories of love

318.04–17　and the first woman. Should the grievous enterprise recall man's dilemma, never fear. May there be no ill omen. Lift the flood from her ancient rites so there will be a remembrance of ALP (as Mother Goddess). Her maiden conjugation alleviates his curse of exile. It was a momentous marriage between the first man and woman which prospered with time.

.18–36　　Eve/ALP now reminisces about how she tried to fulfill her duty as helpmeet, only to be cursed.

319.03–15　I should be shot and throttled, belched God, for bringing you thorns and thistles. Thus conscience does make cowards of us all. In time I will taste My loss. Thus He summarized His Trinity like swallowing a corrosive drink.

.16–17　　Both God and Adam reminisced painfully.

.18–19　　By the pain in my groin, thought captain/Adam, we were here before.

.20–22　　He looks like a hunchback, thought God/tailor, but where are his clothes?

.23–30　　I left them behind the east gate of Eden, said the captain/Adam, turning on the tailor. That double-dealer is drowning in Irish tar water; let it drain down his throat like a Gulf Stream. A curse on that tailor, he said in the vernacular, and whether or not it is going to be, I'm telling no lies. For I cursed his coat and trousers before the flaming sword was placed at the east of Eden [Gen. 3.24].

.31–36　　Smoke and choke, laughed God until tears trickled down to his thighs. You're loafers all. You'll wish to the Lord you hadn't sinned. And Adam, who was being talked to, felt that the fiery furnace was being thrust on him and such a situation would dump him down to the ground.

320.01–17　All right, said Adam. The changed God was deeply hypnotized or half drunk. And curse Him for His monkeyshines, that tailor, addicted to nostrums in his buttonhole society. Which just goes to smoke up the public, said Adam, God boasting He had the latest fashions for a double-breasted navigator. Said Adam, the back of my hand to Him with his penny-bun breakfast when He dances with the doomed. I will put God's sign behind the east gate, the one not well-made, said Adam. The curse of my sore arms [from working God's cursed ground (Gen. 3.17–19) upon this unmentionable being [God could not be named. (Exod. 3.13)]. A goddamned cussed sewer, said he. He is the first cousin to a charlatan who is not fit to light a kettle of fish. He is the worst suitmaker who ever poked a needle in cloth.

.18–22   So that was the second version [from 316.01] of their meeting. How Adam/captain went back to work, from his Druid's dreams to Dublin's round towers, back to thirty hours a week. Ugh!

.23–24   Stop! interjected the Serpent. Come back to Ireland.

.25–31   Ill luck to it, blasphemed the captain/Adam. And he wandered from the African desert to the Bering Strait, baked in the sun, battered by the snow, and soaked in the sea.

.32–36   In the third version of this baffling yarn, it was time for the pair of sinners to be "suitably" punished, as previously,

321.01–18   until they were powerless.
Ignorance is bliss; therefore, they should not have eaten from the tree of knowledge [Gen. 2.17]. But upholding God's law as a sign of welcome to all men of good will (with its halo of virus) was disgusting from Dublin to Australia. God's sign of authority ("wellknown tall hat") was signaling warnings of exile ["east circular route" = east gate of Eden]. That gate was open only to the lucky, thanks to HCE/God with his silver bells and cockle shells like contrary Mary. There will be lots of fun at Adam's demise and Finnegan's Wake until Ireland awakes from its deep slumber. How they succeeded in overcoming

.19   the darkness he who loves will see.

.21   A change of scene.

.22–28   He started out to create me for you, mused Eve/ALP, although we were both His. Now He runs this tavern, serving drinks. See how He scoops up the money like Noah put animals in the ark to save

.29   them. Aside: Like Finnegan, do you think me dead?

.31–   We are in an upside-down world like Australia. Reenter God/tailor.

322.01   Take off that white hat (lo, God the Father is back with his coat dangling over his shoulder).

—Take off that hat while it's hot (ordered God the Son, [Adam] reincarnated, mocking the hollow message in the custom of the new country).

—Take off that awful and wrongly sewn suit (God had cluttered up and misfitted in the most complicated manner the Holy Spirit of His Trinity so that the father couldn't know his own Father.)

.15   Chorus: Here comes God with His coat [Gen. 3.21].

.16   Well, coats in Dublin, how do you do today, my dark gentleman? Search me, said God/tailor. When he had said this for the third time, God reiterated the whole lesson of His training, how the blazing exile occurred from start to finish, and He cursed them soundly. They

.24   peered at Him from behind the flaming sword [Gen. 3.24].

.25   Where were they to go, asked Adam, Eve, and the Serpent, who admitted they had misbehaved?

They lacked resistance ["mho" is the reciprocal of electrical resistance], said the Trinity, which was at the

.34   point of dialectic obsolescence.

.36   That cooked Adam's goose, said God again.

323.01   Now that he is clothed, he is a buggering wanderer, God said, corrupting our language [like Joyce] through the dialect of his arsehole. Confound him, voyaging after maidens; the curse of all tailors besaddle him, God said, I'll spit in his face. One can tell from his vestments that he breached his promise. Where is that old mutineer [Gen. 3.9: "Where art thou"]? Free kicks he'd have from me if I were a few years younger. He'll feel the fall of my fist. That gorbellied hunchback with his pockets full of letters, a disgrace to the Roman Catholic church, he can drop down dead and there is not a tailor in all Ireland that could make a coat and trousers for a fellow with such an error

.23   in his story and a hump on his back.

.25   Upon this call of lightning and thunder the LORD lifted His dizzy pack and returned to his fellow cohorts [Gen. 3.22], who were afraid to laugh for fear the joke of

.36   death might happen to them too.

324.02–   With that old suit on His shoulders with the evil underneath, earning His bread by the sweat of His brow in the
glow of the flame of Eden's gate, God readied to get rid of
the pair from the Garden of Eden even before Adam's lover
was taken from his side. God's cohorts cheered Him:
Empty your bladders and be afraid of HCE/God. Before
God could catch them, the angels were surprised as God
said: Damn the opposites of gods [mortals]. The tree of life
is for Us alone [Gen. 3.23–24].

.17   And they sentenced them to death [Gen. 3.23–24].

.18–36   Radio broadcast: There is one lesson missing for the
good and true believers in the greater glory of God.

Weather forecast: As the Reverend Comcille predicted,
a depression is expected over Scandinavia. A master-builder's
varying precipitation, heralded by false sickness and envel-
oped in an unusual suit of clothes, has filtered its way
toward Ireland and occasioned a sudden wretch of low
pleasure with Lucan drizzles. The outlook for the marriage
of the bride is good. What will happen to them?

325.01–02   News: Giant Fall in Eden. Omens confirm approaching
nuptials. Burial of the hatchet by divine providence.

.04–12   Are you making any sense out of this! Even money says
it is now ALP: I wish an auspicious day for the marriage,
she thinks. There will be 1,001 pities with dreams of bliss
and absolute trust, purity, honesty and love. After which
fishing, dancing, games, and Christian literature while this
palaver is finished.

.13–17   Come here, older man of Eden and tailor-robber of
Ireland [Adam] until I've found you a father-in-law [God
as Eve's father, Gen. 2.22: "God . . . made a woman"] to
become your tailor Lord and Irish ancestor, said God.

.18–26   Then, said the Serpent to God of the scatological story
about Adam's capture, it's either you or him, so let there be
an agreement about who is the conqueror. By my reckoning, he said, they are of one flesh [Gen. 2.24] as sure as
you're first man at the pole. And so even though he must
fall, he's a hardy fucker; for the two will produce Ireland's
toilers and soilers if You are going to save it as You have
said. You have produced too many people [Judg. 7.4–5].

.27–   And the Serpent said unto Adam/captain, who was praying to God that he would "cleave unto his wife" [Gen. 2.4]: come here, said he, my maritime sea dog, you raging whale, into the ship's hold of our four-times-blessed island. Pale Jesus pray. And no more bowing to and believing in our God of revenge with the pope lying

326.01   in wait for you with his persuasive words by the altar. God will rehearse His commandment and make you the first martyr. As sure as St. Patrick picked the shamrock and left the lilies of the field, God in His Trinity will crush you with the doom tree.

.04   St. Patrick carries God's message.

.05   And the Serpent, pouring the water of exile, hailed him with the sign of the cross. I baptize thee Earwicker, the first man of the Irish Vikings, said he, and their savior [ass = Christ]. And let this do for you as a holy puzzle and for all of your descendants out of the hellish sink of foreign language into the Roman Catholic religion. Our pledge is given to the four-Gospel land if not to the Son, for thousands expect the Christian anathema to which I wish them God's battering. For you got caught cold, after a good possibility of a better encore from the ancient fairies' wholesome feud, until Eden. LORD have

.20   mercy on your souls, Adam and Eve. Spit in His hand.

.21   Nonsense, snorted God. He was always against all religious overthrow, so why the hocus pocus would he be taken in by the Godfather Priest of the second-hand suit

.25   in St. Patrick's Cathedral?

.26   Well sir, my admirable rival, said the Serpent to Adam [second-hand suitor of the woman after the Serpent, Gen. 3.1–6], in spite of my being cursed for sponsoring you, let's drink to show you're a scholar. For whether you like it or not, we brought the joy of summer with us and

.31   also Lief Ericson and his discovery of America.

.32   And to let you in on God's anointed daughter, here is that tailor/God of Dublin (said the Serpent while he

327.01   thought about all the juicy fruit he would smuggle by preceding Adam), Who has the nicest little woman in the

.05   house, the daughter of the tailor [Gen. 2.22], commerce for your dangling part. A cutting treasure for you, she will light your lamp when there is a surge at sea. He dotes on the more-than-beautiful foster child, a leap-year girl and future female Trinity, ALP. She will have grit as

.10 hard as a riverbed but a touch as soft as a river flowing and a look as light as hydrogen. You will leap romantically into the evening harbor of the little Irish girl. All this avalanche of foreign words hangs over her

.15 low bed. It will be fortunate if it never falls from the ladder. And when that storm is over until the next time and all the impudent gifts are on dress parade and the tubas are tooting for the glory of their God, every town in Ireland will follow her like a mountain torrent. (Wait a while, blunderbuss, you're much too loud and don't start following the ladies until you've learned to lie in

.20 her language.) When it's hot in the summer and she can hear the soft thunder beyond the beyond in Wales, sleepy talking to the Welsh mountains, peeping out of her dormer window dreaming of the Flying Dutchman over the English strand; when the bell in the ruined church rings out that Sechseläuten be granted with her sailor husband-sinner;

.25 where from Dollymount can be seen the phantom pirate ship; since the winsome Miss made love to her wrecker and he took her to be married. Oh, and playing house in the sexy tower of gold and ivory, he took her as a prize

.30 gift in the pleasure pool like a black-eyed Susan. If she can't work her miracles and give the Norwegian captain/Adam a good Irish time while racing to warm things up for her lover, her spectacular appearance would set old Earwicker on fire, let alone an old fat-ass with water on the brain, as easy as ABC. She would cuckold him as sweetly as a dove (taking his mind and memory like

328.01 a pirate, for there's no fool like an old fool when the beer tap runs to gin) and change his boat into a baby carriage, said the Serpent to God/tailor, who was her co-creator [Gen. 2.21–22].

.05 Talking about cloth and singing about a shirt, I will turn my thoughts above and speak to the Trinity, said the Serpent: You are my truest patron and good founder although we are poles apart. Tied up in enmity, You can do better than Your predestined exile by fire of Your children ["tyler bach" = little tailors].

Although Adam/captain was warned and was laid out like a slain giant among his ships, when it comes to acting honorably, said the Serpent, You should make Your daughter a royal servant [Dickens's "Marchioness"] and

.15 give her everything needed for a layette, from a nursery and shelter down to a doctor's help. In the privacy of that prescriptive night [Gen. 3.16: "I will greatly multiply thy sorrows and thy conception"] and of that hour of birthing, said the Serpent, the first Eve ever so troubled (while the happy husband visited his wife in every port) in the dark before dawn, brings forth the heir and all

.29 the bells ring. She shall have desire, and hopefully forsaking all others, it will be for her husband; and he

.34 shall rule over her [Gen. 3.16].

.35 With my help plus condoms, although the church will

329.01 bless the pain of childbirth, the new God will say: that's enough! She will finish making children's clothes and the urinating child by using birth control. For my old comrade captain/Adam, the husband of her heart, I wish dry dock and upped anchor and one-hundred percent manhood for him (with sensual delight for ten thousand years). He is the best bloody landlubber of an old fool that ever scuttled

.12 a ship.

Buckley and the Russian General (334–54)

The story of how Buckley shot the Russian general is familiar to all Joyceans and is repeated in detail in the Ellmann biography. Ellmann also comments that Joyce had some difficulty in working it into *Finnegans Wake*. Readers, knowing it is there, have also had some difficulty in understanding how it was worked in. The following Generic Paraphrase attempts to show how this was done. The text is extremely elliptical, made worse by Joyce's use of pronouns often in the wrong person and without apparent antecedents. There is also a peculiar development of the Trinity.

Like every episode in *Finnegans Wake* it is based on Genesis 3, but it specifically develops the Joycean heresy that God killed His Own Son, not only Christ but also Adam by expelling him from Eden and denying him the tree of life (Gen. 3.22–23). In addition, by making the setting the Crimean War and using military associations, Joyce includes the claim that God inflicted war on mankind as part of the death penalty. The episode also introduces several other aspects of the New Theology, which are discussed in Chapter 8.

The passage is ostensibly a play, with BUTT and TAFF as the participants. Joyce puts stage directions in italics and encloses them in parentheses. BUTT and TAFF are not, as some have proposed, personalities of Shem and Shaun but of Adam and God reenacting the encounter of Gen. 3.8–13. Like other pairs, the names suggest the old funny-paper characters Mutt and Jeff; their natures seem to be reversed, however, since Mutt was tall and imposing in the comic drawings, and Jeff was a diminutive dwarf. Here TAFF (which sounds a little like "Jeff") is the omnipotent God who imposes His will on BUTT (sounds like "Mutt"), who is the subservient Adam. Yet before the episode is over, we begin to wonder whether TAFF/God has not been belittled sufficiently and BUTT/Adam has become so defiant that the original comic depictions were perhaps not reversed after all. TAFF also embodies Toff, a British dandy—as at 346.36 (which augments God's activity as a tailor). The T in TAFF is the same initial as in Trinity, and deeply hidden at 352.32–33 is HCE. While BUTT suggests Mutt, it is likewise arse or butt end (scape goat), as at 343.25. The Initial B is reinforced by Buckley, whom BUTT/Adam becomes.

The story starts, as it should, with the four characters of Genesis 3: God, Adam, Eve, and the Serpent, as is stated at 335.06. Keep in mind that Joyce's technique of combining multiple personalities into one body is a principal component of the ambiguity, so that there appear to be more characters present. Note also that "the buglar's dozen of leagues-in-amour" (335.06–07) are in Gen. 3.22, by inference, where God speaks to someone there with Him in paradise saying, "Behold, the man is become as one of *us. . . .*" Presumably there were other immortal beings there with Him and Adam and Eve and therefore He had a cohort of "angels," who speak occasionally in *FW* as a Greek chorus.

God assigns BUTT/Adam the further personality of Buckley, an innocent Irish boy like Adam, who is awed (as was the original Buckley in Joyce's father's story) by the Russian general's uniform, described at 339.10 and following. At 340.32–36 God assigns BUTT/Adam the additional personality of the Russian general and, at 343.2–12, urges him to shoot the same; this is to cause illogical consequences as for example as 343.35 where BUTT/Adam himself trembles with fear when he realizes the general's fate and continues to wrestle with his internal conflict from 344.08 to 345.03. God of course knows (at 345.05) that this peculiar combination of personalities means he is proposing that Adam commit suicide by murdering himself; Adam likewise considers this at 346.35. He is mixed up at 347.22. [We were earlier warned, at 101.19–22, "how it was Buckleyself . . . who struck and the Russian generals, da! da!, instead of Buckley who was caddishly {at God's instigation} struck by him when be herselves."]

As in the original story, Buckley makes three attempts to kill the general. The first is at 341.05–17, but God knows it failed at 342.34–35—a fact which BUTT/Adam acknowledges at 343.34–36. The second attempt comes at 345.02, but Adam feels sorry and hasn't the heart to. As the time for the third attempt approaches, Adam at 352.29 says: Let God shoot His own gun (thus conforming to Genesis 3). The shooting occurs at 353.21, but it is confused as only *Finnegans Wake* can be as to who actually did the shooting. It is also confused as to which personalities actually got shot. Of course the general did, as did Adam, in keeping with Gen. 3.24. However BUTT/Adam's penultimate speech at 353.06–21 makes it appear that God also was annihilated because of His treatment of Adam and the Irish race. Since God is immortal, this is of course impossible.

Adam's fate can be rationalized somewhat as follows. Throughout the episode there is continual friction between God and Adam. As early as 340.20 Adam reviles God and relates his grievance in detail in the long BUTT/Adam speech beginning at 350.11. God is usually overbearing but occasionally feels guilty about His behavior, for example at 340.16–18 and 353.02–05. Finally at 354.01 God questions His own behavior and the fact that He killed His Own Son. Following the killing of Adam/general there comes, at 353.22, "The abnihilisation of the etym": the annihilation of the Word. The personality of Joyce is added to BUTT/Adam/Buckley/general to eliminate the biblical teachings of the Old Testament God and to replace the Word of the Bible (which burns at 354.27) with *Finnegans Wake*. At 354.08 BUTT/Adam merges with TAFF/God, "*now one and the same person.*" This results because Adam, who is divine at the start of the episode, has had his immortality deleted. Being now mortal, his Trinity must merge back into God's as the Son entity, as did Christ's.

A word of explication is required for the "twelve-eyed man" (335.01): this is God as two Trinities. Since Adam is God's first son, he is part of the initial, normal Trinity, and at the beginning of Genesis 3, Adam is still immortal and therefore a god in his own right and entitled to his own aspect as a Trinity. Two Trinities contain six personalities with twelve eyes. Later in the story, when Adam is killed, he has lost his chance at immortality and is no longer a god; he therefore merges back into the traditional Trinity at 354.08. In another bit of Wakean logic the twelve eyes add up with BUTT's adding the personalities of Adam, Shaun, Shem, Buckley, and the Russian general.

The Story of Buckley and the Russian General

334.31 After a pause we repeat the story of Adam's Fall, an allegory of killing as in a fox hunt.

335.01 The story tells how, they being sick at heart, two Trinities [3 x Father + 3 x Son = a twelve-eyed man; they will merge at 354.08], one of whom had majesty and the other died down, reigned before the Fall. [See also 340.32–36.]

.05 The story is set for the grim tale of how the four in Eden: God ["deafeeled carp" = deified fish = God], the woman ["mabby" and "sissy," two aspects of Eve = woman = Issy], Adam ["sammy" and "sonny" = Shaun and Shem, two aspects of Adam], and the Serpent ["varlet de shambles"] plus God's cohorts [Gen. 3.22: "we" = leagues-in-amour] were in the right place for the Temptation ("peep o'skirt"), curse ("called a halt"), exile ["vastelend hosteilend" = waste-land hostile end], and death, like Buckley shot the

.14 Russian general.

.17 A storm is breaking.

.19 Warriors are dancing.

.21 Let us see what a boy like Buckley can do to the strong Russian general.

.24 God and Adam were still talking to each other (in Russian) and Adam was minding the garden ("tublin [Dublin] wished on to him with its olives ocolombs and its

.30 hills" [Gen. 2.15]). It was before they fell from grace as told in the prankquean story; before the green wood [Gen. 3.8] where the phallus ("obelisk") rose and the

.33 concubine ("odalisks") fell [Gen. 3.6].

336.01 And it was forever after that God made the sign of the cross and held a mass for His Christian soldiers.

.08 They pleaded with God not to exile them [Gen. 3.24], but when a man marries his troubles begin.

.12 Of this Adam and Eve, who had Cain and Abel and Seth for issue, "nothing more is told until now." Then behold, we are once more like babes in a world remade by the story in *Finnegans Wake*.

.21 The story is of Adam, the grand old gardener, condemned to death by his own Father, presented here as an ideal poster soldier and liberator of his people. But where his peccadillos at his meeting [with God] soiled his chances should be apparent.

.33 About which story there is no photograph or comment by St. Bruno; for that lout Adam, who sold his grace, was only a

337.01 dead pigeon bowled out of Eden on his arse.

.04– God in His Trinity being the dispenser of providence to only the faithful, what matters joy or harm to Adam? Let him just keep on being a banished non-sinner and let ALP take care of God. A truce to temptations presented in war clothes; leave the Bible teachings ("the letter

.14 that never begins") and find ALP in *Finnegans Wake*.

.16 Imagine two creamy roses. Suppose you get a beautiful thought and metonym them silent mothers. Then imagine a stuttering God. Then imagine up to a Trinity of lurking tempters, for instance Crimean officers. Play with them; she will probably smile and He will seem to appreciate it. They are piratical soldiers, sure to participate. Say to yourself (so the flowers can't hear): So this is Dublin! How do you do, dainty daughters? So pleased to pick on you this way. How do you do too, Adam; I hope your woman likes the monkey nuts! And welcome to Tom, Dick, and Harry [Trinity];

.31 who brought you here and how are you?
We want Buckley. There he is in his Borsalino hat

338.01 [like Joyce wore]. The man that won the battle with the belle. We want to hear how Buckley shot the Russian general, demand God's angels [Gen. 3.22].

.04 The scene now shifts to a public place with Crimean soldiers. The conversation continues between God and Adam, but God assumes the personality of TAFF, while Adam becomes BUTT.

.05 TAFF/God *(is smart, looking toward heaven as revealed by the Carmelites prior to announcing the emergency solution to the riddle in His head.)* He says: Everything is ready for the battle. Tell me again, what do you see? [Gen. 3.9: "Where art thou?"]

.11 BUTT/Adam *(an innocent youth who is supposed to behave like his Heavenly Father or be disgraced and die answers):* Yes, Father. I see, as often, a battle like Sevastopol.

.15 TAFF/God *(promptly pulls himself out of the cesspool by making His first point):* Describe him to Us, the Ondt/ God, as though he were the Gracehoper/Adam [see **Ondt and the Gracehoper**]. He is the general of the Baltic Sea, ready to shell us. We will use a military

.20 language which the lilies of the valley [like 337.16, refers to Eve/ALP] do not understand. Shell the world and bombard again. Bring out a strange snake; how little Russians despise her, calling an earwig a snake. Not the Satanic stuff that despoiled the woman. Use good old

.25 fighting swear words for symbols, like tinker's dam. Burning at the stake was the usual procedure when the man of iron was the boss pagan killer. Ejaculate all night! Reassemble the glories of Brian the Brave. And may he be

.30 the valor in our dream which we forgot at waking when the morning cut off our erection and cold breakfast chilled our reverie! Sing praises of Charlemagne, Russian generals, and Ireland.

.34 BUTT/Adam *(drawing forth from his bosom where it is bound in the secret language of the Druids he switches on his Gracehoper personality fed on the green hills of*

339.01 *Erin, gives the horse laugh of the Pope's ring and rambles in what sounds like Japanese):* Irish victorious! Farewell hunchback [see **Norwegian captain/Adam**]. I may have done something dirty, but I was bored. Like old Daddy Dacon, when I say I cooked my eggs in bacon I mean I had intercourse. Like the metaphor, when I cooked I fit

.05 into the woman's cunt and, like all men, spilled my semen. Poor old pissabed. The young cook performs the ritual of eating the sacrificial offering to God, but it turns out to be the meat of curses. God curses damn well, but I am a Shelta Druid. Cannon in front of him with the dogs of the fox hunt behind, baying the warning. His bark is

.10 worse than his bite. He was surrounded by the enemy, Crimean fashion, with all his cannibal insignia in his raglan coat and his sick hussar fur hat and varnished Russian boots and his cardigan hunting blouse and his scarlet cuffs and his three-colored camisole and his Irish raincoat hanging down. Earwigs/Serpents hire

.15 beauties! The famous suit of clothes [Gen. 3.21; see **Norwegian captain/Adam**] from Kersse the tailor. Easy time-payments of several shamrocks. Women will admire.

TAFF/God *(all shooting stars and noise in his ears*

.20 *and full of beans).* Thunder! Life and death! Remember the Norwegian captain and the Gracehoper and their fate. Magnificent!

BUTT/Adam *(as though he had forgotten his deceitful*

.25 *fate among the flowers of the forest* [like 337.16, 338.21, and 354.22, this refers to Eve/ALP; also Gen. 3.8] *his insipid smile giving benefit of the doubt).* Come, all you skirts of women's town that entice men. The Russian bear is raging in his heaven-sent confirmation robes, rainbow colored and violent. Disguise yourself to rescue your

.30 dead lover! First he steps; then he stoops. Look.

TAFF/God *(struggling like a Dubliner to remember by the sickle or the cross who it was that sacrificed people and feeling that perhaps He lived in the Kremlin before He was pope in the Vatican, makes the sign of the Ondt and the Gracehoper, the Father, the Son, the Holy Ghost).*

340.01 Scatterer of guilt, he is notorious on every count! The human son of a bitch! With his erection and his bragging.

BUTT/Adam *(with his tongue in his cheek and his*

.05 *erection pointing routinely to impossible objects beyond the town-of-towns towards woods and meadows of Dublin (and ALP) and the Howth River, where he and his true love may never love again).* The field of stones and that blasted tree [Gen. 2.17]. Forget not the fallen and exiled! For the lamentations of the

.10 Druids! Warfare downed both. Here in the Furry Glen [vagina pun] of Dublin's Eden. No? Their fiery gate. Yes! With "Cherubims and a flaming sword which turned every way" [Gen. 3.24]. And bodies beside.

TAFF/God *(a pessimist, he strives to regulate the*

.15 *struggle for life by the rut of the past, neglecting widows, keening after black sheep, withdrawing too much from decency).* A day of wrath and the murder of My children in Dublin! All My doing! He is the boor of a bear from Oslo looking for his little progeny in all directions!

BUTT/Adam *(back to his rivalry: little rest from*

.20 *God's demands; no more forbidden fruit; an outlaw).* Bearhero, honeymoon monger, and the grizzliest God in man's image in the world! Whose annals live the highest! For He defiled the lilies of the field [namely, Eve/ALP] and armed Samson with the jawbone of an ass. His guards [clergy] strafe Ireland which we all serve.

.25 TAFF/God *(what with the sycophants at the front and the thumb* [penis] *suckers beholding the fair Issy; uncertain between her and the Russian general/Adam; he sees the bishop with his thumb* [penis] *going forth on Rogation Days* [ceremony of abstinence and asking God's blessing] *and Issy just as all our fancies imagined her, with her curves unsheathed and tying her shoe with her*

.30 *leg held aloft to the great consternation of her viewers).* Divulge! Hy-de-dy girls and How-de-do sir! [Gen. 3.9]. Playing Puss-in- Boots. We should let the man [Buckley] seem loony while actually following My example ["ant" = Ondt/God + "folly me line"] while Adam ["post" = Shaun/Adam] drinks his way to become the Russian general

.36 as scapegoat. The first version [Father] of My Trinity is here; the second [Son] is hastily arranged while the

341.01 whole is acting through the earwig/Serpent. We should see him dance the polka. Lead him to the dance [of ridicule], his fly is unbuttoned.

BUTT/Adam *(this signal of the part he is to play seems to cast shrapnel on his inmost thoughts, being central to the coming act of the tailor/God).*

.05 Buckley of the bloodstained massacre! Bang goes the Bomb. The picture of the man he shot was in the Russian Journal, where the girls he loved could see him.

TAFF/God *(obliges with a piano symphony for the two step dance of the boy and girl).* The split Crimean balaleika! I'll rage like the troubadour!

.10 BUTT/Adam *(with the sign of the sickle but the humor of the lobster/earwig/Serpent, speaking through his strangling collar of gold, something to the following effect).* Mortar the martyr with Buckley/Berkley tar water! May his bowels grow bigger so his diarrhea gets worse! The old God makes a virtue out of murder by

.15 encouraging war. I saw him acting like a sergeant under the Turkish flag. By their fruits shall ye know them! Sing the songs of my duplicate personalities: My Life for the Czar and the Rocky Road to Dublin.

.19 *Up to this point we are presenting the Irish Race, who promoted this religion with its public confession and*

.36   *absolutions and the clergy collecting money. Their*

342.01   *tailor/God, if physically present, was morally absent. Addicted*
to boozing, horse racing, gambling, and breeding. To think
that such a thing could happen here! This eerie dream has
been offered as being by BUTT/Adam and TAFF/God, two

.31   *slapstick characters.*

.34   TAFF/God (*aware that the first reports* [about the Russian general] *had been corroborated, takes a different direction and, detecting the fear of malaise after the*

343.01   *poignancy of the man in the woods* [Adam, Gen. 3.8], *turns
Draconian despot*). Call a curse on the corsair; I'll

.05   put him in a tomb. You had just been celebrating the
march of the army's retreat, scattering cannon balls on the
Giant's Causeway, following along the route of the stations
of the cross [to death]. Tell the gospel truth! If you please,
comrade! Perfidious Albion! Think again,

.10   as the tailor/God said to the Norwegian captain/Adam
long ago! Move forward with dispatch like the soldier shot
the hunchback!

      BUTT/Adam (*slipping his coat sleeves over his shoulders
so as to look more like the Russian general as he scents the
anger of annoyance and explaining how the battles were the
valley of the shadow of death and he was in a great state of
fear that an erection on the susceptible side of him would
endanger his posterior*).

.20   Yes sir, I think I did. Never you bother, for I understand,
thank you! No, no, no! Great Jupiter! I speak for the victim
in the spirit of the match. Of all the armor and soldiers in
the tragedy of that ancient Gracehoper, that son of God
with his military epaulets,

.25   smoking the scandal out of his butt end! Disgusting smoke!
I thought back about the time when the fatal itch in his
engine of doom made him walk away from the fighting
and look for a privy to take a French seat and have a
healthy shit for himself so as well as urinate

.30   like the pope on the Druids' stone circle, when I heard his
lewd brogue reciting His cheap, cheating gospels to all and
sundry; I thought he was only just after having his breakfast, but by the Holy Ghost, I no sooner saw the gist of his
fright than I was trembling with fear [Gen. 3.10] some
distance off, feeling for some

.36   stable support. Of man's first disobedience and the fruit!

344.01   TAFF/God *(though the bad-luck-shiver of fear is aiming to get him, joining in is the highly faithful happy-go-lucky soldier sapper with a pain of his fate and a tear in his eye and the constraint of the gods and the croak in his cry and the harm leaning over him).*

.05   There is not a thug who would [shoot him]. Weep on your song of sorrow! Which Goethe and Shakespeare and Dante well know. Papist! Usurer! Take the coward's blow! Yes! Your paradise is lost!

BUTT/Adam *(giving his twin-like twinge in acknowledgment of his accumulated kicks, strafed from the fire trench with cold buckshot, crouched on his heels, he changes*

.10   *uniforms* [lets his pants down in the Russian general mode] *as he is letting the cat out of the bag: his face glows green, his hair turns white, his blue eyes become brown to match his Celtic cult toilet).* But when I saw him come along alone, within hailing distance, that terrible

.15   tall man with his young man's penis and attempting like any bandy-legged Roman Catholic to lay down his life like Christ at the Mass and exposing his naked arse and shitting out in the open, renewing manure with the cows like the Irish peasants, I thought he was recovering his

.20   breath from some headquarters beyond the Caucasus and I didn't have the nerve to tell a lie, not for love or money [in Gen. 3.12 Adam does not lie to God]. But when I got a leisurely full view of his behind in action in the light of the storm clouds and the flare of the battle and

.25   the fierce stink of his offal, a saphead Satrap like the Great Father, my bell forsook allegiance and, this is no

.30   lie, I was babbling and blubbering and wanted to run away. Clemency even if misdirected must be granted. But, my fault, as I love the dear Russian, I confess with out prejudice when I looked on the sword of fire [Gen. 3.24] with the weight of his anger falling on him from the travail of his stomach and recognized the fate of his hump [Norwegian captain/Adam], I was afraid and

.36   wanted to cover his nakedness like Noah's sons, and it was difficult for me, the way I intermingled my Irish Hail

345.01   Mary's with his Lord Have Mercies, I hadn't the heart to shoot him.

TAFF/God *(as a matter of fact, knowing how much a*

.05   *woodman seduced innocent clowns, he is proposing suicide knowing what he is doing is murdering himself, you bet your bloody life, before he does so, surprised though he is).* Fool! You didn't have the heart? What fun!

.10 BUTT/Adam *(hearing someone* [his multiple-personality self] *suddenly give two or three* [Trinity parts] *peevish snores like a knapsack fast asleep, he waits silently to see if he might stir but he goes on sleeping without asking for peace for his soul).* Fuck and shit! I met with who it was [God, general, or Yeats] too late. I hate my fate! Fairwail! Farewell to Ireland. Think of that

.15 when you're near Baggot St., Dublin, or smoke tobacco.

TAFF/God *(who meanwhile at arm's length so as to put a notch in the post* [condemn Shaun/Adam] *by way of sticking out his hand and making room by gathering up the scattered* [souls] *had been lavishing silent words on the*

.20 *repleted speaker's right to keep the tavern* [Adam will become the exiled Porter] *(which if nothing prevents it, there can be little doubt), which right has resulted in a mischanced ministering of another goodness).* Much good may it do you! Someone for the paradise but certainly

.25 not that nipper dandy! Drink this cup of vinegar [as did his other son at Matt. 27.34] and be glad it is offered! Complaining?

BUTT/Adam *(he whipped off his tall hat;* [shed his divinity] *lips opening to the wafer, he takes communion from the hands of the forgiver of tresspassers and sips*

.30 *the wine of the host while predicting his fate of exile but preferring salvation).* There is scarcely known in this gnarled world a valley so sweet that expands for the improvement of the forces of nature by Your solution of acting on me as an evil fiend.

The other forgotten abused people are in the
.36 *Mullingar Inn, Dublin, on a television program during the*
346.01 *interval which tells: How the fashionable world in the frozen crematory are taking off their heavy furs and dressing up in mackintoshes* [symbol of death in *Ulysses*]. *The Nietzsche new God. How the Irish green money is being promoted for the second coming of the Antichrist.*

.05 *Citizens for Roman peace. How Abraham wished his wife, Sarah, a holy hidden motherhood while the Arabian knights executed devil dances around the hemisphere. Learn the nun's*

talk. How the old generation are making plans for the cun-
ning new girls, never aging, still begetting, never trading
mates, and so on, and never to get drunk and never

.10 *to play silly games such as Buckley shot the Russian general.*
Phone for the final Finn tomorrow after mourning and for
your funeral and resurrection.

.15   TAFF/God *(now as in the past with the shillelagh of an*
anarchist, while they are all in the melting pot of Dublin
waiting for old Adam to warm his hands again [resurrec-
tion], *glance at him again, rise up the road, and hike up the*
hill and find him blustering in French and English). Since
you are about to revolt, say your piece!

.20   How Buckley shot the Russian general. A report of Irish
journalism. A breeze from Crimea! And don't leave out
that sod of turf, my son! You haven't got off your song,
have you? Has yesterday not ended? Very good then! Get

.25   after Buckley. Speak Bulgarian. The centuries are calling
you to call the scapegoat's bluff. Somebody, somewhere,
somehow, has blundered. Some fine day in the middle of
the bog two dead men [BUTT/Adam as Buckley and the
general] stood up to fight while three blind men [Trinity]
were looking on. Turn about and try again! Before the
snow storm. It will be the thing to do, yes?

.30   Can you do it?
      BUTT/Adam *(who in his godforsaken heart, ever fonder*
of his woman, an Irish Nihilist, the signal of his Dublin
connection going off all at once lest he should challenge

.36   *himself beyond anguish).* Sure, God! I said I would. It was
the happy fault [Gen. 3.6] first. It was back

347.01   in another time, a holiday where the Devil tempted my
belly, please God, roughly along about the spring equinox,
in a Persian garden as thou goest from Bethel straight
north,

.05   1132 years of blood and death; after a number of drunken
flooded days and nights when we sighted the foe (what a
flood of rainy weather), the most mournful date man ever
held doomsday death with; and I was in the Royal Irish
Fighting Militia under religious military instruction a

.10   good many years, sometimes in Crimea and sometimes in
Ireland, during the dumb truce in the fleshpots of Egypt

and the hanging gardens of London and during my truce in Boston, Mass, and half a league onward. And win against

.15 blackguards or rue the day, to please God the Irish policeman, if the muskets know who's who; the great and dreadful day when St. Patrick came, the grand day, the excellent toastworthy calendar day, according to the ninth book of Sixtus [Sixtus of Sienna wrote eight books of interpretation of the Bible; *Finnegans Wake* is the ninth], with a

.20 seven-hundred-year time lag as told in *The Book of Kells* prophecies; Erin go bragh! But I continue and I'm mixed up. We were lonesome until we disobeyed and were ashamed [Gen. 3.7]. So I began to study the situation and soon

.25 found how to avoid the bloody killers and protect ourselves [Gen. 3.8: they "hid themselves among the trees of the garden"]. But God looked and called to them to come to shelter [Gen. 3.9]. I fell into a heap of ruins! From that Irish policeman. He was angry with me because of the woman [Gen. 3.11]. Boxing and Coxing ["the left hand not knowing what the right hand is doing" = giving Adam the woman and then punishing them]. Arranging with me to consort with the woman like Jonathan Swift, never mentioning the Roman Catholic dance with danger of

.30 falling off the wall. But why was it me who was the victim of the joke?

TAFF/God *(all for letting his thunder and lightning be put to heat in the fire* [of the sword, Gen. 3.24] *and while obedient to the happiness of Dublin's citizens,*

.36 *still smoking his Turkish tobacco in the presence of*

348.01 *ladies).* How do you do, you Yahoo? Whom God has joined, let no man put asunder. Didn't you aid in the joke?

BUTT/Adam *(in his threefold difficulty he feels a bit like a bottle full of stout but falls like a barrel of beer).* And my awful headaches! Between my Irish

.05 association of the recent past and my connection with the sinking future I've a lot of memories in my bosom and my tears run slow, blimy, as I now recall with platonic love

.10 (how the chickens come home to roost) my missionary post for all the old heroes that are now dwelling in Valhalla, my fellow martyrs. I drink to them and their poisoned spirits and associated tricks, even where it's condensed

vodka, with absent melancholy. Gentlemen in salubrity, I
give you our sworn Occupant God, the Unsavory and
.15 Dreadful, the throne filler of all royal believers with the
rest of the inhabitants of New Ireland! One brief word.
And a magnificent one! My old associates the dead (they
would get a kick out of all that has happened to us)
Gormleyson and Adam Don'tshoot and Concubine [Ser-
pent, Adam, and Eve] those were their names for we
.20 were all fellow barracksters in Clongowes Wood [Eden],
Thor's creatures three, with that apple vendor our malady
in the woods [Gen. 3.8], the two fruit-jokesters, the Viennese
Believer [Serpent], and old Daddy Dacon [Adam, see
339.04] who was a great one for playing a game for the
.25 purpose of warmth; that's who we were and the story
mixes the charge of the Light Brigade with our weaving
the end of the disease. For love has a beam in the eye, but
no one knows for whom it beams. Hurrah! Three times
three! Attack the anathema!

TAFF/God *(who still senses that heaven sent*
.30 *concubine that entrapped Adam, who like the senorita from*
Spain played bunny rabbit with his genitals, fatal as the battle
of Waterloo, passing him the fruit to eat in an ironical joke
[Gen. 3.6]. From Adam's rib the scapegoat queen of paradise, Sinner of my Son's dream! You ride cocked whores
that are ready to embrace the bloody
.36 inflamed world! In their seductive talking way. Till they've
rings on their fingers and
349.01 bells on their toes. Where did the penis go? Was the count
mortal or gonorrhea? Mind your P's and Q's if you forge
evidence! Sing the song, dummy! Be a dog [backwards
God]!
.05 Remember old loves! Sing in the chorus to either!

In the heliotrope nighttime following the fading of the
transformed God and pending his new opposite version
.10 *and an energetic reappearance of beaming Adam, the TV*
screen shows the charge of the Light Brigade. The picture
shows them advancing. The machine gun rakes and
.15 *splits them; dynamite bombs kill them; into the valley of death*
rode the six hundred. A gasp of truth leaks out over the
whitewash. And on the TV screen fades in the

.20 *ghostly figure of Pope Don'tshoot* [Adam, cf. 348.19] *the Russian general. The specter exhibits the seals of his orders: the star of the Son of Heaven, the girdle of Isobel the Catholic, the cross of Michael the Apologizer, the tongue of executed Jan of Nepomuk, the powder and ball of Peter and Paul, and the great belt,*

.25 *band and bucklings of the martyrs. It is for the cast-off-mercy muddy-wake-service. The vicar will please not speak what you dread, please not to those about to die. Hell, something's gone wrong with the speech. He anoints his eyes because he confesses to all his vicious*

.30 *vices. He anoints his nose because he confesses to where he was always putting up his fingers. He anoints his mouth because he confesses how often he used to be opening her while wantonly being above her. He binds together his hands and feet because he confesses before all his accomplices and confederates. And, since he*

.36 *can't come back* [to Eden, Gen. 3.24] *and say he wouldn't steal the fruit of the tree* [Gen. 3.22] *he mentioned this*

350.02 *tree of life* [which was not forbidden: Gen. 2.16–17] *because he confessed to it up hill and down dale and in the places the lepers inhabit and in fact, just*

.05 *forgetting how he came to think of it, all over the bloody shop. Bugger old Pompous Dungandshit! ALP will give him salvation after evensong on the field of honor. Bow down ladies and gentlemen. The bells ring.*

.11 BUTT/Adam *(with a gesture expressive of Oscar Wilde with a flower in his buttonhole at his trial, he tells how, when he was first obeying God* [Gen. 2.15], *the wife*

.15 *they both produced* [Gen. 2.22] *was the very thing to alter his mind).* Excuse me! That's enough! Forbidding of every circumstance in debauchery is not right! Stealing back and minding P's and Q's is a putrid way to rivalry!

.20 Take the pains, please, of not forgetting to go to hell! Correct me, please, Commander, but for God's sake I am sick of it. No more Turkish soldiers for this poor leprechaun! Thanks to Oscar Wilde. I had my belly full of Turkish delights the whole fucking time on Romeo and Juliet food, what with taking care of "every beast of the

.25 field" [Gen. 2.19] and Your taking my rib for my helpmeet [Gen. 2.22]; when the Assyrian god came down like a wolf on the fold and we praying players smoking the peace pipe, innocent soldiers all, for the mercenary God to go and leave us and shed the crimson light of dawn on the dark (as directed by the Slob God) causing and ignoring the

.30 massacred (not like Daniel in the lion's den) and promoting martyrdom [as does Revelation] into massacre (Your holy blessing is accompanied by a gun). Yet still and all, as we chanted in Sunday school, "Onward Christian Soldiers," and unless I am forgetful of the rudiments of

.36 savage wildfire I was game and well met; send us

351.01 victorious with guns, Oh Trinity, and all the fun I had at the Fall. Here comes a strange man wearing clothes [Gen. 3.21; see **Norwegian captain**]. And here's a gift of woman and food. And I shall live by working hard [Gen. 3.19]. And beat my gun into a plough. You promised

.05 rainbows! Then were the hell's own days for us, the loyal lovers; we were innocent recruits, your Irish Trinity and we two; an easy time we had in our wayward island [Ireland = Eden], no English around, one long blue streak, the romance of a dark Rosaleen combined with Omar Khayyam as the Serpent,

.10 always wriggling about, encouraging our wooing, our jokester chaplain contriving the black ashes to come. Drink a toast! And we're all tuned in to hear

.15 the topmost novelty, *Finnegans Wake*. Up with the revels, down the drinks and armistice all around! Long live the common man! And tit for tat. Tug at my heart strings. I dream of those days when I loved you with passion. Celebrate the innocent Adam and Issy. It was first rate,

.20 believe me. I was a naked private without authority but did not give in to threat or bribery, touching those engaging genitals from the land of Cornwall [Issy/Isolde], the dearest sweetheart, announcing her very frank actions [Gen. 3.12] in this picture book. It was fine whatever the consequences! I could always take

.25 good care of myself; idols or Serpents, bringers of rain or condemnation, I did not give three hoots for any feeling from my private life on their retrograde leanings because I have the honor of both my respectable sisters [Issy and Eve] and the brothel occupants, the cherubs

.30 minus their drawers; and she can vint her wine and ring the wedding bells and I know her highness the respectable big ass madame would never let the devotees of sexual satisfaction let me down. Not on your bloody life, pimps! No peeking! And, by God, I never went wrong nor let him doom me till, like a risky Russian wolf in charge

.36 of the wake, up came the Serpent (the old contemptible)

352.01 to the Russian general's twin [Adam] with his unreformed brothel and presented him with unopposed nonchalance the same old jokester's story [Gen. 3.4–5] about the apple and the whore who is greatly to be pitied; and I saw his

.05 Britisher's aggression and fatherly advice to the harlot, telling her God would approve [Gen. 3.5] and how he contradicted God's word (Oh just a fly-away flirtation of him and her! Just a mere maid's fling is all it was); and my Ireland for a sordid roll over, when by the splendor

.10 of God, bang goes the enemy. The Serpent really got me, a messenger (as true as there is an almighty God above us) with a blow like the Ondt gave the Gracehoper [which see]. This time it took me! And after me the deluge. We disobeyed [Gen. 3.12], and like the procurer of the Holy Synod before He could tell us about the coats [Gen. 3.21], we were paralyzed, shut out [Gen. 3.24], I and the Mrs. like a white slaver! Fallen like Humpty Dumpty! Tumbled

.15 and heaved out!

TAFF/God *(concluding that since they were shot and lanced, the vulgar boaster was heading toward the red sea* [the Exodus] *but being too conceited not to ignore the unseemliness of his rival's proceedings, in an effort of self-preservation, replaces Himself as a person in favor*

.20 *of the ideology always behind his sodality for self-devotion, which means that if He had joined them mainly to foster their liking Him—shit!—He may* [subsequently] *impregnate one of them* [immaculate conception] *to produce a young heir— comprehend?)* Take communion and believe it's Me! And how very clever of you, you bragging gun fodder!

.25 The grand old spider! It is the name to call Me. Ah, you were Adam clothed [Gen. 3.21] and the victor conquered. You from the race of fishmongers oppose one of the sharpshooters.

BUTT/Adam *(uttering a hasty cry, fearing war, his mus-*

tache bristling, with the jingo ritual of the Mass, he cries out
at his Fall and the foul figures of their chanting!) Bloody
mud face! Let God shoot His gun!

.30 He'll embezzle no more people into their graves with
horns and hounds, the werewolf, for dead companions in
His hills! Captain Backside Black Beard! HCE the frus-
trated Irish, Hebrew, Moslem, Russian general conun-
drum-in-chief.

TAFF/God *(who, as best he can, with the help of gospel*
and with His blizzard maker [Satan/Serpent] *in hell suffer-*
ing Himself all the purgatories of His sin for

353.01 *failing to follow the genealogy of the doomed gods).* [He
should have died long ago like the Greek gods in Hesiod's
Theogony.] Trembling Trinity, who made man the scapegoat! That's the name of the most merciful, the august, the
gracious one! In sober truth and civilian clothes? And

.05 to the detriment and curtailment of all the mankind he
created? Not so?

BUTT/Adam *(momentarily scoffed and unworthily thrown*
out but his bleaching bones will make a busman's holiday out
of the God's holy cynicism of die and be damned).

.10 Yes sir! In sober truth and sober clothes! If it is not true!
That God lives yet is my grief. He endeared me to the
Temptation and he dared me to consummate it, and be
damned, I did dare do it, as the Serpent can tell, and I was
as well victorious over that bear of a Russian general with
all the rats in his attic. As bold and as mad as a

.15 bull in the meadow. Like the violent Vikings. The deaf ear
of former times! For when I saw God and twelve o'clock
rolled all over our Lord's land [time began], tearing up that
sod of turf to wipe himself, Paddy whacked him. Aye, and
death with His pants off for the ex-royal God of Israel. For
that insult to Ireland!

.20 Ready! I gave one Good Night and I upped with my holy
weapon. Aim! Knowing my arms, I made it hit like a Cock
Robin's arrow, and that was the fate of God. Fire!

.22 *The annihilation of the word of the grisly, terrible grinding*
of the founder of the first Lord of Dublin explodes, with the
aid of the Serpent, with an Ivan-the-Terrible-Thor-rumble-
loud-noise amid which a general

.25 *utmost confusion is perceivable, atomic particles escaping with molecules, while the ostracized innocents pretend in the London elegance of Picadilly. Similar scenes are projected from Honolulu, blissful Rome, and*

.30 *dead Athens, but I play pranks. They were precisely at the moment when time began. At some all-day-war-kingdom, but in Ireland by daybreak.*

TAFF/God *(scampering and wool gathering all over Dublin what with the Christian brothers and Isolde's tower and*

354.01 *the fighting and broken homes).* Where is all the enlightenment up in heaven! I shot my own Son? [Cf. 336.22, 468.15, 495.11–14.]

BUTT/Adam *(pulling a last strong denial with a parting drink, being refused pardon, painfully his words*

.05 *diminished to nothingness, he becomes lacking life, faint).* Sure enough! Like Finn MacCool!

.08 BUTT-and-TAFF/Adam-and-God [they merge as consubstantial Father and Son, two-thirds of the Trinity] *(desperate wage slave and feudal foreman, now one and the same person, the right to fight held up for a little,*

.10 *while being battered and tottering, overshadowed by earth's more than mythical God of war; like the capitalists around the world, whose power craven millions had cause to revile, as the Devil did in hell under Moses's burning bush, he falls by the serpent; but saddened by the*

.15 *circumstances of the Serpent in a hurdy-gurdy concert of their dangerous brawl, shaking everybody's hands from all parts of Dublin and, without father or mother or brother*

.20 *or sister, the pledge of friendship, hand to hand, with a communist vow of the strong and best dictator's theology, palms it off like commodity tokens of concatenation* ["of events in the best of all possible worlds," Voltaire's *Candide*]). When the Serpent was in the garden [Gen. 3.1–5] and Issy first spread her legs, wonderful was the way of the world,

.25 where choosing and having were Siamese twins. They had their childbearing instinct and their forecast of murder and God's moldering ire in that vineyard, but there'll be a bright inheritance for mankind when the thieving bird's Bible burns. If they loved the thought of sex and drank the wine, he danced the song of the feminine side and shouted

out to the deaf [wine, women, and song]. And by-and-by
the boys and girls will find a land of milk and honey
[Exod. 3.17] while cutting off Lucifer; and being deaf to
the earwig/Serpent makes coy cousins corollaries [*Finnegans
Wake*] much sweeter to us. So until Buckley again shoots
the Russian general, let God chew the fat of His anger and
Adam abide his toil and trouble.

The Ondt and the Gracehoper (414–19)

This Wakean version of the fable of the ant and the grasshopper combines
the fable with Genesis 3, where Adam and Eve disobey God, Who con-
fronts them and sentences them to toil, trouble, and death. The story is
told by Adam in the guise of Shaun, who in turn assumes the role of the
Gracehoper, appropriately because Adam was innocently cavorting around
the Garden of Eden like a grasshopper and enjoying himself with his
helpmeet, Eve, when God admonished him. In spite of this reprimand, he
still hoped to retain God's grace and is hence the "Gracehoper." The unjust
and righteous God of the Old Testament is relentless, however. He keeps
Eden for himself and throws Adam/Gracehoper out into the cold like the
ant does the grasshopper in the fable. He is therefore the *Ondt,* a name that
means "angry" in Norwegian and "evil" in Danish.

Adam starts out in answer to God's question in Gen. 3.11, "Hast thou
eaten of the tree?"

414.16	—I apologize, Adam began, but rather than a direct an-swer I would rather spin
.17	you a Grimm fairy tale or an Aesop fable,
.18	although a poor excuse. Consider the case of
.19	(God thunders
.20	a cough) the Ant and
.21	the Grasshopper.
.22	The Grasshopper was always dancing an Irish jig, happy on account
.23	of his joyousness (he also had a Dublin partner, Joyce, to succeed him)
.24	or making disgraceful overtures to female
.25	insects (Flea, Louse, Bee, and Wasp) to play making babies
.26	and pushing his antenna into their terminal segment and
.27	committing incest with him, their mouths to his orifice and his

.28   mouth and hands to their hairy region, even if only in clean fun, like

.29   everybody holding a jam pot to catch wasps. He would

.30   maliciously but sweetly, with his hands and muscles, feel her up

.31   and annoy her

.32   till she blushed for shame; he would also furnish her

.33   with silk hosiery from the best shops, in his summer

.34   cottage, which was called familiarly
      Think Again [cf. 343.09].

.35   Or, if he was striking up funny wake dances with

.36   old father time with his halo,

415.01   white robe, and scythe under his wings and

.02   Demeter and Persephone, his offspring, wheedling him,

.03   compound insect eyes on his hornet head, and Puss-in-Boots to

.04   scratch his head and cackle in his throat like a bee (with seven

.05   soap bubbles, a little lime, two spurts of phosphorous, three farts of

.06   sulphur, a shake of sugar, a dozen grains of urine, and a messful of

.07   pitch. Meanwhile this revolving language

.08   is like the song of the Wild Man from Borneo.)

.09   and with tambourines and Spanish-fly castanets, rotating around his

.10   cockroach egghill with their *Danse Macabre* in fear of the past

.11   like fantastic Toulouse-Lautrec dancers, to the

.12   beat of slow heels and toes, attended by a

.13   God-and-Adam fight and myriad

.14   drunken bees singing "Cottar's Saturday Night" and "Humpty

.15   Dumpty Sat on a Wall" and "Finnegan's Wake." For if

.16   science can tell us nothing

.17   about the ultimate being within the universe, perhaps a

.18   concordance of arts might tell us something about the little

.19   people who inhabit the earth. A high old time for the

.20   berated public free all day, thank God. Thunder and lightning

.21 for everyone, any port in a storm; for old Cronus lies emasculated

.22 in the sands of time, but his descendants stumble on. Anything on

.23 earth, as his Holy Book of the Dead [the Bible?] bid him as always, saint

.24 or sinner, seemingly, to kill time.

.25   Gracious, and resurrect my soul! What a trick it is!

.26 Libelous! Insanity! Lousy! Flea bitten! God the Father! What a time for the

.27 barbarians! vented God/ant who, not being a summer fool, was

.28 wisely avoiding His waspy face and icy

.29 voice saying, No, no, and no again.

.30 We will hide ourselves to avoid God, Adam decided [Gen. 3.8],

.31 for he was afraid. Also to avoid Egyptian antecedents

.32 of this God as long as there was a soul in his body.

.33 Nevertheless when he had safely covered himself with fig leaves, he

.34 called God and prayed: May he not void water on me! Please

.35 heaven! May he not pile pig shit on me! But he has. As far as

.36 Pharaoh Pepi's realm shall flourish, my reign shall flourish. As long as

416.01 the leaf-clothed Egyptian god's vengeance shall flourish, my hatred will also!

.02 Yes, flourish even if flogged! Well, maybe.

.03   God was tall, well-built, and able-bodied,

.04 almost as tall as a bell in a steeple. He was very

.05 solemn and looked like a person who was not developing

.06 his soul but who was creating an image that

.07 he was most sacred and wise.

.08 Now when the credulous Gracehoper/Adam had experienced

.09 eating the fruit and realized

.10 afterwards his life was in doubt, then betting with bumble bees,

.11 drinking with water bugs, cheating with daddy longlegs and whoring

.12 after ladybugs, he fell just as

.13 sick as Satan and poor as a church mouse or a Catholic cardinal; and

.14 where to take himself and how to search for food

.15 for his body or find shelter, alas, he didn't know.

.16 Dry as a caterpillar! Spent as a drone! Hungry as a wasp! His whole world

.17 was empty! Nothing! Not a kopeck of Russian

.18 money to buy a little bread! My God! Leaking

.19 basket, what a plight! Oh my God, he regretted with

.20 melancholy. He snowed me! I am hungry of heart.

.21 He had eaten all the wallpaper, swallowed the seats,

.22 devoured forty flights of staircases, chewed up all the tables

.23 and chairs, gnawed the records, made mudballs of the calendars,

.24 and gobbled most glutinously the timepieces of

.25 eternity—not too bad a meal for the nutrition of an insect

.26 chap so small. But when Christmas was about to occur,

.27 off he went from his cottage. He strolled around and

.28 he strolled around and he strolled around again until the

.29 bees in his bonnet and the lice in his hair made him think

.30 he was upside down in Tasmania. Had he gone around twice the seas of the dead

.31 and three times crossed their river source? Had he come to heaven with the

.32 angels or gone to hell with the pope? The June snow [in Tasmania] was

.33 flying in drifts on hailstones, tons of it

.34 and ugly whirling tornadoes, the north wind

.35 blasting tiles off the roofs and gusting sleet off

.36 the coffeehouses, playing havoc with an irritating

417.01 penetrating, sucking water spout. A horror opera!

.02 Horror! Fear!

.03 The Gracehoper/Adam who, though blind as a bat and knowing not

.04 merely a little but a good smattering of entomology, wriggled

.05 without leave or license, promptly tossing himself in the

.06 road, then and there on top of his buzzer, testily wondering

.07 whether his luck would allow him to appease God, and the

.08   next time he made his acquaintance, after they

.09   met and their mutual beholding, it would be

.10   mighty lucky if he did not behold a world of difference. Behold

.11   His Highness the God prostrate on his throne in his

.12   Babylonian costume, smoking a special brand of Hosana

.13   cigars, with unmentionables falling off his unthinkables,

.14   admiring himself in the sun-room, satisfied with the

.15   comfortable philosophy from the minds of Plato and Confucius

.16   (as well as estheticism and Aristotle), as

.17   happy as a honeysuckle and basking with desire, with a flea

.18   biting his thigh and a louse hugging his left leg, and a bee buzzing

.19   in his bonnet and a wasp blowing Mozart's music

.20   up the broad length of his behind. As buggy

.21   as intimacy could pinchably be. Damned ants be jilted

.22   crazy and Jesus wept!, sneezed the Gracehoper, agape

.23   with jealousy and at his wit's end. What have I seen!

.24   God, that true and perfect host [that is, landlord, enemy and eucharistic wafer] like a spider spinning his trap,

.25   making the greatest joke a body could with his woman,

.26   for he was itching all over like anything

.27   for fornication, boundlessly blissful in a bath with Allah's

.28   nymphs. He was amusing himself by dancing around

.29   the maypole, chasing Flo and tickling Lucy with faith, hope and charity,

.30   tackling Bienie as well and grabbing little Vespa

.31   by the chemise. Never did an Irishman dance it

.32   with more deviltry. The peripatetic image of the impossible

.33   Gracehoper/Adam with his head in the mire after his three

.34   ephemeral journeys, without coat or shoes, but with lightened

.35   soul, looking for grace but signifying chronic

.36   despair, was sufficiently and probably crazy for much of his dance

418.01   downwards. Let him be the weeping artist in exile with his parasites

.02   peeling off him; I'll be the highly paid comedian. The flunky

.03   earns little by writing his lies, but the cantor makes

.04   the melody that mints the money. *For the greater money and glory of God.*

.05   Someone darkens the threshold. Who? The god who capsized the

.06   boat in *The Book of the Dead* seeks revenge from the evil Lord of Hosts.

.07   So be it. Whoever you are and gone with the wind,

.08   receive my body. Hail!

.09   *The situation pleased him, all in all.*

.11   *He laughed and he laughed as he made such a noise* [Gen. 3.9].

.12   *Adam/Gracehoper feared he would misplace his voice* [Gen. 3.10].

.13   *I forgive you, grand God, said the Gracehoper, weeping,*

.14   *For the sake of their souls who are safe in your keeping.*

.15   *Teach your children to dance and find what is sweet,*

.16   *And be sure that they all have plenty to eat.*

.17   *As I once played, so now I must pay;*

.18   *So said Mohammed and Abraham on your mountain!*

.19   *Let him who likes ignore you and enjoy life;*

.20   *I could not feel worse if this were gospel.*

.21   *I accept your reproof although it is a gift-horse*

.22   *For the price of your saving is the price of my spending.*

.23   *Like the twins, can your children forsake each other*

.24   *Or Castor feel anxious if Pollux doesn't come for him?*

.25   *A place to love, does that embarrass You?*

.26   *That is what men and women require.*

.27   *You turned things around so much it looks like the north wind goes south*

.28   *Ever since the threat of the Griffin, we are his fairest escape.*

.29   *That man you killed was not conquered with your exile.*

.30   *Since when do long suffering sighs ease the heartache of leaving Eden?*

.31   *We are wasted with want, precondemned, two but true,*

.32   *Come whatever.*

.33   *Before those clergy now defending you, quit your falsehoods; for my gropings*

.34   *Space must extend and time must pass.*

.35   *Of my tactics take stock; my baton will lead and all will be well;*

.36   *As I look at your teaching, you should walk behind me.*

419.01   *You are prejudiced to my thin whims, but my point of view is unbroken, while*

.02   *Your views are widely broadcast as the only right ones.*

.03   *In my laughable universe you'd hardly find*

.04   *Such preconceived ideas which mean so much to the contrary.*

.05   *Your feats were enormous, your writings immense,*

.06   *(May the grace I hoped for celebrate your Godhead!),*

.07   *Your genius is worldwide and heaven is sublime.*

.08   *But, by the Holy Saints, why can't you end death?*

Chapter Eight

The New Theology

Re-creating the Conscience of His Race

Perhaps the most repeated quotation from Joyce is Stephen's diary entry in the penultimate paragraph of *A Portrait of the Artist as a Young Man:* "I go to encounter for the millionth time the reality of experience and to forge in the smithy of my soul the uncreated conscience of my race." Some critics have maintained that Joyce attempted to carry out Stephen's vow in all of his works since the *Portrait.* In none is the effort as evident as it is in *Finnegans Wake.* Disgusted with Dublin life and the restrictive oppression of the Irish priests, he exiled himself and conjured in his soul a vision of his reincarnation of the biblical Adam. In the *Wake* he destroys the Irish conscience and creates a new version based on an autobiographical reinterpretation of cyclopedic scriptures, both sacred and profane, and on all other writings ancient and modern. Indeed, to the extent that *Finnegans Wake* has a dominant theme, the creation of a conscience for the Irish race is it. That was Joyce's purpose and aim in its composition.

There is an abundance of internal evidence that such was the intent, as the following generic paraphrases make clear.

446.27   [In this passage Adam/Shem/Joyce speaks to Eve/ALP:] Come, consider the Irish race and rally around this counsel. We will purify their work and social service, my wife, completing our charitable union by adopting them. Embark for the land of glorious music! Up Irish leaders! Take off unnecessary clothes, and in our shirt sleeves, braces to brassiere, we'll complete our Work in Progress. The union we made in the Garden of Eden will free us from the gaze of the terrible God. We'll civilize all Dubliners by cutting off the restrictions.

.36 Let us, the real people, unite in our condition here on earth as apostles and be instrumental in helping our

447.01 educated sisters clean out that hogshole of Ireland and generally spice things up. Improve the world held down by the Mass; conduct more charitable Irish sweepstakes

.05 until fortune hums like a hymn. Burn everything of the Irish, accepting their own help to do so. You will sooth the dominance of the English and touch the Celtic core. Write your essays, my vocational scholars, but include the coarseness, dipping your nose in the sewage running under the boulevards, about the mortality and birth rate in the

.10 life of the people [like Rowntree; see *FW* 544]. I'd write it myself if I only had a pen. Bear in mind, not by God but by the man who looks like Him [Adam], all the banana peels and garbage in the Dublin streets. Like all the

.15 men God has brought to death like dung or manure for the birds to feed on, our God, with the streets filled with

.20 monks out on a stag party. Compare them with the bridge of sighs which they impose on Dublin. What do you mean by Shaun as a model citizen and Shem/Joyce as a pagan? Compare the real life in Dublin with the humbug of the

.25 poet. Explain why there is such a sea of religious orders. Why do religious orders have preference? Why have religious orders at all now? Where is the greenest island which attracts the black coats of priests? Translated into truth: I (a Dubliner) am a sitting duck. Let us pray! Oh for a way for Dubliners to think for

.30 themselves.

[This segment of the Buckley episode explains its purpose.]

341.19 Up to this point [the *FW* text says] the written, spoken, and visual presentation of the Fall has been given from the standpoint of the Irish race. The huddled masses have shared their religion with the enthusiasm of horse racing. But the winners were announced by the flashing

.25 sword at the gate of Eden [Gen. 3.24]. My God! That was (smoking a pipe) HCE/God confessing how Buckley shot the Russian general as though it was an amusing horse race.

.30   The perversion of confession and absolution tells a story of successful romping home by a lot of priests and nuns with flesh and blood collecting boxes. One ought to spare the faithful to be fair and provide condoms for the children. That thief and tailor, HCE/God, physically

342.01   present with them but morally absent, was "slooching" about in His fine clothes asking Adam, the Serpent, and woman to set up the Temptation scene. As the Trinity, however, in His unrelenting form, God was sulking in His

.05   silken tent, bawling out the curses [Gen. 3. 14–19] and setting up the baleful day [Gen. 3.24]. And the flocks of pious sheep in their fashionable ensembles! You see: a chiefsmith, several scandle makers, a madam from the Whitehouse, and of course the Tempter. Bare ass! Pardon

.10   the inquisition, but doesn't that bring up a question? It is the mercenary Dominican Brothers. Why do they wear that weird hood? Because under no circumstances whatever is the patronage of the Governor General to be lost. Great Jupiter, what was that? Our lucky number. On the

.15   thousand-to-one horse race. [The next fifteen lines describe the horse race intermingled with an erotic description of the Temptation of the woman by the Serpent.]

.30   This eerie dream is being offered you by the Father and the Son of the Trinity [see 354.08] as believed by the Irish race.

188.09   [Shaun/JUSTIUS in this paragraph condemns his twin Shem/MERCIUS for abandoning his early religious training and establishing a new conscience.] "You were bred, fed, fostered and fattened from holy childhood up in this two easter island [Ireland]" with admonitions of heaven and hell, and now you have formed your mind against God and

.16   "you have reared your disunited kingdom on the vacuum of your own most intensely doubtful soul. . . . must I too nerve myself to pray for the loss of selfrespect. . . ?

.24   I shall shiver for my purity while they will weepbig for your sins." [There are echoes here of Shem/Joyce's abandonment of an old conscience and creation of a new and puzzling one.] "Away with covered words [*Finnegans Wake*], new Solemonities [the new conscience]. . . ! That inharmonious detail, did you

.26   name it?" [It was called *Finnegans Wake*.]

189.30   "you with your dislocated reason, have cutely foretold . . .

the reducing of records to ashes," and by chopping and peeling [transforming] all figurative meat and vegetables [food

190.09 of the Fall], have created a "new Irish stew."

374.16 "Wait till we hear the Boy of Biskop [Joyce, the novice director of a new conscience] reeling around your postoral lector! Epistlemadethemology for deep dorfy doubtlings." [*Finnegans Wake* is the epistle to make a new theology for Dubliners.]

472.34 The Irish people await the day that Adam/Haun/Joyce "retourneys postexilic . . . to joyful Ireland . . .

473.01–02 to mind us of what was when and to matter us of the withering of our ways."

597.01 [The first part of this page explains how *Finnegans Wake* is the rewriting of Genesis; It is paraphrased in "Internal Correspondences" in Chapter 2. Then comes this rhapsodic vision of the new version]:

.30 Time has begun again.
The weather is perfect. The jackdaw does not scold. The clouds promise spring rain. Anemones are emerging and the world is waking up. Human nature is feeling at ease with life. The signs of spring are an aphrodisiac. Listen to what they say. You have eaten the forbidden fruit. So what. You have talked to the Tempter and

.36 accepted the knowledge of good and evil. How can you tell which is which?

598.01 Every person wheresoever has just been doing what all the human race does without being bound to the affliction of death. The Old Testament God has disappeared. You heard Him at the start of time but not a solitary syllable of sound since. Instead of caring and steering, He has set us adrift. We were

.05 walking in the night toward the void. The source of order was a riddle. It was a very long, very dark, all-but-unending, scarcely endurable, quite variable, and somewhat stumbling night. Yesterday He sent us out of Eden. It is a new day! The old God has gone; the new

.10 one is coming. Hail the ghostly yesterday with a greeting to the new morning. Let the old destiny sleep. The fasting is doomed. It is well done with; replace it with the good new order. The new day is divided from the old slow day by the delicate and divine. The lotus goddess of the universe, ALP, brighter and sweeter than the old God is the flower goddess, who rings our hour of arising. She will tickle you [see 21.29, 76.28, 198.12]. Let us pray to her coming. Today!

.15   Take thanks in this theme and bring the Sanskrit-Hindu goddess concept into European religion.

There was something perfidious in whatever you called Him. To call a spade a spade, there is no transubstantiation of bread and wine; they are simply and solely what they are. Adam was the same as Christ. Both

.20   were God's sons. The old Easter story is stale and falls apart. Matthew, Mark, Luke, and John now support Adam as the Son. And your last words on hearing that story, which is going to stretch your imagination through strength and joy, colleagues, is Adam's resurrection in *Finnegans Wake*. Ally with your neighbor; do not ask an eye for an eye and a tooth for a tooth [agrees with Matt. 5.33–48].

.27   "Tim!" [almost Time].

579.10   On the diamond anniversary of Adam and Eve's Fall, *Finnegans Wake* lists proverbs for a new conscience. Here are some: Remove the old Bible. You will never control the grasping clergy unless you keep your money on your own plate. Keep holy beggars outdoors. You will be a goat until your end if you let your guard down. Mind the monks and their grasping ways. Be responsible for your own soul; do not accept absolution. Don't depend on God's help ("Commit no miracles.") . . . Let loose the doves of

.15   love to enjoy sex. Love thy neighbor but take care of your own ("Hatenot havenots. Share the wealth and spoil the weal. . . . Earn before eating.") . . . No Old Testament

.20   Gods before ALP . . . Let the Serpent's advice to the

.25   woman/ALP teach you the proper way of life.

Thus, as the title of the book indicates, Joyce created a new conscience for his race. Finnegans are not only the Irish descendants of Adam; they also carry his patronym. *Finnegans Wake* tells all the Irish people to wake up!

They are to abandon the old God of their corrupt religion and adopt ALP as their Savior.

The Evil God

The religious essence of *Finnegans Wake* has been noted by many critics, but the hermeneutics have not been very enlightening. "You see I have read your theology for you" (189.04), says Shaun/Adam to Shem/Joyce; "[and you are the] seeker of the nest of evil in the bosom of a good word" [you seek the evil God in the words of the Bible] (189.28). On the face of it Joyce's theology is highly heretical, but before he can introduce a new salvation, he must destroy the old. His hatred of the clergy and disgust of the Irish submission to it has produced an eruption of vituperation unmatched among twentieth-century authors. He succors those heretics who held that the God of the Old Testament was wicked, vengeful, and corrupt.

Heresies

Joyce's rewritten Bible contains a number of heresies of his own invention, including the one that God established killing as a human activity. Numerous historical heresies which resulted in a multitude of deaths of their proposers are also included and are reviewed below. When Shem/Joyce discusses the sources of *Finnegans Wake* at 172.28–34, he tells us that "he was in his bardic memory low" and that "delicate tippets were thrown out to him touching his evil courses . . . vainly pleading by scriptural arguments with the opprobrious papist." The "arguments" for the most part are no longer of any great importance except to *Wake* readers, to whom all "tippets" are relevant:

173.13   "Albiogenselman." The Albigensian heretics are mentioned by name only. The sect was wiped out in southern France in the thirteenth century during the Inquisition, and now no one remembers exactly what they disbelieved. They were one of a widespread Catharist group who generally were anti-church reformists and shared the concept of a dualistic nature of God with the Marcionists mentioned below.

75.02   "shall Ariuz forget Arioun." Arianism, named for Arius who died in 336, held that God is one and alone and therefore Christ is not God since there is no Trinity.

424.36   "lowbrown schisthematic robblemint." Giordano Bruno is implied, and Browne and Nolan are mentioned numerous times. Joyce used the "union of opposites" theory as a compositional principle. That is a corollary of Bruno's general thesis that God is universal and unifying, from whom all things must come; another corollary, that God must know and contain evil, got Bruno burned at the stake in 1600.

4.36   "erigenating." Erigena was known as John the Scot, but he signed himself as being of Ireland. He was among the first of the scholastics in France of the ninth century. Many of his ideas would have appealed to Joyce; he held that (1) the universe or God is a unity which contains all things, including man; (2) the Eucharist was merely symbolic and therefore transubstantiation was false; (3) God's free will allows all activities of man; (4) if God knew evil, He would cause it because His knowledge and His will are identical; (5) the Trinity is composed of Father as substance of being, Son as wisdom, and Spirit as life; (6) only after God introduced sin did man lose his spiritual being and acquire physical sex; (7) the result of punishment is the redemption of all, including animals and devils. John the Scot-Irish influenced Nicholas of Cusa, who influenced Bruno.

173.12   "Jansens Chrest." The Jansenists, named for Cornelius Jansen, 1585–1638, were opponents of the Jesuits. They maintained doctrines of predestination—therefore no free will, therefore total depravity, therefore limited atonement, and therefore irresistible grace.

472.20   "manipulator." Adaline Glasheen's *Second Census* lists this reference for "Mani, a Persian heretic." The connection is a tribute to Glasheen's astuteness, for it is deeply buried in the context. Mani, who was born in Babylonia in A.D. 216, founded the Manichaean Gnostic sect (which is covered under "The Gnostic Texts," in Chapter 3, where many of his teachings which found their way into *Finnegans Wake* are discussed). It is sufficient to point out here that Mani preached freeing of Light caught in Darkness which he equated to divine spirit caught in the human body. The heresy comes from his holding that the Jewish God Yahweh was actually the Prince of Darkness, who wickedly created man but had no Light to form his soul—Light which

Sophia ultimately supplied. The following line references on page 472, which occur within the context of Haun/Shem/Adam's death by exile, support the Mani/"manipulator" reading: "touch the light theorbo!" ["theorbo" = musical instrument] (472.08); "Musicianship made Embrassador-at-Large!" (.10) [see the relationship of music to Spirit under **Trinity**]; "Gone is Haun" [Adam exiled by God] (.14); "'Tis well you'll be looked after from last to first as yon beam of light" [Mani's soul as Light] (.16); "mansuetudinous manipulator" [Mani the manipulator is gentle with Sophia's feminine Light] (.19); "Thy now paling light lucern [from the Latin *lux* = "light"] we ne're may see again" [your soul = light we may not see again on earth] (.23); "For you had . . . the nucleus of a glow of a zeal of soul" (.26).

192.01   "hereticalist Marcon and the two scissymaidies." Marcion attempted the first reformation of the church in the second century. He saw the God of the Old Testament as just but stern, jealous, wrathful, and variable, whereas the God of the New Testament was goodness and love. He accepted the Gnostic position of the Jewish God as the Demiurge and the discovery of a higher God who took pity on the condemned race of men and sent Christ to save them. The "two scissymaidies," while they may include Issy and Eve, also means the God which Marcion split in two.

156.11   "monophysicking." The Monophysites believed that Christ had but a single nature, the human and the divine in one composite. There was a lot of suppression and fighting over the issue in the sixth century throughout the East, but the issue became moot with the rise of Islam.

161.08   "the system, in the dogmarks ["dog" = *God* backwards] of origen on spurios." Origen developed a sort of Platonic logic of Christianity in the third century called "subordinationism," which meant that the persons of the Trinity were subordinate to the ones named higher in the hierarchy: that is, the Son was subordinate to the Father, and the Spirit subordinate to the Son.

525.07   "Pelagiarist!" yells one of the four evangelists at Yawn, who has just defended Adam's behavior. This statement accuses Yawn not only of plagiarism but of stealing the arguments from Pelagius. Like Erigena four hundred years later, Pelagius was either a Scottish or an Irish monk who felt the call to preach true reform to the depraved church of the fifth century. Joyce, with "his pelagiarist pen" (182.03) devotes more space to this than to any other heresy. He appropriates six of the charges on 358–59 as Roland McHugh discovered in 1970. Pelagius's teaching that not only do we not inherit original sin from Adam but that there is no such thing as Original Sin, of course, fits right in with Joyce's theology. Pelagius apparently escaped excommunication although he promoted a lifelong opposition to St. Augustine. It was actually his disciple Coelestius, who was charged with the six errors. HCE/God repeats the charges: "I am highly pelaged" (358.10), He says, introducing the heresy; "I am, I am big altoogooder" (358.15) He adds, introducing Himself. "From whose plultibust preaggravated, by baskatchairch theologies" (358.27) [His charge against Pelagius and Adam was aggravated by what He had already ordained and expressed a disabled low-church theology]. The six numbered propositions at 358.36–359.20 are stated by HCE/God as the opposite of those held by Coeletius or Pelagius, whose version is given first in the following discussion; then HCE/God's version is in brackets. (1) Since Adam was created a mortal man, he would have died whether he had sinned or not. [He had to die because I exiled him {as told in the Ondt and the Gracehoper}.] (2) Adam bore the consequences of his actions himself and did not pass them on as Original Sin. [He killed himself {as told in episode of Buckley and the Russian general.] (3) Children are born innocent and free of Original Sin. [The pelican feeding her young children with the blood plucked from her breast is symbolic of Christ, whom I sent to redeem mankind from Original Sin. Adam, who suffered the penalty because he took his own life, thought up, over and over again, under his shield of heraldry, a personal law which is outside his territory. He forsook his children with mumbojumbo heresy.] (4) Mankind is not damned by Adam's Fall, nor will they necessarily rise just because Christ was resurrected. [Adam was a man like that Irishman Finton, and just because Finton survived the flood doesn't mean he is not damned or will be saved again.] (5) Christ was not the first man to be without sin. [Well, it wasn't Adam, who wasn't any better before the Fall than he should have been, and he could have been better afterward.] (6) The law of the Old Testament can bring men into the kingdom of heaven just the same as Christ's gospel. [Adam, Pelagius, and Joyce are three aspects of the same person, and you can clean and bleach him down to the original ashes and dust, but he's the same old windbag. What we want to hear is the cry of the soul to "Swing Low, Sweet Chariot," and you can punish that hypocritical speaker of religious heresy.]

It is apparent that Joyce embraced his predecessor heretics in disestablishing the Irish conscience.

Original Sin

Furthermore, God was a liar Who went back on His word and is not to be trusted. "Certified? As cad [God] could be. Be lying!" (88.13). Not only did He not honor His rainbow but after creating woman as a helpmeet, He reneged when Adam and Eve did only what He had created them for. By changing His mind God, not Adam and Eve, became the creator of Original Sin. God's sin was the conversion of the natural relationship of man and woman into a sinful one. The creation of Issy as woman is repeatedly referred to as a practical joke which God played on Adam. "Mere man's mime: God has jest" (486.09–10). The Prankquean does not instigate the prank (as her prototype Grace O'Malley might be considered to have done), but as ALP she rectifies God's bad judgment.

Gen. 3.21 is greatly amplified in the *Wake.* The statement that God made coats of skins to clothe Adam and Eve turns God into a tailor. The fact that there was actually a tailor in Dublin named Kerse (see Ellmann 22) helped Joyce to expand the farce. Indications of clothing always imply God's involvement in imposing the first couple's shame and are a reminder that God was really at fault.

God the Killer

One of the salient propositions is that when God sentenced Adam to exile and death He was Killed His Own Son. This position is presented in greatest detail in the Buckley and the Russian general episode but is expounded throughout the *Wake.* For example, at 495.11, "Lynch Brother . . . prepared to stretch him sacred by the powers to the starlight, L. B. W.

Hemp." [A Galway warden named Lynch hanged his own son with a hemp rope.] Another historical precedent is "Publius Manlius" (336.22), a Roman consul who condemned his son to death. At 515.21–25 St. Patrick wants St. Luke to explain why God killed His Sons: "I want you to reconstruct for us . . . how these funeral games . . . massacreedoed as the holiname rally round took place." Furthermore, by permitting the crucifixion of Jesus, God also killed His other Son. Although HCE/God defends His actions at 534.07–535.21, He does say, "Let me never see his waddphez [face] again! And mine it was [Adam in God's image] . . . immitiate my chry!" [an imitation of Christ] (535.01–03). Some theological problems arising from God's killing His Son(s) are discussed below under **Trinity**.

Joyce is not content with this accusation but extends it to charge that by introducing death on earth, God is also responsible for war, all battles, floods, disasters, drownings, and misery. In fact God promotes such calamities as an efficient way to impose His death penalty on mankind. Mention of such woes in the *Wake* always occurs in the presence of an HCE personality, or at least His initials. In this guise "Allhighest sprack for krischnians. . . . And it is as though where Agni araflammed and Mithra monished and Shiva slew" (80.20–24) compares the Christian God with the Hindu gods of fire and destruction, and the Gnostic God of Light admonished Him.

Time: 1132

Joyce may not have been the first to use numbers as a fictional device, but he was certainly the most prolific. A glance at Hart's *Concordance* shows a plethora of numbers, with 1132 having by far the greatest occurrence. Even so, the thirteen listings fall short of the thirty-five included in the following Generic Paraphrases. That is easy to understand since many are as obscure as only Joyce could make them.

Why is 1132 scattered so often throughout the *Wake*? The first two references (at 13.33 and 14.11) are given as "1132 A.D." and therefore seem to be dates. Many readers have sought for an authentic historical anniversary, but none has been found. Harry Levin (146) states that 1132 was the date of accession of St. Malachy to the primacy of the Irish church and eighteen years after the battle of Clontarf, which, *Finnegans Wake* points out, was "a slip of the time between a date and a ghostmark" (473.8–9). In other words, 1132 is a "ghostmark" not a date. Also, in the *Annotations*, Roland McHugh suggests that if we multiply by 4 the date of Finn MacCool's death, the product is 1132. Finn does not seem to be anywhere around these first two references in the *Wake,* nor is any announced reason for such a strained calculation apparent. An internal clue that a date is not the intention exists in the reference to whales cast ashore at Dublin: this did not happen in 1132 but in 1351—close and deceptively inaccurate.

Joyce carefully gives the key for the proper identification in the very next occurrence (at 19.20–21). The number 1132 is the code for all the active personages in *Finnegans Wake* as well as for the plot. It should be read: First there was one, then another one, then there were three, and finally two. It has the same characters and plot as Genesis 2 and 3: God made the first one, Adam; then the second one, woman; then He brought them together with the Serpent and caused the three to interact and as a finale expelled and sentenced to death the two, Adam and Eve. Thus 1132 is shorthand for telling the reader that *Finnegans Wake* is really Genesis rewritten. From the beginning to the end, we are reminded of it at least thirty-five times.

Another interesting aspect is that at least sixteen of the occurrences are linked to time, either directly or in context. It may be that Joyce's purpose in the initial misdirection to the number as a date is to emphasize that time had not yet started. One of the important motifs of *Finnegans Wake* is that time started at the Fall of Man. While Adam and the woman were forbidden to eat the fruit of the tree of knowledge of good and evil (Gen. 2.17), they were allowed to eat from all the other trees (Gen. 2.16), including the tree of life. After disobeying God they were banished so that they could not "take also of the tree of life and live forever" (Gen. 3.22). Prior to this they were immortal and, like all gods, timeless. After the Fall their mortality made them start counting time as their descendants still do. Thus 1132 also reminds us that it was the evil HCE/God who imposed death on humanity.

When Adam meets the cad (HCE/God) in the park, he asks "how much a clock it was" (35.18), and finally (at .33) cad/HCE says, "by Jehova, it was twelve of em" and thus started time counting. At 96.22, "oooooooo Ourang's time" means it had not yet started; nor had it at 513.03. At 517.24–32 Luke is discussing the exile with St. Patrick; their dialogue, in paraphrase, runs:

St. Patrick: Do you mean it happened about half noon?
Luke: I wish you hadn't asked me.
St. Patrick: Does that mean twelve thirty?
Luke: And eleven thirty too, before.
St. Patrick: "Tick up on time"—that is, start counting time.

In the freemason ritual, time is stopped at twelve o'clock, exactly between the two saints' comparison of Irish and German time: At 353.30 we find that it was "*precisely the twelves of clocks, noon minutes, none seconds.*" Such references to time, its measurement and pervasiveness, abound in the *Wake*.

The following Generic Paraphrases show how 1132 is spaced throughout *Finnegans Wake* to remind readers not only that they are rereading Genesis but also that the start of time was a result of the evil God's sentence.

13.33–	1132 A.D. and [half of that number] 566 A.D. These first references seem to be dates; however, A.D. is an abbreviation not only for *anno Domini* but also for *Adam.* One half of Adam is Eve, who was taken from his body. "Men like to ants" refers to man, Adam, in the image of God who is the ant in the Ondt and the Gracehoper. The crone who had a wicked wish and found herself with a sackful of shoes [used by God to kick Adam and Eve out of Eden] and was rich in sweat [from God's curses] is Eve, who also grieved because her loved one was ravished "by the ogre Puropeos Pious" [God/HCE]. Two sons Caddy and Primus [Cain and Abel] were born to Adam and Eve "at an hour"— that is, after time began at
14.12	their exile.
19.20–21	Not only is 1132 obscure in these lines; the explanation of its meaning is hidden as well. "One by one place one" means that God placed woman beside Adam; "be three dittoh and one before" means that God placed one Serpent who existed before [not created by God] by Adam, and the woman to make three. "Two nursus one" means that Adam and Eve, as a couple versus God, were plainly free to go from Eden but they left a dim future behind. The rest of the paragraph indicates that the ancient, meandering, tall tale that was to become *Finnegans Wake* starts off with snakes and prophetic curses [Gen. 3.14–19] and applies to all us sons and daughters of Adam and Eve.
36.16–18	It is doubtful that "ellboge" means eleven, but if it does, it goes with "thirty two." It is more likely that here 32 = g, the acceleration of speed of a falling body (g = 32 ft. per second per second) and therefore refers to the Fall.
69.32–	"Herr Betreffender ['the person in question' is the Serpent]

... digging in number 32" joins Adam and Eve, who are "the Sockeye Sammons ... at the time orange fasting [not yet eating the fruit]"; "prior to that" the Serpent was a salesman of condoms earning 11 shillings a week in conscience money, which establishes him as a tempter. Grouping Adam, Eve, and the Serpent with 32 and 11 justifies the connection.

70.33   The phrase "from eleven thirty to two" reinforces the link with Adam, who is about to be executed by HCE/God. The phrase also includes time.

73.10   References to "two and thirty" (straws) and "eleven" (hundred years) substantiate "the first heroic couplet from the fuguall [fugue and fugitives] tropical, Opus Elf

.15   [German for "eleven"] Thortytoe: *My schemes into abeyance for This time has had to fall,*" which clearly establishes 1132 as a fugue [repetition with variations] on Adam and Eve's

.20   disobeying God and their resulting Fall.

77.06–12   The phrase "eleven and thirty ... to" is linked to "clocks" and "nobody appeared to have the same time. . . ."

95.14   "Wall by the 32 to 11" connects 1132 with the wall of the Fall and with the start of time.

119.25–26   "sansheneul" is 32 in a French transliteration of Chinese, and "ninth from the twentieth" = 11. "our own vulgar 432" (St. Patrick's landing in Ireland) is "irrespective . . ." of "1132" which excludes St. Patrick's date from 1132 [see also 347.19].

256.22   [The explication of "eleven in thirtytwo" is given in Chapter 2.]

274.12–13   "Number Thirty two West Eleventh" brings 1132 into a paragraph discussing the Cherubims at the gate of Eden ("the death ray stop him"), the fruit tree ("datetree doloriferous"), and so on.

310.03   The "magazine battery . . . patent number 1132" is the source of energy for God's science-fiction machine, which will bring about the Fall.

338.05   At the start of the conversation in the Buckley and the Russian general episode, "*thirty two eleven*" is inserted in the description of TAFF/God to establish that the action is posited in Genesis.

347.04   "elve hundred and therety and to years." [For the explication, see **Buckley and the Russian general**.]

347.16–20 McHugh's *Annotations* finds 700 + 432 ("the druidful day come San Patrisky" = St. Patrick's landing) = 1132. However, since it is stated that "the heptahundread annam dammias" are "the timelag," it seems equally logical that they should be subtracted, not added; thus Wakean logic makes St. Patrick's historical aversion to sex and women likely to separate him from the Fall. Likewise at 462.35 the decimal point in 4.32 may separate the 32 = g from St. Patrick's date by the same reasoning.

348.32 "11.32." [See **Buckley and the Russian general.**]

386–87. The discussion here is about HCE/God and the violence and disorder He caused, such as earthquakes, volcanoes, and the

.13 creation of Ireland; "his three andesiters" who were sighted in Ireland/Eden [Adam, Eve and the Serpent] "and the two pantellarias" [Adam and Eve thrown out of Eden as from a volcano] establish the 3 and the 2 in the 32

.23 for "the year of the flood 1132 S.O.S." which the "explutor" [rain and disaster maker] caused.

388.12–391.02 This cluster of 1132s (five occurrences including the preceding one at 387.23) serves to connect the discussion of the four New Testament evangelists with the Old Testament Genesis. The first [388.12] repeats the flood reference, and the other three [388.20, 389.13, 391.02] refer to ALP/Eve ("Notre Dame," "Bride street," "Bambam's bonniest"). At 391.02, the number occurs with two actual dates to heighten the false connection as well as references to ALP/Eve.

397.30 "1132" continues the connection with ALP/Eve and the evangelists.

420.20–23 In a list of addresses of a letter carried by Shaun the Post, 1132 occurs twice. The first appears to be a date, while the second may be an address; both, however, refer to Adam: A.D. as in the 13.33 occurrence, and then a simple "a." Some of the addresses mock where Joyce lived.

448.03 "eleven" and "thirtytwo" remind us that the message in *Finnegans Wake* is found in Genesis.

516.17 God/HCE is "counting as many as eleven to thritytwo seconds with his pocket browning," relates 1132 to time ("seconds") as well as "forecursing hascupth's foul" [forecasting the Fall of Adam {who has a cup which "runneth over"}] by relating 32 ft. per second per second, the speed of falling bodies, to killing with a Browning pistol.

517.30 Again we have "eleven thirstytoo" just as time is about to start at the Fall.

544.26 Here the "one . . . three . . . two" goes back to line 20 for the first "one." Although the page describes the miserable, poor people in Dublin, the 1132 connects them with Genesis.

574.26 The discussion (574–75) makes a case for condoms' being as effective as the Serpent in providing temptation for intercourse. The "cheque, a good washable pink" is numbered "11 hundred and thirty 2," but it appears to be a check = condom as well as the Genesis signifier.

617.24 "twentyeight to twelve" is 11:32 but also the time when "Femelles will be preadaminant." In other words, before time started at the Fall of Adam, and even before Adam himself existed, ALP existed in the Gnostic story and will again become predominant.

The Mother Goddess

HCE vs. ALP

One of the puzzling features of Joyce's New Theology is that God Himself appears to be killed. When the Russian general was shot, "The abnihilisation of the etym" (353.23) annihilated not only the word of God but also HCE/God himself. If the Son in the Trinity is killed, and if part of the One God is killed, the whole must therefore also have been killed. (This dilemma is discussed in detail in the sections on the Trinity below, and in the section on Buckley and the Russian general in Chapter 7.) At any rate, from this point on, the powers of HCE wane, and ALP becomes the ascendant. At 349.07–08 a TV shows the fading of a transformed God and the awaiting of His new opposite version, ALP: "if you've tippertaps [revenge] in your head or starting kursses, tailour, you're silenced," says ALP at 594.35–36. In her Kate personality, she comforts Adam (or one of her children) at 565.20: "No bad bold faathern, dear one." This signals the death or at least the permanent sleep of HCE, who must be the giant buried under the hills of Dublin. Creating a new conscience requires the disposal of the old God and the substitution of a new one. Notice that the one who is buried cannot be Earwicker/Adam, who was not a giant. In fact ALP's letter says that HCE/God is buried under the Hill of Howth and that Earwicker/

Adam will be resurrected (619.12–15). The revelation is that the new Savior is ALP, the Mother Goddess, who prophesies: "Kilt by kelt shell kithagain with kinagain" [The dead whom God has killed shall kiss again and live again through their descendants] (594.03).

The paragraph at 598.17–26 explains that the old God of Darkness ("supernocturnal") no longer exists, even in transubstantiation. The message at 614.14–18, paraphrased, is: The new religion will be joyous and uplifting. Discard those old coats of skins and put on new clothes you will not be afraid to soil. At 614.20–23: "Begin to forget it [the old Bible and religion]. It will remember itself from every sides, with all gestures, in each our word. Today's truth, tomorrow's trend. Forget, remember!" A joyous religion is introduced by ALP, the new Mother Goddess. After her letter dismissing HCE, Eve explains to Adam: "He's for thee what she's for me. . . . If you spun your yarns to him . . . I was spelling my yearns to her" (620.33–36), thus establishing her connection with the ancient mythological Mother Goddess. (Her derivation from Demeter and other "geomaters" is given in detail in **ALP, personalities of.**)

Those goddesses certainly are part of her makeup, but the dominant presence is probably the Gnostic Sophia. Such would explain her antipathy to, and final domination over, HCE/God. The Gnostics had already absorbed Astarte, Cybele, and other Eastern earth mothers into their Sophia and delineated her role as the opponent of the Judeo-Christian God. Her personality was thus already developed, awaiting Joyce's adoption. Some Gnostic sects considered Sophia to be the Holy Spirit and, as explained in **The Trinity** below, there is some evidence of her presence as such in the *Wake*.

Both Aphrodite and Sophia are prototypes of ALP's river symbolism, the Greek having been born in the sea and the Gnostic being equated to the waters. Since the scene of *Finnegans Wake* is Dublin, the river Liffey is the body of water of choice, and it is, of course, incorporated in Anna Livia's name. The well-known presence of hundreds of other rivers in her Chapter I,8 emphasizes the life-giving fecundity of the Mother-Water-Earth Goddess.

The phrase "an old story, the tale of a Treestone" (113.18–19)—which is repeated by the washwomen, "Telmetale of stem [trunk of tree] or stone" (216.03)—introduces the symbolism of the tree and the stone. When BUTT/Adam says, "The field of karhags [stones] and that bloasted tree. Forget not the felled" (340.07–08), the significance becomes a little clearer, for he is referring to the antagonism between God's barren ground and ALP/Sophia's tree of knowledge, which perhaps was felled along with

Adam and Eve. But there were two trees in the Garden of Eden, and the other one was the tree of life. At 503.30 St. Patrick asks: "There used to be a tree stuck up? An overlisting eshtree [an everlasting tree of life]?" St. Luke's answer, paraphrased, is: The tree of life used to be ALP beside the ford in the river. Her hair waving from one little beer-bough and crowning the phallic symbol (maypole) of the renewal of life. She is still the source of life. and the leaves of her tree lecture us like the leaves of a book (503.31–504.01). St. Patrick notes: "Remounting aliftle towards the ouragan of spaces" [Renewed by ALP it becomes the origin of our species] (504.14). So ALP as the new Mother Goddess replaces or becomes the tree of life.

The stone part of the image represents the harsh, crushing, throwing, killing HCE/God. The dialogue between St. Patrick and St. Luke at 505.21–25, which elucidates the image, may be paraphrased thus:

St. Patrick: A tree free from restraint indeed. But that stone of the law of death, what is its meaning?
Luke: Death, death, the hard stone parts us.
St. Patrick: I understand now, Doctor. A finite mind of infinite truth. The form of God may be masculine, but the gender is feminine.

Earlier, Luke says: "The flagstone. By tombs, deep and heavy. To the unaveiling memory of. Peacer the grave" [Gravestone monuments are evidence of God's harshness, that cannot help those forgotten] (503.26–27). Note that one of the names of ALP's "mamafesta" is "*As Tree is Quick* [life] *and Stone is White* [death] *So is My Washing Done by Night* [I overcome death by sex]" (106.36–107.01).

The tree-stone allegory of the battle for supremacy between ALP and HCE is an echo of the Gnostic struggle of Sophia with Yahweh, Prince of Darkness. In fact the question asked at 573.32—"Has he [HCE] hegemony and shall she [ALP] submit?"—is the fundamental crux of *Finnegans Wake* theology. Does the God of the Old Testament have dominion over women? Or should he be replaced by ALP, the new Mother Goddess? An obscure, almost indecipherable discussion of the problem occurs at 572.19–573.32, of which the following is a Generic Paraphrase.

ALP's Trial

This convoluted discussion comes in the middle of the episode which ostensibly relates an intimate scene in a Dublin family. It is, however, essential to the theology of the *Wake* and, in that respect, connects the prankquean episode and the letter. The preceding lines (572.07–17) are usually considered to be the conversation between the parents whose intercourse was intruded upon on earlier (559). That may be. But the lines are more certainly a rephrasing of Gen. 3.8–10, where Adam and Eve hid under the trees—indeed, after their own interrupted lovemaking—and heard God and were questioned by Him.

The passage starts with the procurator (governor of the province of Eden—that is, God), whose name is "Interrogarius Mealterum" [Questioner of Mealtaking—that is, of fruit eating] (572.19) and who puts forth the "proposer" of Gen. 3.11, where God asked, "Who told thee that thou were naked? Hast thou eaten of the tree, whereof I commanded thee that thou shouldest not eat?"

The question is now examined as though it was an ecclesiastical inquisition, which indeed it is. Resorting to pre-biblical precedents, it invokes the Gnostic versions of the Fall story as well as the biblical one. The passage ends with the fundamental question: Who is to be the major deity, HCE or ALP?

Before we start this interpretation, it is necessary to identify the multiple personalities whom Joyce has disguised, even more obscurely than usual. They are, in order of appearance:

> Honuphrius = God/HCE
> Felicia = woman/Issy/ALP
> Eugenius [Shaun] and Jeremias [Shem] = Adam
> Anita = Lilith/Issy
> Fortissa (she who is strong) = Zoë-Eve/ALP
> Mauritius (Mauritanian slave and sailor) = Adam
> Magravius (he who is heavy, or on the ground) = Serpent
> Gillia = Lilith
> Barnabas (who helped Paul proselytise) = Shaun
> Poppea (red), Arancita (orange), Clara (shining: sun, yellow),
>   Marinuzza (pertaining to the sea: green), Indra (indigo blue),
>   and Iodina (violet) are six of ALP's Rainbow Girls, who with
>   Lilith make the Seven
> Michael (like God) = Shaun/Adam
> Sulla (Roman dictator) = Gnostic God of Darkness
> Gregorius, Leo, Vitellius, Macdugalius = Gnostic angels who
>   raped Zoë-Eve and are members of the Sullivani

Guglielmus (William) = probably Shakespeare
Canicula (little bitch) = Issy/woman

572.21 HCE/God [*Honuphrius* means "bearer of an ass." The ass
is Christ, whose bearer or Father is therefore HCE/God] is
a lustful ex-soldier who makes dishonest propositions to
all [Joyce's indictment of God's behavior in Genesis]. He is
considered to have committed, by involving the help of
the Serpent, simple infidelities with the woman/Issy, a
fertile virgin; and to be practicing making unnatural coats
[not coitus] of skin [Gen. 3.21] for Adam [Shem and
Shaun, the two brother personalities and lovers of Issy]
and Eve [the third lover who loved the brothers].

.25 HCE/God, woman/Issy, and Adam are related because
God created the other two. Lilith/Issy, as the wife of HCE,
has been told by her derived personality, Eve, that HCE
has blasphemously confessed under voluntary chastisement
that he has instructed His slave, Adam, to urge the Serpent, a

.30 hired servant of HCE/God, to solicit the chastity of ALP.
ALP is informed by some illegitimate children of Zoë-Eve
and Adam (as supposed by an Irish historian) that Lilith,
the castoff wife of the Serpent, is visited clandestinely by
Shaun, the advocate of HCE/God who had been cor-
rupted into an immoral person by Shem.

573.01 Lilith with the six other Rainbow Girls has been tenderly
debauched (in a Dublin historian's view) by HCE; and the
Serpent knows from spies that ALP has previously committed a sacrilege with the Shaun/Shem double personalities of Michael[looks like God]/Adam [note that the
prankquean kidnapped the two jiminies]. The Serpent

.05 threatens to have ALP/woman molested by the Gnostic
God of Darkness [See notes 17 and 18 pf the **Prankquean**
Generic Paraphrase], who desires to procure woman/Zoë-
Eve/Issy for four of His angels if she will not yield to Him;
and also if she will not deceive HCE/God by having
conjugal

.10 relations when such are demanded [Gen. 3.16]. ALP/
woman, who claims to have discovered incestuous temptations from Shem/Shaun/Adam [incestuous because the
woman was derived from Adam's body and could techni-

cally be called his daughter], would yield to the lewdness of HCE to appease the savagery of the God of Darkness and subjugation of His twelve angels; and (as another Dublin historian first suggested) to save the virginity of woman/Issy for the

.15 Serpent when converted by Shaun/Adam after the death of Lilith; but she fears that by allowing the Serpent marital rights, she may cause reprehensible conduct between Shaun and Shem. Shaun/Adam, who has formerly debauched ALP [see **Prankquean**], exempts woman/Issy from yielding to HCE, who pretends publicly to possess His connubial rights to thirty-nine ways of

.20 carnal union (shamefully affirmed by the ecclesiastic authority) whenever He has rendered Himself impotent to consummate by painful cunning. ALP is disturbed, but Adam threatens to reserve (exchange) her case tomorrow for the ordinary Shakespeare tale, even if she should practice a

.25 faked orgasm during copulation, which she knows from experience leads to nothing. Zoë-Eve, however, is encouraged by the Angels of Darkness to warn ALP by describing the strong chastisements [Gen. 3.14–19] of HCE/God and the filthy depravities of Issy/Lilith (the deceased wife of Adam) with the God of Darkness, who is

.32 unwilling to repent. Has HCE the authority, and shall ALP submit?

ALP's Ascendancy

The verdict is predicted at 146.12: "Blessed Marguerite bosses . . ." And at 614.24 it is stated: "A plainplanned liffeyism assemblements Eblania's conglomerate horde" [ALP's theology will dominate and absorb HCE's Irish followers]. In spite of Shaun's disclaimer of writing *Finnegans Wake* (425), he is obviously affected by the Shem/Joyce author, for at 426.01–04 he expostulates an "oath by the awe of Shaun (and that's a howl [hell] of a name!) that I will commission to the flames [of hell] any incendiarist whosoever or ahriman howsoclever who would endeavor to set ever annyma roner moother [mother ALP] of mine on fire" [So, like Shem/Joyce, he will send to hell anyone who condemns ALP]. In one of the few instances where HCE/God expresses remorse, He reacts to Shaun's outburst: "And, with that crickcrackcruck [thunder] of his threelungged squool [Trinity school of God's teachings of death by gallows] from which grief had usupped every smile, big hottempered husky fusky krenfy strenfy pugiliser [vengeful HCE/God], such as he was, he virtually broke down on the mooherhead, getting quite jerry [teary] over her, overpowered by himself with the love of tearsilver that he twined through her hair [overcome by the thought of her as a Mother {Machree}] for, sure, he was the soft semplgawn [weak] slob of the world with a heart like Montgomery's in his showchest and harvey loads of feeling in him and as innocent and undesignful as the freshfallen calef [sacrificial calf]" (426.05–13).

Early in the book, when ALP is only Issy, she anticipates her letter (112.28–113.22) and warns that she is not merely a midget majesty but will become a Mother Goddess when she puts on the cloak of maturity. She defends Adam and then utters a thunderword in presumption of her Godhood. All she wants, she writes, is to tell the truth about HCE/God: "Kapak kapuk. No minzies matter [German *kaputt*. He produced ruination and death, not to mince matters]. He had to see life foully the plak and the smut. . . . There were three men in him . . . [God as Trinity saw only the dirty side of life]" (113.12–14). Her declaration continues (in paraphrase): Having fun and sex were just foibles to Him. Shame on him who thinks evil of that. It is an old story, the tale of Adam with Eve, of God the unshakable mountain and his Pal the Serpent; but as Venice defeated Genoa, ALP/woman will take charge.

There are other early endeavors to write the letter, but only ALP's final version completes her triumph. It is announced as the "Mamma Lujah" (614.28), which ALP wrote as the new gospel, as Elijah the prophet did. The new Mother Goddess promises redemption and everlasting life through sex. She also puts the old God to rest so that mankind can produce immortality through procreation without sin. She as woman will retrieve what the old God and his clergy took away. ALP speaks for herself, as the following Generic Paraphrase (615.12–619.19) reveals.

ALP's Letter

615.12   To: His Majesty, HCE/God
          Dear Reverend: As we leave Eden for Dear Dirty Dublin,
    .15   we have frankly enjoyed sex more than anything (we thank
          you for it) and it was delightful at nighttime. Clergy and
          detractors who try to wreck our hours of joy will come to
          know better. Yonder clouds will soon disappear, and it
          looks like a fine day coming. They should be like the first

man, Adam, who got knowledge [Adam from the tree; Finn from the salmon]. It was in Dublin/Eden that I

.20   still think of him looking at me in ecstasy as we merrily rolled along. When he woke up in a sweat beside me, I pardoned him, my having my own way, but he daydreamed

.25   another lovely embrace. Back we were in a flash, back to the paradise lost long ago; the man who never ejaculated but naturally. That was the start of sex, which gave me the keys to heaven [compare 628.15]. The Serpent isn't necessary. If I were to bruise his head [Gen. 3.15] but

.30   whisper for his help in intercourse, what is the harm in sex? It's the anointing of the Fall. It is only forbidden with your neighbor's wife. Your clergy suggest it is shameful. Never! So may the Lord forgive them

616.01   their trespasses against the Serpent. The hardiest Finn is about to be resurrected. An out and out Irishman called Earwicker by his first wife. May all the

.05   daughters of our old-time story [Eve's descendants] have such a husband. For a small fee we could hire someone to make a corpse of somebody [God] by shooting with the greatest of pleasure. And in contravention of the laws

.10   of chemistry, not enough of Him would be left to form a Trinity, God knows! How offensive for the Trinity, but what a worthwhile price for two superhuman nuns [Issy and Eve]. Poison for the despots! Peace! Adam possessed since he was a child the highest attractiveness one could behold,

.15   complete with hairy chest, muscular legs, and affectionate eyes. He had real devotion. Serpents take notice! We exclude all such tempting snakes. They are pests although we agree with their suggestion! Couldn't God see that?

.20   About that man and his knowing the size of a vagina. At first he looked around the Garden of Eden before God expelled him. He was knowledgeable about penises! Statistics show that for intercourse a firm erection is

.25   to be appreciated. We should also call attention to our orgasm. The attraction between the sexes was noticeable in a plethora of examples [among the animals]. Did God permit bad examples to be set before Adam as a mitigation

.30   of the king's evil? He only pictured himself in their actions.

His giant erection made him understand. No weak objections wanted either! Once you understand the intent of the Serpent, you are impervious to his message. Get things in order now before we reach the conflict. We must now close, hoping St. Laurence of Dublin all best wishes.

.34 Interruption from God. To Mrs. Adam: So you are expecting trouble perhaps, from the actions I took? As for Adam: Just as there is good and evil [the tree of],

617.01 ALP, I bare my ass to you. Thumb and fingers up his. Whereupon our best of III plus 1,001 blessings will now conclude the 1,001 nights as well as your kind letter you

.05 took the trouble to write. We [the Trinity] are all at home in old Ireland; for our sake that dearest husband will be true and loving as long as the church has money. It is impossible to remember all the persons [whom God created] in various places. Who would bellow his head off to

.10 create a particularly mean stinker like Adam, mystery man of the Park murders? The revolter! St. Thomas and St. Laurence are both My twin sons; now they've changed their

.15 character after they died. Conan Doyle will be the medium to reveal them if they are correctly contacted. Music, Maestro, please! We'll have a band rehearsal. Sing! One must simply laugh. Catch him again! Revenge! Well, this ought to make him wake up. He'll want his furious murderer [God] to make him new clothes [Gen. 3.21]. The Serpent will help. The big bad sprawling uttering fool!

.20 He has now stuffed his last pudding [intercourse]. His funeral will take place when time starts today. Kings welcome. Also brewers. Exiled Adam's picture in Dublin shown in the newspapers as multiple personalities. Females will be with Adam as in Genesis 3. To hear that person laid low by love, of course a born gentleman, will

.25 need further miracles. Don't forget! The grand funeral will now shortly occur [Exile: Gen. 3.24]. Remember. The remains must be removed before time begins. With earnestly conceived hopes. So help Us, God; witness My hand. From: My illusion of God; the day is now closed.

.30 [From ALP] Well, here's the continuing letter erroneously concerning other clerical devils alleged herewith. I wish I were that dumb youth [Adam] and he'd wish I were his twin [Genesis 25.26]. How about it? The sweetest song in the world! My figure when I was young was much admired—me with my red hair [twin Esau had red hair]. Perhaps improper in a married woman, the fashion of hair hanging down straight denotes innocence. O happy fault

618.01 and vagina! If only the Serpent would handle wakes like newspaper reports! Talk to us instead! God with Lilith, who became the wife of the Serpent to preserve her good

.05 name after he tempted her, will now pay attention. Just a pinch for tonight! Best bacon for sale [see Daddy Dacon, 339.04]. The thugs by the cemetery were organized by God. The Dublin kicking brigade. And she was given

.10 an aphrodisiac. Trinity Shame! We are advised that the One Who made the boots [for kicking Adam and Eve out of Eden] is at present in the Irish Sweepstakes Hospital and may He never come out! Only look through your letterbox [or book = *Finnegans Wake*] one day along with the past Chief Patriarch St. Patrick, with the court of sessions masters and clerks and the bevy of Mary Restoresses, for a good all-around full

.15 view of St. Patrick's purgatory; you will be surprised to see under the ground [grand piano = big plain; purgatory is underground] Lilith reclining seductively on the sofa and then he'd [St. Patrick] begin to jump a little bit to find out what goes on when love walks in, aside from the Temptation business, by kissing and behaving like a man.

.20 We were not treated very well when the Cherubims [Gen. 3.24] directed us to dance out of Eden. And personally speaking, they can make their bows to my arse as the old poem sang about Finn MacCool. Item: we were

.25 never chained down, and no one forced us to eat the fruit. Meet a great man [Adam] (proud lives to him!) who is as gentle as a mushroom and very affectionate when he sits over me for his coitus; while to whom it may concern, God/Sully is a thug for all He drank though He is a rattling fine kicker-outer in his profession. Would we

.30 were here on earth to lodge a complaint on the God who stole paradise; if we did, his health would be constantly broken into small change, which would be the change of His life by a Norwegian captain [Adam] who was expelled by the Christian God.

Well, our talks are resumed by more polite conversations with human beings over natural goodness and

619.01 pleasure rather than God's scabrous humbug. While for whoever likes women it is one apiece [Gen. 2.24], thanks to Adam, our former first man, and to our ribald father, Joyce, for his

.05 beautiful crossword puzzle [*Finnegans Wake*].

Well, we simply like their undulating gluteal cheeks [demb = damped, refers to restricted or gradually reduced oscillation], the Dublin maidens walking here about with rhythms of a water bed [Joyce the prognosticator]; and God being as deaf as He possibly could to the Fall.

.10 Certain religious people are profitably, agreeably deaf. Here is your answer, pigs and scuts! Because we've lived in two worlds [paradise and earth]. God is in another world under the Hill of Howth. The Earwicker [Adam] of our home fame is God's real namesake [God's image], who will get up erect, confident, and heroic when he is acting young as

.15 of old, for my daily orgasm; he woos his little wife.

ALP (School of Love, Beautiful Spring)

P.S. Adam's sweetheart. And she's about fed up with the reams of religious nonsense. And all that dressing up in ritzy clothes in ornamental churches. The costumes are

.19 worn out. But she's the proposed alternative.

The Trinity

References to the Trinity abound in Joyce's rewritten Bible but, as one would expect, they are apt to turn up in unexpected ways. The word *Trinity* is not used in the Bible; rather, the concept arose early in the Christian church in an attempt to reconcile a divine Christ with a monotheistic Jewish God. The triple aspect was carried over, I suspect, from the Gnostic efforts to rationalize the problem. The church fathers have contended with the paradox over the ages, but explanations remain illogical, and if accepted, must be done so on faith. The Trinity is "those who, would it not be for that dielectrick, were upon the point of obsoletion" [The Trinity is at the point of dielectic obsolescence] (322.30–32). At 608.01–04 it is explained as a spiritualist fraud [to paraphrase: It is a mere mannerism of uncertainty, visible, according to the meteorologist of the Ancient Irish Sorcerer's Association for the Advancement of Séance, because mentioning it under the breath is the essence of pure bunkum!]. But obsolescence or fraud only enhances the presence of the Trinity in the *Wake* "when style, stink and stigmataphoron are of one sum in the same person" (606.27–28).

In one of the guises, the three soldiers become the Trinity. They are exemplary of the killing nature of God (since that is a soldier's job) and always appear in threatening situations, especially when the encounter of Adam with God (Gen. 3.8–13) is the *generic* basis of an episode. For example the mystery of what happened in the park seems to have been observed by the three soldiers, under various names but always referring back to God as the Trinity accosting Adam (35.01–36.34).

The Joycean heresy that God killed His own Son(s) poses a dilemma for the Trinity because that would require God in a sense to commit suicide, since killing part of Him is to kill all of Him if he is One. He "killed his own hungery self in anger as a young man," according to 126.22–23. This is the theological issue confronted and admitted in the Buckley and the Russian general episode (354.01–06). It is resolved by having Buckley/ Adam be resurrected back into the Son after his death (354.8). But this solution generates the second horn of the dilemma because if God admits both Adam and Jesus, then He has two Sons, who will not fit into the Trinity. The answer to this is provided by the multiple-personality concept of having Shaun and Christ present as two personalities of Adam in III, 1 [see **Adam: personalities of**]. This of course would require that God kill His Son twice—an idea which does not violate Wakean logic or morals. The ancient Irish clans are willing to "pay their firstrate duties before the both of him" (497.21).

Another perplexity now arises, for if Adam is part of the Trinity, did He instigate His own Fall? *Finnegans Wake* says "yes." God's thunderword at 314.8–9 announces the Fall, which is immediately explained by the three Persons: (1) he dived, (2) fell like a barometer, (3) slid. The three are then identified as "the lad at the top of the ladder" (Father, at 314.17), "sohns of a blitzh" (notice the plural Sons, 314.28), and "thonder alout makes the thurd" (Spirit, 314.29). The triple involvement is confirmed by identifying the parts of God (appearing here in the Norwegian captain episode as Kersse the tailor [Gen. 3.21]) as (1) "top gallant," (2) "scum of a botch," and (3) "confiteor" [present as the Spirit in the Mass] (322.03–09).

The identity of the Holy Ghost or Spirit is perhaps the most perplexing part of the Trinity. Wakean logic solves the problem neatly: if Adam is the Son, then Eve/ALP is the Spirit. Such a reading has been proposed by no less an ecclesiastical authority than Father Robert Boyle, S.J., in his contribution to *A Starchamber Quiry,* an essay titled "James Joyce and the soul": "Joyce seemed to find no difficulty in judging that a woman can far better represent the Spirit than could any male," says Boyle (135), who himself finds no such difficulty as a priest. He traces Joyce's assignment of a feminine Spirit from *Chamber Music* through *Ulysses* and thinks that Molly can be the Madonna as well as the Holy Spirit. He bases his argument on the following points:

1. The use of the male pronoun in prayers is a grammatical convention.
2. Sex applied to any person of the Trinity is a human, extrinsic attribution.
3. Throughout the centuries the "anthropomorphic representations of the third person as a third male" have been avoided; the imagery is usually the dove or the heart.
4. It is easier to treat the Spirit as feminine.
5. In the Hebrew text of Gen. 1.2—"And the Spirit of God moved upon the face of the waters"—*ruah* is a feminine noun.

Boyle cites little textual evidence from *Finnegans Wake* to support his proposal, mentioning only that when ALP says "give me the keys of me heart" (626.30–31) (150), she is a goddess like Isis, expressing the heart as the symbol of the Spirit. He feels that ALP's last words, "as they strike my ear, suggest an analogy with Dante's ecstatic openhearted union with the infinite Trinity 114."

There are, however, textural reinforcements to this argument. St. Mark, in his quest for the history of Adam and Christ, says: "Those [ALP's accounts of the Fall] were the grandest gynecollege [lessons from the feminine tree of knowledge] histories . . . for teaching the Fatima [highest feminine ideal] woman [Issy/ALP] history of Fatimiliafamilias [prediction of a family or group] . . . on which purposeth [proposes, purposes] of the spirit of nature [Mother Goddess] as difinely [divinely] developed" (389.09–17). To put it coherently: the Fall was the grandest basis for teaching that the highest feminine ideal, woman, would be the Spirit in the divinely developed group, the Trinity.

When the Trinity reviews (360.17–25) the killing of the Son in the Buckley episode, three persons speak, as the following Generic Paraphrase makes clear:

360.17–19　(1) Nasty rogue and loud bragger, how can a vile father be high? Yes he did kill his own son was the answer.

.20–22　(2) And used his son as a soldier to do the shooting. The noise rang out like a fart.

.23–25　(3) [ALP emerges as Mother Goddess:] Don't shilly shally. It is the hour of the golden sickle's castration ritual. I am the Holy Moon Priestess.

Father Boyle says (123) that Joyce deified woman as "That image of the Dove, the constant and almost sole image of the Holy Spirit." There is linking of ALP with birds in *Finnegans Wake*. Aphrodite's sacred lovebirds, swans or doves, accompany the prankquean. At 359.32 the "song of the naughtingels" is of nightingales and also of the naughty girls who are perhaps Issy's collective chorus but more likely are Issy + Eve. The twit-twin-two-sing like a sweetish-sad nightingale to provide "their terce that who(e) betwides them" to the "jemcrow, jackdaw, prime and secund" [the nightingale is the third part of the Trinity chorus]; and the organ accompanies them "when we press the pedal (soft) pick out and vowelise your name. A mum" [ALP is vocalized as Mother Goddess] (360.02–07).

At the end of the Norwegian captain episode the Serpent forecasts the ascendancy of ALP as Goddess. At 327.8 he comments that Issy with all her charms is "tramity trimming"—that is to say, she is training for the Trinity. He then tells God what He should do to help ALP assume Godhead.

Yawn/Adam/Christ, as the Son in the Trinity, is able at "to hear with his unaided ears the harp in the air, the bugle dianablowing . . . the mocking-bird" (475.36–476.01). This passage also combines music, birds, and the Mother Goddess (Diana) into the Holy Spirit, which the Son in Trinity can easily hear. Jaun/Adam in two pages (449–50) containing a profusion of allusions to birds and music, would rather pass up joining "with any tristys blinking upon this earthlight" (449.07), since he realizes he will have to die to do so, and "stay where I am" (449.13) with Issy "to guide me by gastronomy" [teach him to eat the forbidden fruit] or go fishing and "singasongapiccolo" about the "chthonic solphia" [the divine ghost Sophia] (450.18–19). It seems likely that Joyce did intend bird-words to imply at least ALP, if not always the Holy Spirit; the linkage with music raises the possibility that the hundreds of echoes of songs throughout the *Wake* may also be a signal for ALP's presence.

At 504.20–505.13 the bird image is transformed into its natural habitat, the tree; St. Luke explains the Gnostic origin of ALP to St. Patrick as the tree of knowledge and says she has "triliteral roots" (505.04). Inasmuch as St. Patrick drove the Gnostic Ophites out of Ireland because of their snake worship, he must have known that the Ophite Trinity included *Sophia*—whose name in Greek means "prudence" or "wisdom"—as the Holy Spirit. And Joyce must have known the general Gnostic belief that the Father of Light was the highest divinity with Sophia, the Mother of Life, as second in the hierarchy.

One must be cautious about interpreting groups of three, since they are not always the Trinity. At 387.13, for instance, "three andesiters" are Adam, Eve, and the Serpent, as are the "one by one place one be three" referred to at 19.20–21. Note also that the prankquean asks her riddle three times because she must address HCE/God in his Trinity. When the Trinity speaks, as mentioned above at 314.10–12 and 360.17–23, Joyce's convention of using a dash instead of quotation marks can be confusing because the utterance of the Three Persons looks typographically like a conversation among different individuals.

ALP the Savior

ALP the Mother Goddess is also the new Savior. As she revives Adam after his Fall and exile, so she resurrects all mankind. Once before, when she was Nuvoletta/Issy, she saved the quarreling Mookse/Adam and Gripes/God and took them back to heaven (158.25–159.05). Then she was only a brook, about to become a river (159.16–18). Now at the end of *Finnegans Wake* she is a full-grown river and Savior carrying mankind's burdens away to the sea of eternal bliss: "Ourselves, oursouls alone. At the site of salvocean" (623.28–29).

The long paragraph starting immediately after her letter at 619.20 and ending in the final "the" (628.16) is the most lyrical and inspiring in the *Wake*. The river gives herself in sacrifice to the sea, and the human joins the divine. The primeval conception of Persephone's death and resurrection as Mother Goddess is renewed; and the Gnostic notion of Sophia, Mother of Life, joining the supreme deity Father of Light and His Son as a propitious Trinity is revived.

The message of the New Conscience is that not the sons of Adam but the daughters of Eve will make humanity humane.

Bibliography

Atherton, James S. *The Books at the Wake.* New York: Viking, 1960.

Barnstone, Willis, ed. *The Other Bible.* San Francisco: Harper and Row, 1984.

Beckett, Samuel, et al. *Our Exagmination Round His Factification for Incamination of Work in Progress.* Paris: Shakespeare and Co., 1929; New York: New Directions, 1939; rpt., 1962.

Benstock, Bernard. *Joyce-Again's Wake.* Seattle: University of Washington Press, 1965.

Bishop, John. *Joyce's Book of the Dark: "Finnegans Wake."* Madison: University of Wisconsin Press, 1986.

Boyle, Robert, S.J. "James Joyce and the soul." In *A Starchamber Quiry: A James Joyce Centennial Volume, 1882–1992,* edited by E. L. Epstein. New York: Methuen, 1982.

Campbell, Joseph, and H. M. Robinson. *A Skeleton Key to "Finnegans Wake."* New York: Harcourt, Brace, 1944.

Clark, Hilary. "Networking in *Finnegans Wake.*" *JJQ* 27 (Summer 1980).

Connolly, Thomas E. *The Personal Library of James Joyce: A Descriptive Bibliography.* Buffalo: University Bookstore, University of Buffalo, 1955; 2d ed., 1957.

Cumpiano, Marion. "The Boots at the Swan." *JJQ* 16 (Summer 1979): 517.

Ellmann, Richard. *James Joyce.* New York: Oxford University Press, 1959; rev. ed., 1982.

Epstein, E. L., ed. *A Starchamber Quiry: A James Joyce Centennial Volume, 1882–1992.* New York: Methuen, 1982.

———. "The Turning Point/Book I, Chapter vi." In *A Conceptual Guide to "Finnegans Wake,"* edited by Michael H. Begnal and Fritz Senn. University Park: Pennsylvania State University Press, 1974.

Gillespie, Michael Patrick. *James Joyce's Trieste Library.* Austin: Harry Ransom Humanities Research Center, University of Texas, 1986.

Glasheen, Adaline. *A Census of "Finnegans Wake": An Index of Characters and Their Roles.* Evanston: Northwestern University Press, 1956.

———. *A Second Census of "Finnegans Wake": An Index of Characters and Their Roles.* Evanston: Northwestern University Press, 1963. All Glasheen page references in the text are from this book.

———. *A Third Census of "Finnegans Wake": An Index of Characters and Their Roles.* Berkeley: University of California Press, 1977.

———. " *Finnegans Wake* and the Girls from Boston, Mass." *Hudson Review* 7 (1954): 89–96.

Hart, Clive. *A Concordance to "Finnegans Wake."* Minneapolis: University of Minnesota Press, 1963.

———. *Structure and Motif in "Finnegans Wake."* Evanston: Northwestern University Press, 1962.

———. "Afterword: Reading *Finnegans Wake.*" In *A Starchamber Quiry: A James Joyce Centennial Volume, 1882–1992,* edited by E. L. Epstein. New York: Methuen, 1982.

———. "Notes." *Old Series A Wake Newslitter,* no. 4, July 1962.

Hayman, David. *A First-Draft Version of "Finnegans Wake."* Austin: University of Texas Press, 1963.

———. "Nodality and the infra-Structure of *Finnegans Wake.*" *JJQ* 16 (Fall 1978): 135–49.

Joyce, James. *Finnegans Wake.* New York: Viking, 1939; Penguin, 1982.

———. *Letters of James Joyce,* vol. 1. Edited by Stuart Gilbert, New York: Viking, 1957.

———. *Letters of James Joyce,* vols. 2 and 3. Edited by Richard Ellmann. New York: Viking, 1966.

———. *A Portrait of the Artist as a Young Man.* Edited by Richard Ellmann. New York: Viking, 1964, 1982.

———. *Ulysses.* New York: Random House, 1961, 1992.

Joyce, Stanislaus. *My Brother's Keeper.* Edited by Richard Ellmann. New York: Viking, 1958.

Levin, Harry. *James Joyce: A Critical Introduction.* Norfolk, Conn.: New Directions, 1960.

MacManus, Seumas. *The Story of the Irish Race.* New York: Devin-Adair, 1921, 1973.

McCarthy, Patrick A. *The Riddles of "Finnegans Wake."* Rutherford, N.J.: Fairleigh Dickinson University Press, 1980.

McHugh, Roland. *Annotations to "Finnegans Wake."* Baltimore: Johns Hopkins University Press, 1980; rev. ed., 1991.

Mercier, Vivian. *The Irish Comic Tradition.* London: Oxford University Press, 1962.

Morford, Mark P. O., and Robert J. Lenardon. *Classical Mythology.* New York: Longman, 1977.

Moseley, Virginia. *Joyce and the Bible.* DeKalb: Northwestern Illinois University Press, 1967.

Norris, Margot. *The Decentered Universe of "Finnegans Wake."* Baltimore: Johns Hopkins University Press, 1974.

Senn, Fritz. "In Quest of a *nisus formativus Joyceanus.*" In *Joyce Studies Annual 1990,* edited by Thomas F. Staley. Austin: University of Texas Press, 1990.

Simpkins, Scott. "The Agency of the Title: *Finnegans Wake.*" *JJQ* 27 (Summer 1990): 735.

Skrabanek, Petr. "Cunniform Letters." *"Finnegans Wake" Circular* 3 (1988): 75.

Slocum, John J., and Herbert Cahoon. *A Bibliography of James Joyce.* New Haven: Yale University Press, 1953.

Strong, L. A. G. *The Sacred River.* New York: Pellegrini and Cudahy, 1951.

Tindall, William York. *A Reader's Guide to "Finnegans Wake."* New York: Farrar, Straus and Giroux, 1969.

Index

Entries in boldface type are the cross references mentioned in the text that provide the interwoven explanation.

Adam: in the prankquean episode, 134; miscellaneous names, 92ff., 155, 209
Adam: personalities of, 78ff.
ALP: ascendancy of, 206; Goddess, 127, 169, 195; versus HCE, 208ff.; origin of letter of, 66; miscellaneous names, 209; as Prankquean, 135; the Savior, 220; trial of, 208ff.
ALP: personalities of, 94ff., 206ff.
ALP's letter, 212ff.
Ambiguity, 5
annihilation of the word, 206
Aphrodite, 207
apostrophe omission, 1
ass, naming 81
Atherton, James S., xii, 7, 8, 10, 11, 16, 28, 67, 75, 76 81, 96, 98, 109
Atkins, Tommy, 75
Augustine, 33

Babel, Tower of, 18
Ballad, 143ff.

Barnstone, Willis, xii, 34ff.
Becket, Samuel, 10
Benstock, Bernard, 8
Bible, 7ff.; rewritten, 8, 9, 15ff.
Birds, 219
Bishop, John, 8
Boyle, Robert, 217
Box and Cox, 177
Brawn, 83
Bruno, Giordano, 33, 68, 83, 196
Buckley and the Russian general, 165ff., 192, 217
BUTT, 169ff.

cad, 77
Campbell, Joseph, xii, 75
Carroll, Lewis, 2
circularity, 9
Clark Hilary, 4
claybook, 21
cod, 71
Connolly, Thomas E., 27
conscience, re-creating, 191
creation: Bible reference to, 28; Manichaean myth, 34
Cumpiano, Marion, 103
curse, 31, 168
Curses, 126ff.